Deer Hunters' 1998 Almanac

FROM THE PUBLISHERS OF DEER & DEER HUNTING MAGAZINE

Published by:

krause publications

700 E. State Street • Iola, WI 54990-0001
Telephone: 715/445-2214
fax: 715/445-4087
World Wide Web: www.krause.com/outdoors

Please call or write for our free catalog of outdoor publications.
Our toll-free number to place an order or obtain a free catalog is
800-258-0929. Please use our regular business telephone
715-445-2214 for editorial comment or further information.

Library of Congress Catalog Number: 92-74255

ISBN: 0-87341-549-3
Printed in the United States of America

Deer Hunters' 1998 Almanac

FROM THE PUBLISHERS OF DEER & DEER HUNTING MAGAZINE

FEATURES

What factors determine how a buck is scored for the Boone and Crockett and Pope and Young clubs? Find out by turning to Page 147.

FAST FACTS

Deer Hunters' 1998 Almanac

FROM THE PUBLISHERS OF DEER & DEER HUNTING MAGAZINE

Editorial Director: Patrick Durkin   **Associate Editor:** Dan Schmidt

Cover photo by Dan Schmidt

Short End of the Stick

■ *Mike Moutoux*

The north wind picked up just after sunrise, making Tim shiver each time it found an opening in his parka. The coat was another hand-me-down from his father, just like the old pump shotgun he cradled in his arms. The blueing was worn off the barrel, and the stock was scratched, but he could hit a paper plate easily at 25 yards, which was about as far as he could see in this thicket anyway.

With two older brothers, Tim was always the last to get anything new. When deer season came around, Dad made sure everyone was equipped, and after two years Tim was familiar with the drill. Dad went through the same routine as they prepared for the trip to Pennsylvania's central mountains. After unloading the groceries at their two-room cabin, they would sight-in their guns on a sheet of plywood nailed between two trees.

This year was no different. Dad uncased three guns and passed out two to Jeff and Paul — both rifles. Of course, the final gun was the more weathered of the three. He turned to Tim and said, "Well, I guess you got the short end of the stick again, son, but this old shotgun will kill a deer out to 40 yards — if you shoot straight."

Settling in

Tim kept hearing Dad's words as he settled into his stand. "The short end of the stick." How many times have I heard that? While Tim contemplated his fate, he heard two quick shots off to the north.

Trying to shake off his disappointment, he pulled down the hood of his parka so he could hear better. He thought of what might be happening with the rest of the hunting party.

The family owned 20 acres adjacent to the Allegheny National Forest, and each family member had his own stand. Dad and Paul were at the north end of the family's land. Both killed deer from their stands last year. Jeff had a stand along a small creek that ran through a cedar swamp. He killed a deer there two years ago.

Tim's spot was the only stand on the south end of the property. Although the stand was close to a gravel road, he watched an old field that bordered the woods.

Behind his stand was a ditch that fed into the swamp where Jeff hunted. Tim felt like he got the short end again when stands were assigned. His uncle supposedly killed a buck from this stand five years ago, but

Short End of the Stick

Tim had hunted out of it for the past two years and didn't see a deer.

A Familiar Drill

Twenty minutes passed — long enough for any deer to come his way if they intended to. Even this part of the drill was becoming familiar.

Another shot rang from the north. Tim wasn't sure if it was Paul or Dad. If it was Paul, he would blow his whistle, which meant he had a deer down. Almost on cue, the cold wind carried the sound of the whistle to Tim, who heard it clearly, and then gritted his teeth. He pulled the hood back over his head.

At 10 a.m., he pulled out a sandwich and chewed it slowly. Nothing seemed to be out in this wind, and the only other sound was the dried beech leaves that rattled with every gust. The dry sandwich needed to be washed down, and as Tim was unscrewing his thermos, he heard three shots from the other side of the road. He set the cup down beside him, pulled the hood down and turned to see the road. He did not have long to wait.

He heard it coming before he saw it. "A buck," he whispered to himself. It paused at the opposite side of the road, giving Tim enough time to work up a good case of the jitters. He had never seen a buck this close before. The barrel of the gun jumped up and down as he tried to calm his nerves. It was no use.

In two leaps, the buck crossed the road and angled past the boy. Tim looked for a place to shoot and saw an opening about 70 yards away. "Too far," he thought as the buck picked its way through the trees. The buck continued on its path, heading straight toward Jeff and Dad. When it was out of sight, Tim listened for a shot until his ears burned. He heard nothing.

Dejected, he turned back to his lunch and knocked over the cup, sending it 12 feet down to the ground. When it hit, he heard a deer snort behind him. Tim froze. A second deer must have been following the buck.

Waiting Patiently

The wind rattled the curled leaves and nipped at Tim's ears and nose, but the boy became a statue. Only after it was satisfied the noise was harmless did the heavy-beamed 8-pointer move again. Slowly, it walked toward Tim's tree.

When it was 20 yards away, Tim slipped off his right mitten and lifted the shotgun to his cheek. He slid the gun's

Leonard Lee Rue III

safety forward as he centered the front sight in its notch. It was almost automatic the way the sight found the buck's shoulder. Just as the boy began his squeeze, the buck stopped behind a tree. From his perch, Tim could only see the buck's neck and head.

"Come on boy, take one more step," he thought, but the buck stayed put. The gun grew heavy, and when the buck looked away, Tim brought the gun down.

A single shot broke the silence and the spell. The deer and the boy snapped their heads in the direction of the sound. Tim raised the gun and settled the sights where the tree trunk intersected the deer's neck, but the buck didn't move. Another minute passed, and Tim had to take the gun down again. "Come on, move, darn it."

Jeff's distant shooting eventually unnerved the buck, and it took one step in the direction of the swamp. Tim could now only see the deer's tail. "Should have shot him before. I blew my only chance," he thought.

A Change of Fortune

Tim's break came when the wind shifted and carried the sound of Jeff's jubilant holler. The buck turned away from the swamp and began walking parallel to Tim. Again, Tim shouldered the gun, released the safety, and nestled the sight on the buck's shoulder.

The next gust of wind carried the sound of a shotgun blast. Tim watched as the buck fell and lay still. Shaking visibly, he lowered his gun to the ground and climbed down. When he got to the deer, he knelt beside it and studied every detail. It had a silvery-gray muzzle and dark, knurled antler bases. The brow tines were short, but the main beams were heavy and long with ivory tips.

By the time Dad got there, Jeff and Paul were already admiring the buck. "Good shot," he said as he tussled the boy's hair.

"Thanks." Tim said, bashful yet proud.

"Jeff, you can get back on stand. Paul, you go back to the cabin and get the camera. Tim and I will meet you halfway."

After field dressing the buck, Dad lashed a sturdy branch to its antlers to use as a drag handle.

"Which side do you want?" Dad asked. Tim eyed the branch and noted that one side was longer.

"I'll take the short end. I don't mind," he said with a big grin.

The Russians Are Coming!

And They Want Your Fur.

And so do the Chinese. And the Koreans. And many more.
The fur market is up. Supply is down. Prices are rising.

Stay In Touch.

Read

1 Year (10 issues)
$16.95

Subscribe Today!

Credit Card Orders Toll-Free
800-258-0929 Dept. ABARAP
Monday - Friday, 7 a.m. - 8 p.m.; Saturday 8 a.m. - 2 p.m.; CST

☐ **YES!** Please send me one year (10 issues) of **The Trapper & Predator Caller** for only $16.95.
☐ New ☐ Renewal (attach mailing label) ☐ Payment enclosed

Name ____

Address ____

City ____

State/Zip ____

Send with payment to:
The Trapper & Predator Caller
Circulation Dept. ABARAP, 700 E. State St., Iola, WI, 54990-0001

Insights into Deer Behavior

What is it about white-tailed deer that has allowed them to capture our interest and hold it for so long? Many elements, we're sure, but perhaps the answer lies in their behavior. Although many hunters spend years trying to "pattern" deer, the truth is that deer behavior is never understood by simplistic philosophies, and successful deer hunting requires more than routine tactics.

Each year, we ask our readers to provide their insight on deer and deer hunting. This accumulation of knowledge allows us to not only better understand deer hunting techniques, but it allows hunters to improve their skills by learning from their peers. This chapter includes the results from our 1995 Readers' Survey. Readers responded to several common, yet complex, behavioral, biological, ecological and management hunting situations that we asked about in a survey. From the letters we received, these questions caused readers to think and integrate information from many sources, including the "school of hunting experience."

We hope this information will help us understand how a diverse group of people can share such a deep interest in deer and deer hunting.

Insights into Whitetail Behavior

> *"As a serious hunter, some of your questions surprised me. I probably got them wrong, but these are things I never considered really important to know in deer hunting. Since you have sparked my curiosity, I will do more studying."*
>
> — *'95 Survey Respondent*

■ *Jay McAninch, with Patrick Durkin*

When we published our 1995 Readers' Survey in the October 1995 issue of *Deer & Deer Hunting*, we hoped the questions would challenge even the most well-read hunters, and be educational for everyone. Our intent wasn't to ask tricky, vague or irrelevant questions, even though some respondents hinted that we were out to trip them.

Perhaps Mike Parsons of Coloma, Mich., summed up our

Readers' Survey, Part I:

purpose best when he said, "The quiz made me think, and made me want to learn more about the best sport in our country!"

We hope the comments above, and similar feedback we received, indicate the quiz succeeded in passing along some insights into white-tailed deer.

Since the survey was published, many readers called and wrote to ask for the answers in advance, whether out of curiosity or to settle friendly bets. To be fair to everyone, we held the answers until now. During the next three issues of *Deer & Deer Hunting*, we'll share them with you. Part 1 of the series, which follows, concentrates on questions we asked about the whitetail's biology and management.

Deer Biology and Management

Our survey on the whitetail's biology and management began with, "How many different species of white-tailed deer exist?"

Although most reference books name 38 subspecies of white-tailed deer, there is only one species of whitetails, *Odocoileus virginianus*. Nearly 27 percent of our respondents correctly answered the question. The other choices, and the percentage of respondents choosing them were:

✓ Two species, 8 percent.
✓ Three species, 19 percent.
✓ Four species, 23 percent.
✓ Five species, 13 percent.
✓ 10 species, 10 percent.

Some respondents considered this a tricky question. But we simply wanted hunters to know that — despite the great variation and adaptive qualities of whitetails — they're all of the same species.

Question: *Which animal is the closest relative of the white-tailed deer?*

Most readers, 41 percent, knew sheep were the whitetail's closest relatives. The other choices, and the percentage of respondents choosing them were:

- ✓ Llama, 32 percent.
- ✓ Oxen, 9 percent.
- ✓ Horse, 8 percent.
- ✓ Pig, 7 percent.
- ✓ Donkey, 3 percent.

None of the animals listed are in the deer family, *Cervidae*. The closest group to *Cervidae* would be the *Bovidae,* which includes sheep and oxen. *Cervidae* are browsers, and they're considered more primitive than *Bovidae,* which are grazers.

Sheep are considered the closest relative of white-tailed deer because both species thrive best in mixed open and forested habitats. Oxen would have been a good answer, but this species lives exclusively in grasslands.

The next closest relative to deer is the Llama, which is in the *Camelidae* family. This family shares the same suborder as whitetails, *Ruminantia,* which includes all species with a four-part stomach. The pig is loosely related to whitetails, with both belonging to a branch of the *Artiodactyla*. This group includes the even-toed ungulates, meaning they all have a two-toed hoof. The horse and donkey are distant relatives of whitetails, and belong to the group *Perissodactyla*, or odd-toed ungulates.

Question: *Can hunters determine a deer's sex by its tracks?*

Despite the opinion of 36 percent of our respondents, the deer's sex cannot be determined solely by its tracks. Many hunters rely on track depth to determine if a deer is heavy, which is only possible on soft ground. These hunters usually assume all heavier deer are bucks, which isn't always true. Regardless of track depth, there is no definitive sex determination in all cases.

The 64 percent of our readers who believe sex couldn't be determined from tracks acknowledged that in some circumstances — such as light snow — it might be possible. Perhaps Kathryn Collister of Falls Church, Va., said it best: "You can make an educated guess about a deer by its tracks — taking into consideration length of stride, width of stance, splaying and dragging — and temper it all with terrain, weather factors, and the type and condition of the

Readers' Survey, Part I:

ground. No concrete factual answer, though."

Ron Shoup of Olean, N.Y., summarized the most accurate answer when he wrote: "Some authors say they can; others do not. So maybe at times, yes; most of the time, no."

Question: *Can hunters determine an adult deer's age by its tracks?*

We thought this question might draw a response similar to the previous question, but more than 87 percent of our respondents correctly answered that age cannot be determined from tracks. Many acknowledged they could tell fawn tracks from adult tracks, but only when the size difference is easily noticed. As Shoup said: "Once the deer becomes an adult, it's probably less likely to tell the exact age. No one should have problems distinguishing a fawn track from a doe track. This is my opinion. I might be wrong!"

Several readers noted that older deer have worn hoofs, which leave rounded prints. However, detecting rounded prints, like other specific track observations, requires good surfaces such as snow or soft ground.

Question: *In which locations can you find white-tailed deer in the wild?*

More than 97 percent of our respondents correctly said white-tailed deer were found in North America, but only 71 percent correctly indicated whitetails live in Rhode Island. Some respondents might have thought we were being tricky in saying North America. Maybe they believed whitetails had to live throughout the continent. Slightly more than 12 percent of the respondents believed Hawaii had whitetails, and more than 36 percent said whitetails live in Alaska. Both states have never been home to whitetails.

The remaining correct choices, and the percentage of respondents choosing them were:

✓ Alberta, 80 percent.

✓ Central America, 46 percent.

✓ South America (Columbia, Peru, Ecuador and Bolivia), 23 percent.

✓ Europe (Finland, central Europe), 16 percent.

The remaining incorrect choices, and the percentage of respondents choosing them were:

✓ Greenland, 8 percent.

✓ Asia, 6 percent.

✓ Africa, 4 percent.

✓ Australia, 5 percent.

✓ China, 4 percent.

✓ Middle East, 3 percent.

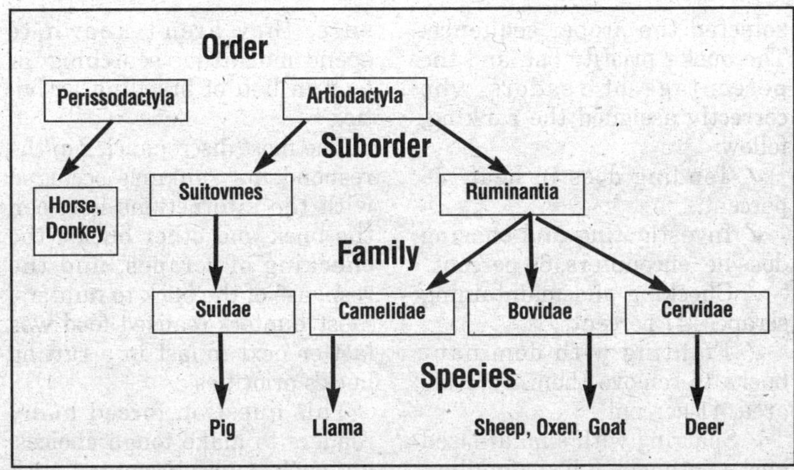

This chart shows where the deer fits in under the Artiodactyla order. Its closest relatives are sheep, goats and oxen.

Whitetails haven't been transplanted to any of these locations, but they have been established in New Zealand.

Question: How many times each year does a deer shed its coat?

Deer shed their coat twice a year, which was correctly selected by 55 percent of our respondents.

The incorrect choices, and the percentage of respondents choosing them were:

✓ One time, 31 percent.

✓ Zero, 12 percent.

✓ Three times, 1.5 percent.

✓ Four and five times, less than 1 percent.

All adult deer have a thin, reddish-brown summer coat of hair, which they shed between August and September. The summer coat gives way to a winter coat, which features brownish-gray hair with black tips. The winter coat has long guard hairs that cover a layer of short underfur, which insulates the deer and keeps it warm. The winter coat is shed in April and May as summer nears.

A fawn's coat is a set of white spots on a reddish-brown background. This coat remains from birth until the autumn shedding period, at which time it's replaced by the whitetail's standard winter coat.

Question: What are a buck's priorities during the rut's peak?

Many readers correctly

Readers' Survey, Part I:

selected the proper sequence. The buck's priority list, and the percentage of readers who correctly assigned the ranking, follow:

✓ Tending does in heat, 76 percent.

✓ Investigating and chasing does he encounters, 66 percent.

✓ Checking and maintaining scrapes, 47 percent.

✓ Fighting with dominant bucks to remove them from his area, 41 percent.

✓ Sparring with similar-sized bucks with whom he is familiar, 46 percent.

✓ Spending daylight in secluded areas to avoid hunters, 44 percent.

✓ Searching for food to store energy for winter, 57 percent.

This sequence recognizes the intent of a buck to breed does, find and tend does in heat, communicate with does and bucks in his area, defend does in his area from competing bucks, and maintain his place in the bucks' hierarchy.

The order of the final two choices is more open to discussion, but bucks search for food only when they have nothing else to do during the rut. In addition, during heavily hunted firearms seasons, bucks often reduce movements during daylight. Although bucks will sometimes pursue breeding activities despite hunting pres-

sure, they aren't known to spend much time searching for food in lieu of breeding activities.

The most discrepancies in the respondents' rankings occurred with the interactions between the buck and other bucks, the checking of scrapes, and the response of the buck to hunters. Most hunters realized food was last or next to last in a rutting buck's priorities.

This question forced many readers to make tough choices, although it also prompted Nick Godwin of Weidman, Mich., to ask, "Great quiz, but how does anyone know what is a priority to a buck?"

Question: *What is the most important factor determining the size of the antlers of all 3-year-old bucks in a particular year?*

The most important factor is the quality of the herd's nutritional intake, which was correctly picked by 57 percent of our readers. If bucks find ample quantities of excellent food, they could easily grow a thick, impressive rack. If they're forced to live on poor quality or low amounts of food, they could grow mere spikes or thin 4-point racks.

Genetics were believed to be the critical factor by 27 percent of our respondents, while 10 percent believed minerals and calcium were important. While arguments are long and strong on the role of genetics in antler development, recent work by researchers such as Harry Jacobson at Mississippi State University have shown genetics ultimately influence less than 5 percent of the buck's antler growth in any particular year.

Question: *Which mortality factor has the most impact on deer populations?*

Nearly 38 percent of our respondents correctly agreed that hunting is the most significant cause of death for whitetails. Across the whitetail's range, hunting accounts for more than half and sometimes more than 75 percent of a herd's annual mortality. Hunting is also important because it's the only cause of death that can be controlled. That means hunting is the management tool that determines the herd's composition, density and distribution.

Other factors that readers deemed important were weather, 21 percent; and starvation, 20 percent. Although these factors can be important in a local population, their effects in most regions rarely rival hunting mortality.

Question: *What time of day is deer vision most accurate?*

If we had a trick question in the survey, this one fit the description best. The most popular answer, which was marked by 52 percent of our readers, was that deer vision was equally accurate all the time. Only 11 percent correctly answered that the whitetail's vision is most accurate at night.

As most hunters know, the whitetail's vision is one of its weaker senses when compared to smell and hearing. Why? Consider the attributes vital to an animal if its activity is greatest during darkness. It needs a well-developed sense of smell, followed by good hearing and night vision. These are exactly the key features of the deer's sensory system.

The key to answering this question, then, is understanding the general features of the whitetail's eye, as well as the deer's activity patterns.

Deer are a night-adapted species, and their vision functions best in nocturnal situations. The pupil of a deer's eye is bigger than the pupils of day-adapted animals, which means the eye can receive large amounts of available light when the pupil is dilated (wide open). This is a major reason deer can see well in low light and at night.

Another feature of deer

Readers' Survey, Part I:

vision is a large field of view. The eyes are monocular on each side of the head, meaning that each eye covers an area of nearly 180 degrees. When a deer looks forward, it has binocular vision over a span of about 90 degrees, similar to humans. This combination of monocular and binocular vision gives deer a wide range of view.

Finally, an important feature of the deer's night vision is its ability to detect movement. Motion vision is a result of the eye's retina having many more rods than cones to act as photoreceptors. With their eyes providing a wide field of view, deer can easily catch movements in their peripheral vision. Because whitetails have a habit of moving slowly and — when alert — standing still for long periods, they have a distinct advantage over intruders, especially those less patient than themselves.

Nearly 30 percent of our readers thought deer vision was most accurate during daylight. Relatively speaking, deer likely have limited color vision, which is important in daylight. Still, they are thought to be capable of detecting changes in tones between some colors. Many hunters have sat motionless in the woods while deer have walked literally over their position. If deer had good daylight vision, and could associate the colors of certain objects with danger, then the sight of a still human would — by itself — send deer into flight.

Question: At what age will a white-tailed doe quit reproducing?

This question tricked few people. Nearly 73 percent of our respondents indicated that, as long as a doe is healthy, she will reproduce. Research from around North America has repeatedly shown that the oldest groups of does not only reproduce but typically have the highest rates of fawn production. With the advent of "reading" cross-sections of deer incisors to age older whitetails, biologists have discovered does 10 to 15 years of age and older that were pregnant.

Question: Which time of year is the most nutritionally stressful for a doe?

This question tested our readers' knowledge of the doe's caloric demands in a typical year. Despite variations in the quality and quantity of nutrition available throughout the year, does are most nutritionally stressed during late fawn-raising, or shortly before the fawns are weaned. Only 7 percent of our respondents picked this answer.

The most popular answers were:

✓ during late pregnancy, 34 percent.

✓ early pregnancy, 30 percent.

✓ early fawn-rearing, 19 percent.

Clearly, most readers believed pregnancy was the doe's more difficult time.

The stress experienced by a doe is greatest during pregnancy and fawn-raising, and is directly proportional to the total weight of the fawns she supports. The fawns' demands on their mother are greatest during lactation, and their needs grow as they increase in size and activity. The offspring are largest and most active during late fawn-rearing. Therefore, shortly before they're weaned, they demand the most nutrition from their mother. When a doe has two fawns to suckle that might be 40 to 60 days old, she is supporting nearly 50 pounds of additional deer. Research has shown that her nutritional demands might be 2 to 3 times that of a doe's without fawns.

Question: *What time of year is most nutritionally stressful for a buck?*

Most respondents, 61 percent, knew the most stressful time for bucks is the breeding season. At this time, bucks commonly lose 10 percent or more of their pre-breeding season weight. This weight loss is mostly caused by bucks increasing their home range from a few hundred acres in summer to up to a few square miles during the breeding season. While moving, the bucks spend their time in stressful pursuit, tending and courting does, maintaining scrapes, and interacting with other bucks. These priorities leave little time for feeding. Most bucks feed only when they aren't busy pursuing other breeding duties.

The second most common answer was "after the breeding season," which was picked by 34 percent of our readers. That's a reasonable answer because many bucks are in a rundown condition after the breeding season and, in the North where winters can be stressful, the post-breeding period can be difficult. In all cases, though, the post-breeding period is only stressful if environmental conditions create stress. Except for severe winters, bucks won't slip much further than the condition in which they ended

Readers' Survey, Part I:

the breeding season.

Question: How long does the deer's breeding season last in your area?

This question was designed to distinguish the rut — when peak breeding activity occurs — from the breeding season. The breeding season for white-tailed deer begins when the buck's testosterone levels rise, and it ends when testosterone levels fall.

In nearly all white-tailed deer populations, the breeding season lasts four months and, often, longer. In Northern ranges, the breeding season begins in early September and ends sometime after early January. It varies much more widely in the South. In some Southern regions, the breeding season could run from early September through February.

Given the above, the best answer was four months, which was selected by 3 percent of our respondents. We detected much indecision on this question:

✓ Two weeks, 22 percent.
✓ Three weeks, 17 percent.
✓ One month, 21 percent.
✓ Two months, 20 percent.

We expected many hunters might think the rut — the one or two weeks of peak breeding activity — constituted the breeding season. The wide distribution of answers suggests hunters knew the breeding season differed from the rut, but weren't certain when it began and ended.

Question: After being born, how long will it take most fawns to walk?

The most popular answer was five minutes, which was picked by 47 percent of our respondents, but 45 percent of respondents correctly chose one hour. A few readers, 4 percent, thought it would take six hours.

The best answer is one hour because, after a fawn is born, it requires more than a few minutes before it's ready and able to walk.

Question: How many sections are found in a deer's stomach?

Of our respondents, not quite half, 48 percent, knew whitetails had a four-part stomach. Other answers and the percentage of response were:

✓ Three sections, 21 percent.
✓ Two sections, 22 percent.
✓ One section, 7 percent.
✓ Five sections, 2 percent.
✓ Six sections, 1 percent.

As we discussed earlier, deer belong to the suborder *Ruminantia,* ungulates with a four-part or compound stomach. The common name for ruminants is "cud-chewers." This refers to the process by which animals consume food quickly, and later regurgitate and further chew it to improve microbial decomposition.

The whitetail's stomach is comprised of the rumen, reticulum, omasum and abomasum. The rumen is a large storage container that holds microorganisms which produce high-energy food. After being eaten, food spends the most time in the rumen, where fermentation occurs and fluids wash between the reticulum and rumen, suspending small particles. Eventually, the particles in the rumen fluid move into the omasum, where the fluid is absorbed. Finally, the particles move into the abomasum, or true stomach, where further breakdown occurs.

The whitetail's four-part stomach provides the species with highly evolved advantages. For one, it allows the deer to survive on low-quality diets. It also allows them to quickly consume large amounts of food and then retreat to protective cover to fully digest it over long periods of time.

Conclusion

As we expected, many topics

> *The whitetail's four-part stomach provides the species with highly evolved advantages. For one, it allows the deer to survive on low-quality diets. It also allows them to quickly consume large amounts of food and then retreat to protective cover to fully digest it over long periods.*

in Part 1 of our survey brought a mixed bag of answers. Some respondents apparently read more information into certain questions than was required to pick the correct answer.

Fortunately, most respondents took the survey in stride, and liked the challenge of testing their knowledge of the whitetail's biology. As reader Mike Dault said: "As a serious hunter, some of your questions surprised me. I probably got them wrong, but these are things that I never considered really important to know in deer hunting. Since you have sparked my curiosity, I will do more studying."

It's Easy to Misread Deer Behavior

Before leaping to conclusions about a deer's actions, logically apply some basic principles about deer biology and behavior.

■ *Jay McAninch, with Patrick Durkin*

After publishing our annual Readers' Survey in 1995, we were fascinated by the discussions — or debates — that grew from the hunting scenarios we asked about. In some cases, we even disagreed among ourselves on the right answer. Therefore, if you still don't like some of the answers that follow, feel free to write and share your thoughts with us. While we believe there is one best answer for each question, we have no doubt some hunters will interpret situations differently than we did.

Enough said. Let's get into it:

Question: *You're hunting early in the breeding season from a tree stand at the edge of a wooded area. The stand overlooks a pasture. A doe and fawn appear in the woods and move cautiously but steadily toward you. Both deer pass under your stand and head toward the pasture. At the pasture's edge, both deer stand erect, look in all directions, and move slowly into the pasture. As you glance back into the woods, you notice a buck on the same trail the doe and fawn traveled. The buck moves steadily along the trail, pausing occasionally to look intently ahead into the pasture. After the buck passes under your stand, you shoot and kill it. Check each of the following explanations that is most likely true, based on information in the preceding paragraph.*

Discussion: The most popular answer, 48 percent, was that the buck had been with the doe and fawn, and stayed behind to be sure they had moved safely into the pasture. Another 26 percent

Readers' Survey, Part II:

believed the buck was following the same trail as the doe and fawn, while 24 percent said the buck was scent-trailing the doe and fawn, and was obsessed with the doe being in heat. Less than 2 percent of the respondents said the buck was chasing the doe and fawn.

This question was tough for many avid hunters because they have experienced this situation, and likely drew on firsthand observations in forming their answer. The key to this question was to stick solely to the information in the scenario. Many readers injected their beliefs about deer behavior into their answers.

Let's start by breaking down several key points. First, an important factor in the relationship between the buck and doe is that the incident occurred early in the breeding season. Remember, the breeding season lasts several months in most areas, or for as long as bucks are capable of breeding. That means the incident happened weeks before the rut, which would mean the doe is not in heat.

The scenario we described offered no evidence, nor did it describe any behavior to imply the buck had been with the doe and fawn. Had the buck been with them, and if the doe had been in heat, the buck wouldn't let the doe move without being on her tail. Further, if the buck was following the doe from some distance down the trail, he would have had his nose on her trail. Either that, or he would have exhibited some behavior associated with courting the doe.

The most popular answer, however, was based on the belief that a buck will stay back while watching a doe and fawn "test" the safety of the trail ahead. The idea that a buck stays back to let a doe and fawn check for danger has been around a long time. Unfortunately, nothing could be further from the truth.

This notion is unfounded for many reasons.

First, hunters often see lone bucks following does or appearing on the same trail as other deer. Bucks following does is a common and natural behavior because bucks during the breeding season are consumed with finding and courting female deer. In fact, when bucks are not checking scrapes for signs of does and competing bucks, they'll be on the move, investigating any does they intercept. The fact bucks are often alone and usually on the move during breeding season could easily lead to the described scenario.

Second, if bucks routinely orchestrated "testing" behavior by does and fawns, the bucks would have a lower mortality rate than antlerless deer. But as we know, the reverse is true. In addition, buck mortality during the breeding season is higher than any group of deer because the rut causes bucks to lose much of their wariness. The preponderance of does and fawns in many deer populations is caused largely by the bucks' higher mortality rate.

Third, the impossibility of the manipulative buck belief is apparent if you try to figure out how a buck can make a doe and fawn enter the field first. We don't mean to be funny, but how could a buck tell a doe: "You go first. I'll wait to see if you get shot or attacked." The fact is, many bucks die while following a doe, but usually it's because they have lost all concern for their safety while pursuing a doe in heat.

Fourth, deer don't have a long-distance communication mechanism that would allow a doe and fawn far away from the buck to relay to him the location and degree of danger they detect. If, for example, the doe and fawn had passed you and then smelled you in your stand as they neared the pasture's edge, they likely would have flagged and moved closer to the pasture. How would the buck, who was some distance away, have known where the danger was located? And, more importantly, which direction would the doe direct him to go to avoid the danger? To flee safely, a deer must know the direction and approximate distance of danger, and the relative degree of alarm to exhibit.

Based on the above discussion, the best answer is that the buck was simply following the same trail as the doe and fawn. If you carefully read the information and make no assumptions, the only reasonable answer is the one that's least interesting.

The take-home lesson here is, when hunting, don't jump to hasty conclusions about what you see. Study each situation carefully, absorbing every detail you can about the deer's movements and body language. Realize that experience can occasionally make us "see" something that might not be happening in the current situation.

Leonard Lee Rue III

Many of the hunters who completed the 1995* Deer & Deer Hunting *Readers' Survey believed bucks allow does and fawns to "test" the safety of a trail ahead. In fact, the idea that a buck stays back to let a doe and fawn check for danger has been around a long time. Unfortunately, nothing could be further from the truth.

Question: A buck emerges from the woods on your left and walks down the wooded edge toward your stand. When he's about 40 yards away, he stops, stands erect, looks in several directions, and continues to move slowly toward you. As the buck moves, he frequently picks up his head to look around, and sharply flicks his tail side to side with every few steps. Which description of the buck's behavior is most likely true?

Discussion: Most respondents, 51 percent, correctly decided the buck was alert and was prepared to flag its tail and run. The remaining hunters were almost split. Many readers, 17 percent, said the buck had detected your presence, while 15 percent said the buck is alert but bothered by flies. Further, 12 percent said the buck had detected the presence of another buck, and 6 percent said the buck had detected a doe in heat.

The belief that the buck was alert was evident from several behaviors. He stopped frequently, stood in an erect posture, looked in several directions, moved slowly, frequently picked up his head, and sharply flicked his tail. All of these behaviors are tip-offs to a deer's high degree of alertness.

The single best clue to answering this question was the sharp tail flicking. This behavior is given moments before a deer flags and runs. To other deer, the tail flick is a sign the buck has determined something is not right in the area, and that he is about to flag and run once he locates the danger. A deer flicks its tail with the white hairs under the tail in a semi-erect position. When combined with the tail's sharp movements, the bright white hairs draw the attention of other deer and relay a danger sign.

A deer doesn't sharply flick its tail to deal with annoying flies. When bothered by flies, a deer lazily slaps its tail back and forth, not unlike the tail action of cattle. Also, when slapping at flies, the

> *When hunting, don't jump to hasty conclusions about what you see. Study each situation carefully, absorbing every detail you can about the deer's movements and body language.*

deer's tail hairs aren't erect.

From the information we provided, it wasn't possible to determine if the buck had detected and identified you, another buck, or a doe in heat. If the buck had detected and identified your presence, he would have flagged and run in a safe direction. At the least, he would have riveted his attention in your direction the moment he detected you. This is a behavior many hunters have unfortunately observed!

If the buck had detected another deer, his behavior would have differed from the scenario described. He would have fixed his attention directly on the other deer, stopped the alert behaviors, and taken some action after identifying the other deer. He likely would not have slowed his pace, would not have sharply snapped his head up and down, and would not have flicked his tail. If the deer he detected was a doe in heat, the buck would have demonstrated the behavior of a buck courting a doe. If he had detected another buck, he would have exhibited defensive behaviors or aggressive actions intended to determine the other buck's status.

Question: You're standing in your back yard in a city of 5,000 residents. You turn from working in your garden, which is about 50 yards from the house, and you're startled to see an 8-point buck about 30 yards away. The buck is standing erect and looking at you. He snorts a couple of times, and then stomps his left front hoof. What will likely happen next?

Discussion: Nearly all respondents, 77 percent, knew the buck was about to turn and run. The buck's behavior indicates he knew something was wrong, and that the source of his concern was in your direction, but that he wasn't certain what threat you represented. Usually, if a buck knows danger's location, but is uncertain what it is, he will stamp a hoof to alert other deer that danger is near. The buck is likely to hesitate only a moment longer because he has decided danger is nearby.

For the reasons outlined above, it's unlikely the buck would stay frozen in position, which is what 9 percent of our respondents believed. A deer that has stomped a hoof will not stay near a source of danger.

Almost 9 percent of our respondents thought the buck might take steps toward you to scare you, while 2 percent believed the buck might rush you to bluff you into moving. If the buck took any steps toward you, he wouldn't be trying to scare you. He would only be trying to determine what you were. Deer rarely become aggressive when confronting danger and, except for a doe protecting a fawn, deer never take chances to defend other deer. This buck is clearly in a state of high alarm, and is ready to escape as soon as he determines the danger's location and identity.

Question: You shoot a deer from your tree stand, and the deer runs out of sight. You get down and find the spot where the deer stood when you shot. You follow the trail 3 to 5 yards, and find blood in a spot about 3 to 4 inches in diameter. You follow the blood trail about 100 yards and, during that distance, the

It's Easy to Misread Deer Behavior

blood spots get continually smaller.

As you get about 100 yards away from where you shot the deer, the blood appears in small drops, and you can find them only every yard or so. As you take another step, the deer bolts from its bed 20 yards ahead. The deer runs out of sight without any obvious signs of injury. You walk to the bed and find a 3- to 4-inch blood spot. As you follow the deer's path from the bed, you find only a few blood spots for about 10 to 15 yards, and then nothing. Based on the information given, where was the deer hit?

Discussion: The keys to this situation are the small blood pool found just after the deer was hit, the diminishing size and number of blood drops for 100 yards, the fact the deer bedded within 120 yards of the shot, the splotch of blood in the bed, and the lack of a blood trail shortly after the deer left its bed. Another important consideration was that the hunter didn't appear to wait a specific amount of time before getting down from the stand. As a result, we can assume the deer bedded down in the amount of time it took the hunter to get within 20 yards of its bed.

> *Why will a white-tailed buck usually be last in line behind a doe and her fawns? Contrary to a long- and widely held belief, the buck isn't manipulating the other deer to check the area ahead.*

The pattern of an initial large splotch of blood, followed by a rapidly diminishing number and size of blood drops, is typical of a gut-shot deer. The initial splotches occur because of blood rushing to the surface wound. In such wounds, bleeding diminishes quickly because of clotting. Also, the body of a running deer is pumping blood to the heart, lungs and muscular areas, and not to the digestive tract. This shift in blood flow results in less blood in the gut as compared to the legs, neck or muscular areas.

Because of cramps in its gut, much like a severe stomachache, a gut-shot deer beds down as soon as it puts some distance between itself and the source of its concern. Its bed often contains blood splotches or blood pools because the priority for blood in a bedded deer is the wound, not the heart/lungs or muscular areas. Usually, the shorter the distance from the shot to the bed, the more critical and life-threatening the gut-shot wound.

The lack of a trail after the deer leaves its bed is caused by clotting and reduced blood flow to the wound. As the deer begins running again, blood flow is maximized to the heart, lungs and muscular areas, leaving little for the area around the surface wound or gut. The effect of this condition is a poor and difficult-to-follow blood trail.

The least likely answers to this scenario were that the deer was hit in the lower front legs, 9 percent of responses; or the deer was hit in the lower hind legs, 2 percent. A shot in these areas might break a limb, but it wouldn't cause bleeding that would produce the blood trail described. If the leg were broken, the blood trail would be continuous.

A few hunters, 9 percent, thought the shot grazed the deer's back, but that wound usually leaves large quantities of hair and little or no blood where the deer was standing. Remember, no hair was reported in the scenario. Also, such wounds usually cause superficial bleeding, which clots quickly. As a result, after an initial splotch of blood, the blood trail is usually short and poor.

Some hunters, 4 percent, believed the deer was hit through the liver. Based on the information provided, that would not be possible. A liver-shot deer will bleed continuously, whether running or bedded. That's because the liver never stops processing red blood cells. In addition, most liver-shot deer would be dead or seriously weakened by the time it went 120 yards from where it was shot.

A popular answer, 15 percent, was that the shot hit the deer through the front shoulder, but missed the chest cavity. Again, these circumstances don't fit the scenario's bleeding pattern. Muscle wounds bleed best while the deer is running because the blood flow to muscles is highest when the muscles are being used.

Although some clotting occurs, the jarring of the deer running leaves the wound open, and it will bleed continuously. Muscle wounds tend to leave little blood in a bed because this is when the wound is clotting and able to close up. Once the deer is jumped from its bed, the wound reopens because it's jolted again and begins bleeding with the rush of blood to the muscles.

Many hunters, 19 percent, believed the deer was hit through muscles high on the back. This hit would share many characteristics with the front-leg wound described above. Although this is a muscle, a wound high on the body reduces the blood flow to the ground, leaving a trail of blood drops rather than larger splotches. In addition, clotting is likely to have a greater effect on the blood trail because the wound is so high. The key here is that blood flow from this muscle wound would be continuous, and would have resumed after the deer got up from its bed. In fact, many muscle wounds leave a large blood splotch after the deer jumps from its bed because the clot breaks.

A reasonable but incorrect answer is that the shot passed through the rear of the chest cavity, missing the lungs and heart. This response was chosen by 21 percent of our respondents. That wound would likely produce an initial splotch and then bleed in diminish-

> *Deer rarely become aggressive when confronting danger and, except for a doe protecting a fawn, deer never take chances to defend other deer.*

ing amounts as the deer ran. The blood trail from wounds in the rear of the chest cavity don't involve major muscle groups, and could miss all organs. Therefore, they often don't bleed continuously and, in fact, might not bleed at all after the first 30 to 50 yards. Poor blood flows result because the only damaged tissue is the entrance and exit wounds.

This question frustrated many readers. They believed we didn't provide enough information to accurately assess the situation. Marty Wolf of Mankato, Minn., asked: "What weapon was I using? How far was the shot? What sound did the deer make when it was hit?" Donald Shaeffer Jr. of York Haven, Pa., and Gordy Bogner of Dewitt, Mich., wanted to know what type of hair was found at the site where the deer was shot. Also, David Uchtmann of

It's Easy to Misread Deer Behavior

Sparta, Ill., wanted to know the blood's color.

Perhaps Barry Schriver of West Lawn, Pa., had the best response: "This question surely stirred up some heated conversations among myself and my hunting partners."

Although this question was tough, our intention was to provide the limited information hunters often encounter in the field. Many times we don't have the luxury of having all the clues we would like to help determine the wound's type and severity. Our hope is that when facing a tracking challenge, hunters will logically apply some basic principles to lead them to a correct analysis.

Conclusion

One of our survey's objectives was to stimulate thought and discussion about relatively common hunting situations. Often, we have incomplete information when we need to make decisions, but must go with what we know at the moment. In addition, some hunters seek advice from others, yet offer only scant information about a situation.

We hope our survey made you look carefully for information in each scenario. We

> *A liver-shot deer will bleed continuously, whether running or bedded. That's because the liver never stops processing red blood cells. In addition, most liver-shot deer would be dead or seriously weakened by the time it went 120 yards from where it was shot.*

also wanted respondents to use the facts we provided, and couple them with some basic knowledge of deer behavior, biology and management to make the best judgment about a situation. We wanted you to scratch your head, get a little frustrated, and maybe do some reading to form an answer.

Allan Lonas of Summerville, Ga., summed it up best: "I have not had an exam since 1970! I think you got a very good point across with this survey. We think we know a lot about hunting and the whitetail. Thanks for the gut check!"

Chapter 2

Deer Browse

Anyone who spends much time in the woods knows deer are unpredictable. Whether it's their behavior, travel habits or physical traits, no two deer are exactly alike. As soon as you create labels such as "typical" or "normal," the next deer that comes along will shatter your notions.

Years ago, the editors of *Deer & Deer Hunting* decided to devote a special section in the magazine to short articles that discuss unusual occurrences, naming it "Deer Browse."

Recently, the scope of this section was expanded to include news briefs on deer and other interesting stories on deer hunters. The articles come from all corners of the United States.

Your *Deer Hunters' 1998 Almanac* includes the most interesting "Deer Browse" articles from the past year. We're sure these tidbits and unbelievable photos will become popular conversation items in your deer camp.

Deer Browse

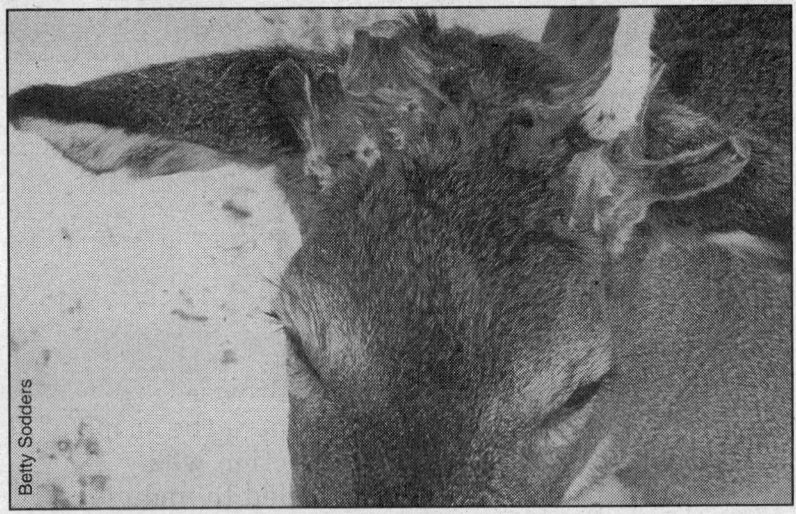

This antlered doe, killed in Michigan in 1991, had two pedicles that sported eight spikes. The deer also had about 12 hardened bumps underneath the skin on its forehead.

■ Michigan Doe's Skull Riddled with 'Bulbs'

As a manager of a hunting club, I have seen several antlered does over the years. However, the most unusual antlered doe I've seen was killed by Jim Meffers of Gulliver, Mich., in October 1991.

What made this doe different was the fact that multiple tines grew directly out of her skull. The doe had five spikes growing from the right pedicle and three on the left pedicle. However, she also had about 12 other mini-spikes, or hardened bumps, on her skull. The bumps were just below the skin's surface. While most of the bumps were small, some were as long as a half-inch. It was as if this doe's head resembled a bed of sprouting flower bulbs across the front of her skull.

The doe field dressed at 185 pounds. Game managers estimated the deer was 7½ years old.

Meffers killed the deer during archery season. He and other hunters saw the doe during summer and — by the appearance of her headgear —

thought she was a large buck. Meffers said the doe appeared as though it sported two huge bumps on her head, unlike anything he had ever seen.

— *Betty Sodders*

Editor's note — *For more on the mystery of antlered does, see John Ozoga's deer research article in the January 1997 issue. The issue will appear on newsstands Nov. 5.*

■ Deer Hunters Helping Fuel Tourism Economy

Skiing, boating, camping and sightseeing are popular tourist activities in Vermont, but they pale when compared to deer hunting.

The state's deer hunting season generates more than $68 million annually in tourism.

"It's a large chunk of change, and it comes after the leaves are off and before the skis are on," said John Hall of the Vermont Fish and Wildlife Department. "And to top it off, the money spent by deer hunters is distributed throughout all the communities in Vermont."

Hall said most of the expenditures are made on food, lodging, gasoline, clothing and equipment.

■ Video Teaches Responsible Shot Placement

In an effort to promote bow-hunting ethics and responsibility, the National Bowhunter Education Foundation and Precision Shooting Equipment have released a video titled, *Responsible Shot Placement for Bowhunting*.

The video provides information consistent with the International Bowhunter Education Program. The video also incorporates high-tech graphics and classroom interaction with impressive wildlife footage to communicate successful strategies for proper shot placement.

"We were glad to do this," said Pete Shepley, founder of PSE. "The future of our sport depends on effective bowhunter education."

Also helping with the video were *Deer & Deer Hunting* magazine, Haas Outdoors and Safari Club International.

For information on how to obtain copies of *Responsible Shot Placement for Bowhunting*, contact the National Bowhunter Education Foundation, 249B E. 29th St., Box 503, Dept. DDH, Loveland, CO 80538.

■ Whitetail Drops in on Alabama Motorist

Lots of people hit white-tailed deer with their vehicles, but it's doubtful many motorists have had encounters like the one experienced by Alabama's Kenny Pinn.

In February 1996, a 6-point buck:

✓ jumped through the windshield of Pinn's pickup truck,

✓ sat dazed in the passenger seat for a couple of seconds,

✓ kicked Pinn in the head, and

✓ smashed out the rear window and fled.

"It all happened in the blink of an eye," Pinn said.

Pinn was traveling at about 50 mph when the buck leapt onto the highway and ran toward his truck. The deer didn't touch the hood. It jumped straight into the windshield.

Pinn said the deer landed sitting upright in the passenger seat. Pinn quickly stopped the truck, got out, and tried to open the passenger door to let the deer out. However, before he could get his door open, Pinn was kicked by the flailing buck. Pinn tried to shield his head with his hands, but the buck kept kicking until it smashed through the rear window.

"I was bleeding very badly from the glass and the deer's

Kenny Pinn of Guntersville, Ala., displays the antlers of a buck that smashed through the windshield of his pickup truck.

hoofs," he said. "In a matter of a few short minutes, this deer messed up my truck and beat me up pretty good."

After he got home, Pinn realized the buck left behind its headgear. Looking down at the floorboard of his pickup, Pinn discovered the buck had broken off both antlers during the melee.

— *The Advertiser-Gleam, Guntersville, Ala.*

This New Jersey buck fawn died while trying to squeeze through the bars of a wrought iron fence.

The deer's hind leg became caught in front of the bar of an adjacent wrung and it was unable to free itself.

■ Buck Fawn Dies in New Jersey Cemetery

A buck fawn that wandered into a New Jersey cemetery died when it became caught in an iron fence.

Kevin Kyle found the deer in December 1994 after it been dead several days.

Kyle said the incident was odd because the deer must have walked a long way to get into the predicament. The cemetery is surrounded by a busy highway and a lake, and it is far from the nearest woods.

■ Oregon Man Cited for Attacking Buck Decoy

An Oregon man was cited for several game violations in October 1995 after he tried to "kill" a deer decoy with a knife.

Wardens had placed the decoy near a road where poaching was a problem. On Oct. 22, the decoy caught the attention of Michael Clarke, 34, who stopped and shone his car's headlights on the buck.

Clarke got out of his car and told his wife the deer was probably in a trance. With wardens watching from nearby bushes, Clarke grabbed a knife and crept up to the decoy and attempted to stab it.

The wardens quickly came to the decoy's rescue and apprehended Clarke.

— *The World, Coos Bay, Ore.*

■ Bow-Hunter Survives 3 Days in Woods

I looked up at my backpack, which was hanging from my tree stand 17 feet above me, and knew I was in trouble. The pack held everything I needed for survival. It might as well have been on another planet instead of in northeast Georgia.

I lay on the ground in excruciating pain. My right hip was broken and out of place. As I squeezed my right shoulder, it sounded like I was crushing a bag of potato chips.

I had felt nauseated the night before, but awoke early anyway to go bow-hunting. I was still feeling sick when I got into my stand that morning. I was not wearing a safety belt, and fell out of my stand when I vomited.

Although I had told my wife, "I'm going deer hunting in Banks County," no one knew exactly where I hunted. I figured when they found me, I'd be dead.

So there I lay, on a cold Saturday morning in October 1995, waiting to die.

I continued to vomit all day and long into the night. The only time I felt afraid was when three wild dogs headed toward me. "Man, I'm in big trouble," I said out loud. I hollered, and they growled at me but ran away.

I dragged myself on my left elbow and knee, which became

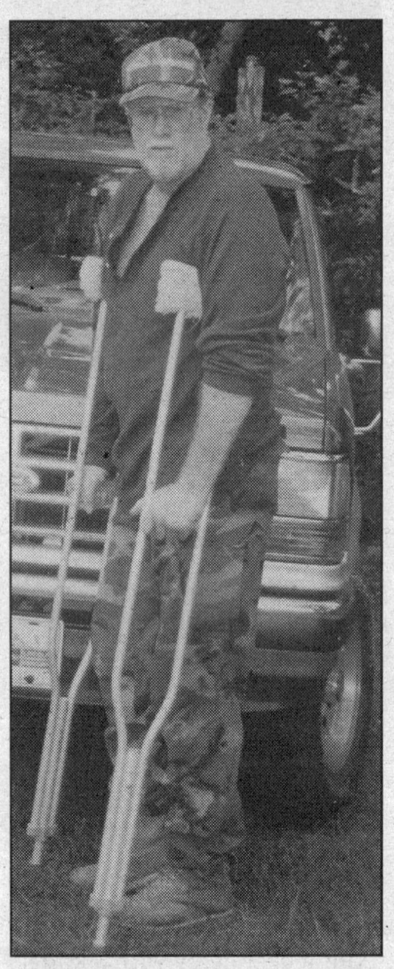

Harold Roebuck, 56, was bow-hunting in Oakwood, Ga., when he became sick and fell from his tree stand. He lived on worms and lake water for three days before being rescued.

a painful, bloody mass, downhill to a lake to get water. I cringed in pain with each movement.

I knew I stood a chance of surviving. I had to find some food. Based on my survival training in the Army, I pulled bark off pine logs and ate grub worms and red ants. It surprised me how much strength they gave me. I felt something stinging my leg. A centipede was hauling off one of my dad-blamed worms! I felt angry. I thought, what are you doing, stealing my worm?

Although the lake was only about 100 yards away, I didn't reach it until Monday evening. I drank 10 cans of delicious, cold water from the lake, using an empty soda can I found. "Thank you, God," I said.

I felt cold and was shaking. A light rain started splashing on the lake so the night would be cold. I figured I would have a peaceful death. After making a bed of leaves, I prayed for a few minutes. My main concern was for my family.

A beaver swimming near me had become relatively tame. He splashed water on me, and I said, "Can't you let a man die in peace?"

On Monday night, the silence was broken by human voices. I was rescued! A son-in-law had brought others to look for me. They strapped me to a board, and 12 men took turns carrying me 1½ miles around the base of the mountain to an ambulance.

In the hospital, I had surgery on my shoulder and hip. Doctors said I had gotten food poisoning when my wife and I ate out the night before I went hunting.

I lost all my teeth from the fall out of the tree stand, and I have chronic pain in my legs. I had hip replacement surgery last fall.

Looking back, I wish I had obeyed the warning signs when I felt sick before going hunting, and I wish I had told someone exactly where I was going.

— Harold Roebuck, told to Sara Hines Martin

■ Pope and Young Upholds Let-Off Rule for Bows

The Pope and Young Club has upheld its long-standing rule that limits the let-off of compound hunting bows to 65 percent for purposes of record-book entries.

The widespread marketing and use of high let-off compounds prompted numerous questions and concerns about the club's policy. After reviewing the 10-year-old rule, the P&Y board of directors unanimously voted to uphold the 65 percent let-off stipulation.

Deer Browse

This Pennsylvania whitetail died after getting its leg wedged in the crotch of a hemlock.

The fawn was reaching for low-hanging branches when the bizarre accident happened.

■ Whitetail Dies Reaching for Branches

I was grouse hunting near my Selingrove, Pa., home on Jan. 20, 1996, when I found a buck fawn that must have endured a long, painful death.

The fawn was lying at the base of a hemlock, with it left leg wedged in the crotch of the tree. The deer obviously became trapped when it was feeding on low-hanging branches.

Although this photo was taken one day after most of our snow melted, we had more than 4 feet of snow on the ground up until Jan. 18.

— William Sordoni

■ Buck Rescued from Underground Trap

Michigan conservation officer Dwayne Painter has observed some odd encounters with wildlife, but a recent experience with a white-tailed deer might be the oddest of his career.

Painter was called to an apple orchard in Honor, Mich., to investigate an emergency call concerning a a 6-point buck. Aaron Meade, a town resident, said his father had been picking apples when he heard an unusual underground noise. He searched the area and discovered the noise was being made by a 6-point buck, which had fallen into an abandoned well and was trying to jump out of the underground trap.

When Painter arrived, the buck was thrashing in the 6-foot square well. To make matters worse, the well was holding more than 3 feet of water. Painter said the deer probably stumbled into the hole at night, falling headfirst.

The rescue proved to be a difficult job. Painter, another conservation officer and Meade tried to rescue the agitated buck by pulling him up with a makeshift winch. First, they made a tripod from 2-inch saplings and dropped a noose over the buck's head.

The men intended to merely

This Michigan buck became trapped after falling into an abandoned well. Conservation officers rescued the deer by building a tripod out of saplings and using a rope to hoist the buck from the 6-foot-deep hole.

pull the buck part way through the opening, then grab his antlers to complete the rescue. However, when the buck reached the surface, it lunged suddenly and began thrashing. Painter quickly grabbed the buck's antlers and wrestled the 115-pound buck to the ground. Luckily, Meade pulled the rope free before the buck could get up.

The exhausted buck ran about 100 yards and collapsed. After a brief rest, however, he jumped up and bounded into a nearby woodlot.

Deer Browse

■ Deer Work to Rid Raccoons from Feedlot

I've managed several hunting clubs in Michigan over the past two decades and have observed that deer herds in remote areas often tend to be territorial and aggressive. However, I've never seen deer behave as aggressively as they do when forced to share food with other animals.

At a Menominee County, Mich., hunting club, I helped manage a herd of about 40 whitetails. During early fall it was not uncommon to see more than 20 raccoons vying with deer for food the club supplied. At times, the deer so resented the raccoons they would escort the raccoons out of the area.

Three does would usually work together to shoo the raccoons from the feed. Forming a reverse arrow point, with two deer on each side of the raccoon, the third doe served as "pointman," walking just behind the raccoon and forcing it to slowly move away from the feed. The does would escort a raccoon 500 to 1,000 feet away from the dried corn, oats and apples.

It was also not unusual for the deer to chase the raccoons and tree them in a nearby apple orchard.

— Betty Sodders

■ Doe Crashes in on Funeral Visitation

A doe fawn, which had been hit by a car, crashed through the chapel window of a Manitowoc, Wis., funeral home during a funeral visitation in April 1996.

The doe broke through a storm window and an interior double-hung window in the south chapel of the funeral home while a visitation was in session in a nearby room.

An owner of the funeral home heard the crash and found the deer bleeding and tangled in some curtains. The deer stopped thrashing when the owner turned off the lights. The semi-conscious deer remained calm until wildlife officers arrived. The officers removed the deer after shooting it with a tranquilizer gun.

Almanac Insights

Antlers & History

Aside from the hide, deer antlers were the most useful parts of the carcass for American Indians. They relied on antlers for arrow and spear points, needles, and other essential tools.

■ Hunter's Patience Pays Off with Record Buck

Dennis Mackeben of La Crosse, Wis., has hunted the same farm for 15 seasons. Although he's bagged several bucks from the property, Mackeben hoped that someday the farm would produce a record-class buck.

His patience paid off last fall.

On opening day of the gun-deer season, Mackeben bagged one of Wisconsin's all-time largest non-typical bucks, which scored 197⅛ on the Boone and Crockett system. The 17-pointer ranks No. 76 on the state's all-time B&C list.

Mackeben and his hunting party hunt from tree stands on the hilly property, which is located in Buffalo County.

"I've shot four very nice bucks on the ridges," Mackeben said. "But this is certainly the granddaddy of any deer we have seen up there."

After a rather uneventful day of hunting, Mackeben saw the buck just minutes before the end of shooting hours. Mackeben's son was walking to meet him when he jumped two deer out of their beds. The buck eluded the shots of another hunter before it approached Mackeben's stand.

Dennis Mackeben killed this non-typical buck on opening day of Wisconsin's 1995 gun-deer season. The buck scored 197⅛ on the Boone and Crockett system.

The buck then appeared about 30 yards to the left of his stand. He killed it cleanly with a slug from his shotgun.

The 4½-year-old buck had a rack with an inside spread of 19¾ inches.

— *Kathy Dugan*

Life in the wild can appear cruel, but everything serves a purpose. In June, and especially during years when fawn production is high, bears prey heavily on fawns. In fact, fawns become a major source of the bear's protein during these times.

■ Death of Fawns Depicts Nature's Reality

Life in the wild can be cruel by human standards. However, much of what happens has a purpose, no matter how gruesome it might seem. Bear researcher Terry DeBruyn of Marquette, Mich., witnessed such an event recently between black bears and two white-tailed deer fawns.

Through the use of radio collars, DeBruyn tracked two bears, a 10-year-old sow and her 5-year-old daughter. DeBruyn followed the bears throughout their day-to-day activities, photographing them and keeping track of their behavior.

The bears' predation of white-tailed fawns is something DeBruyn has documented since the beginning of his research six years ago. He has seen both bruins catch and kill fawns each year.

When fawns are abundant, as they were in 1995, the bears added a significant amount of protein to their diets by preying on small whitetails in June.

Two for One

For the first five years of his research, each time DeBruyn saw a bear kill a fawn, it was a single fawn. This is partly because does with twins usually hide the fawns apart from each other to reduce the chances of losing both to a predator.

However, last year DeBruyn watched as the 5-year-old bear and her cubs found and killed twin fawns.

DeBruyn was filming the threesome as they walked along the edge of a wetland when they jumped doe. The adult bear rushed toward the spot where the doe had been and pounced on a fawn that was bedded near its mother. He said the fawn was only a few hours old.

When DeBruyn stepped up on a log to get a better vantage point, he spotted a second fawn hiding on the forest floor in front of him. The bear carried off the first fawn and fed on it for a while, then returned to the area and eventually spotted the second fawn. Amazingly, the fawn remained motionless, even as the bear sniffed it. The close proximity of both fawns indicates they were born shortly before the bears wandered into the area.

Life's Lessons

While their mother was killing the first fawn, the cubs climbed a tree. They called for the sow from their perch after she grabbed the second fawn. Upon hearing them, the bear dropped the fawn and went to the base of the tree to make sure the cubs weren't in danger.

It was at least 15 minutes later before the bears returned to the second fawn, which was still alive. To train her cubs how to kill, the sow allowed them to paw and bite the struggling fawn. After a few minutes, the mother bear led her cubs a quarter-mile away to rest.

Their lessons with the still-living fawn resumed 2½ hours later. DeBruyn said the bears chewed the fawns ears and nose off before finally killing it. He said the incident was difficult for him to watch, but he knew it was not his place to intervene.

— Richard P. Smith

Almanac Insights

The Rumen Factor

As ruminants, white-tailed deer are highly adaptable. For example, during severe Northern winters, a deer's digestive system can draw enough nutrients from woody browse and cedar fronds to help the animal survive.

■ Absence of Testes Caused Buck to Grow 'Cactus' Rack

Although I've killed some dandy bucks near my home in eastern North Carolina, it will be hard to top the trophy I killed the day after Christmas in 1995.

My son and I were hunting near Maysville, N.C., when we decided to set up in a swamp. My son decided to hunt one area with his dogs, which is legal in North Carolina, while I set off in another direction.

By the time I settled into my stand, the temperature had fallen to 22 degrees, and the wind picked up. I held tight about an hour before hearing the first activity of the day — my son's beagles had picked up a deer's scent and were chasing it my way.

Unfortunately, the deer passed through a thicket about 150 yards from my stand, and I never got a glimpse of it. The dogs stayed on the trail, but were soon out of earshot.

With the cold wind biting through my clothing, I decided to move toward a stand of cedar, sweet gum and maples. I set up my portable seat on a tree limb and vowed to stay put at least three hours.

I didn't see or hear anything

The absence of testes in this North Carolina buck caused it to grow its unusual rack.

the rest of the morning. However, as I stood up to stretch shortly before 1 p.m., I saw a deer's tail moving through the brush about 40 yards to my right. I quietly raised my rifle and waited for the deer to enter a clearing. When it did, I couldn't believe my eyes. The deer was not only big, but it appeared as though its antlers were covered with moss.

After making the shot, I realized the buck sported a velvet "cactus" rack. As we began to field dress the buck, my son and

I discovered the cause of the unusual antler growth — the buck had no testicles. Other than that, the buck appeared healthy. It weighed 180 pounds field dressed.

The rack has 24 points that measure 1 inch or more, and our wildlife biologist aged the deer at 5½ years.

Besides testicular injuries, antler growth can be affected by a combination of factors, including malfunctions of a buck's thyroid and/or pituitary glands.

In cases of testicular injuries or absence of testes, antlers develop in the velvet but rarely calcify. Therefore, these deer won't shed their antlers, and the antlers experience continuous growth. The result, as documented in German research, is an antler "wig."

— *Joe S. Cunningham Jr.*

■ Boy's Hard Work Pays off with Huge 13-Pointer

Gavin Sisson had to take a summer job to prepare for his 1996 deer hunt, but his hard work paid off big.

Sisson, of Tisdale, Saskatchewan, needed just one shot to bag an impressive 13-point nontypical buck. The buck's rack scored 191⅜ on the Boone and

Gavin Sisson bagged this 13-point buck near Tisdale, Saskatchewan, in 1996.

Crockett system.

In anticipation of his Oct. 4 birthday, Sisson took a summer job helping a beekeeper. He saved his earnings and bought a .30-30 and a hunting license. He even stocked up on magazines so he could learn more about deer and deer hunting.

Then, just 46 days into his hunting season, Sisson's persistence paid off. Armed with his new gun and a set of rattling antlers, he set up in a wooded area near a gravel pit. He clashed the antlers together a few minutes, then stopped to listen. Within moments, a large buck responded.

Deer Browse

Sisson responded too — dropping the buck with a double-lung shot from his iron-sighted rifle.
— *Dan Schmidt*

■ Late March Storm Kills Piebald Fawn

A snowstorm that struck Mighigan's Upper Peninsula during late March 1996 was the last straw for some whitetails. The storm, which dumped about 2 feet of snow in parts of the region, killed hundreds of deer.

A piebald buck fawn in northern Marquette County was one of them. The fawn had been feeding irregularly on food Carol and Terry Brady of Marquette placed at their camp. Because of the deer's unique coloration, the Bradys were able to track its progress.

The deer had a pink nose and hoofs. Its lower legs were white, and there was more white than normal on other parts of its anatomy, including a band extending from its nose to its forehead.

Carol Brady said she first saw the piebald on Jan. 4. It was with its mother, which had a normal pelt.

The fawn's behavior was as odd as his pelt. Brady said the fawn was extremely aggressive, fending off all but the largest deer while feeding.

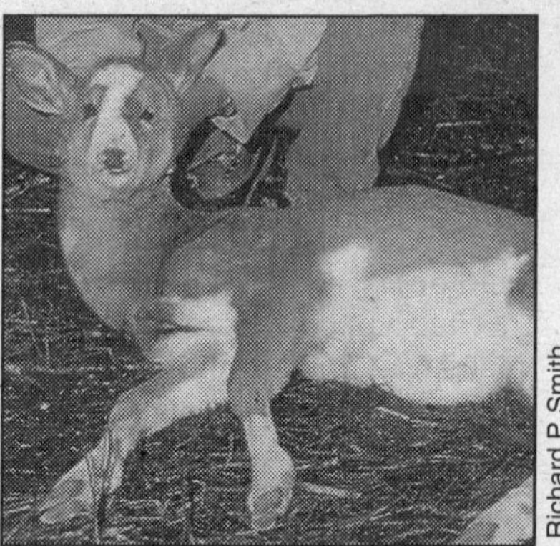

This piebald buck fawn died in a brutal March 1996 snowstorm in Michigan's Upper Peninsula.

That behavior enabled the buck to get his share of food.

Ironically, the Bradys saw the fawn several times in March, and it appeared healthy. They saw it three days before the storm when it was one of 47 deer to show up at the feeder.

After the storm, the piebald didn't show for six days. When it did, it was sick and weak. It died the next day.

Despite the handouts, several other deer died in the area of the Bradys' camp. This is a good example of how many whitetails rely on natural food sources for survival during Northern winters.
— *Richard P. Smith*

Chapter 3

Tips, Tricks and Other Helpful Information

There's more than one way to skin a deer, and there's many ways to prepare for deer season.

If you're looking for new ways to improve your deer hunting skills, they're all here.

We've packed this chapter with everything from a comprehensive how-to section to tips and tricks to make you a better deer hunter.

You'll learn new ways to attract deer to your hunting area, and you'll discover how to make your hunting equipment perform more accurately and efficiently.

You'll also learn quick and easy ways to field-dress, skin and butcher deer.

The chapter also includes several informative short articles from manufacturers of deer hunting equipment. Their contributions include insightful articles on everything from mounting riflescopes to selecting ideal camouflage patterns.

We're confident this chapter includes all the information you'll need to prepare for deer season.

Field-Dressing Tips

Field dressing a deer doesn't have to be a tedious, messy chore. Do it the easy way. Follow these five simple steps the next time you field-dress a whitetail:

1) With the deer on its back, carefully open the deer's abdomen.

2) Place a small log under the rump to get it off the ground. Cut deeply around the rectum, being careful not to cut off or puncture the intestine. Pull to make sure the rectum is separated from tissue connecting it to the pelvic canal. Do not split the pelvic bone. Lift the animal's back quarters a bit, reach into the front of the pelvic canal, and pull the intestine and connected rectum into the stomach area.

3) If you want to make a full shoulder mount, do not cut open the chest cavity. Reach into the forward chest, find the esophagus, cut it off as far up as possible, and pull it down through the chest. If the buck won't be mounted, split the chest and sever the esophagus at its lower end. Or, simply cut into the deer's throat patch deeply enough to sever the esophagus. After it's cut, reach into the chest cavity, find the lower end of the esophagus and pull it through.

4) Roll the deer onto one side and cut the diaphragm away from the ribs all the way to the backbone area. Roll the deer onto its other side and finish cutting away the diaphragm.

5) Leaving the deer on its

Carry Tree Steps the Easy Way

A rifle or shotshell belt works great for transporting tree steps. The belt keeps the steps from hitting each other, and it makes them easily accessible when you climb a tree. This trick eliminates the noise and bulk caused by carrying steps in a fanny pack or pants pockets.

Most one-piece steps have a larger diameter than a shell casing, so the steps fit snugly in the belt. Otherwise, sew the slots to get a closer fit. To

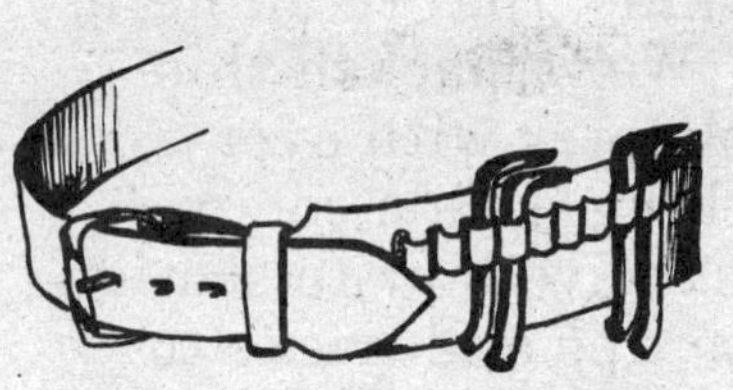

organize steps in your fanny pack, sew a 10-loop section of the belt into the pack.

Use this trick this season, and the only noise you'll hear walking to your stand will be the leaves under your feet.

— *Steven E. Colf, West Valley, N.Y.*

side, grab the esophagus with one hand and the rectum/intestine with the other. Pull hard. The deer's innards will come out in one big package with a minimum of mess.

How to Cape a Trophy

Caping — the process of skinning out a trophy deer's shoulder and head — is best left to the taxidermist. In a remote setting, however, storage problems may require you to cape a deer if you want to preserve it as a full shoulder mount. Follow the illustration above when making your cuts.

1) With a short, sharp knife, slit the skin from the top of the withers, up the back of the neck to the midpoint between the ears. Now, going back to the withers, circle the body with another cut. This should leave plenty of hide for the taxidermist.

2) Peel the skin forward up to the ears and jaws, exposing the point where you want to cut through the neck. The easiest way to separate the head from the neck is to make an encircling cut through the neck to the atlas joint, the first vertebra under the skull. This is the only joint on the neck that has no interlocking bones.

3) Remember, when field dressing a trophy to be mounted, don't cut into the chest or neck area. If blood gets

Keep Gun on Shoulder

Rifle and shotgun slings allow hunters to free their hands when they drag a deer out of the woods. Slings also make things lighter on a hunter at the end of a long day. How many times have you been walking or dragging a deer out of the woods when the gun slips off your shoulder?

There is an easy solution: Find a good-sized button and sew it on one of the shoulders of your hunting coat. With a button in place, the sling will stay put and allow you to concentrate on dragging the deer or getting back to camp.

— Matthew Stinson, Ardsley, Pa., and Ronald Shialabba, Pittsburgh, Pa.

on the area to be mounted, wash it off with snow or water as soon as possible. Also, when taking the deer out of the woods, place it on a sled or rickshaw. All it takes is one sharply broken branch on a deadfall to damage the hide.

Skinning Made Easy

Skinning deer does not have to be a laborious chore that leaves hair all over the meat. Using a car, truck or come-along, you can winch off the hide in about 5 minutes of work.

1) With the deer hanging by its neck, slice the hide around the neck as close to the head as possible. (Don't cut into the meat. The neck muscles bear much force later as the hide is pulled off.)

2) Cut down the front of the neck to the opening made during field dressing.

3) Saw off the legs slightly above the knee joints.

4) Pull the neck hide down until about one foot of it is free. Take a golf-ball-sized rock or 1.5-inch section of 2-by-2 and wrap it into the hide's end. Make a tight package and cinch it off with high-quality nylon rope of about 3/8-inch thickness. A double half-hitch works well.

5) Tie the rope's other end to a car, truck or come-along hook. Back up the vehicle until the hide is pulled to the brisket and shoulders. It will bind slightly here. If necessary, have someone work the hide around the brisket. With tension on the rope, the hide will slide over fairly easily.

Skinning a deer accelerates cooling of the meat. Normally, skinning a deer is easiest when the carcass is still warm, so experienced hunters normally skin the deer as soon as possible, or practical.

In extremely cold weather, immediate skinning is not necessary. In fact, it is beneficial in some circumstances to leave the hide on the carcass to prevent the meat from freezing. As a general principle, meat quality depends upon rapid and uniform cooling of meat. Quick freezing, or repeated freezing and thawing can cause meat to be tough.

Silence Noisy Chains

To silence and camouflage tree-stand chains, I conceal them in bicycle inner tubes.

First, take a rubber inner tube, cut it into one piece, and remove the air valve. To feed the chain though the inner tube, tie a piece of string to the end link, and snake it through the tube.

This trick is easy and inex-

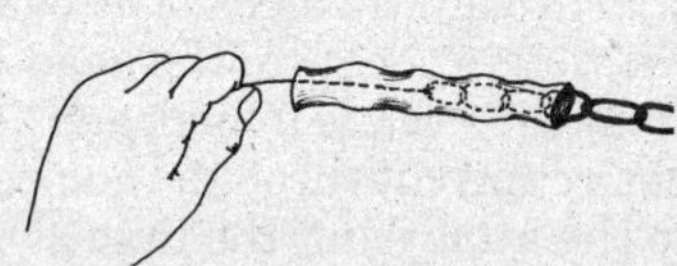

pensive. Most bike shops will give you punctured inner tubes for free.

— Henry Holt,
Lawrenceville, N.M.

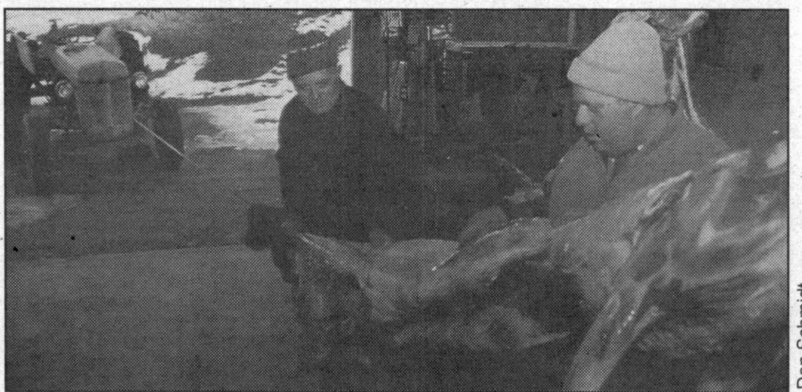

It's easy to pull a hide from a deer carcass when using a tractor or automobile. This process also helps keep hair off the meat.

If you do not immediately butcher the skinned deer carcass, cover the meat with a white, commercial deer bag made out of cheesecloth. Such bags permit further cooling and air circulation, while also keeping out insects. You can discourage flies from attacking the exposed meat by liberally sprinkling black pepper on it.

After a deer is skinned, the surface meat dries to the touch, a condition known as being "glazed." In this condition, such meat will stay in good shape for two to three days if the temperatures stay moderately cool (not hotter than 40 to 50 degrees).

Put Deer at Ease

The problem with bow-hunting in areas without large trees is that it's hard to stay hidden. I've found that mesquite trees make good tree-stand trees, but it's difficult to find one that allows you to place a stand high enough off the ground to stay hidden.

To improve your odds, camouflage yourself as best you can, and place one or two dove decoys in a nearby tree. Doves are wary, and usually won't stick around when humans are present. I've found the dove decoys seem to put skittish deer at ease.

— James Tassin, Santa Fe, Texas

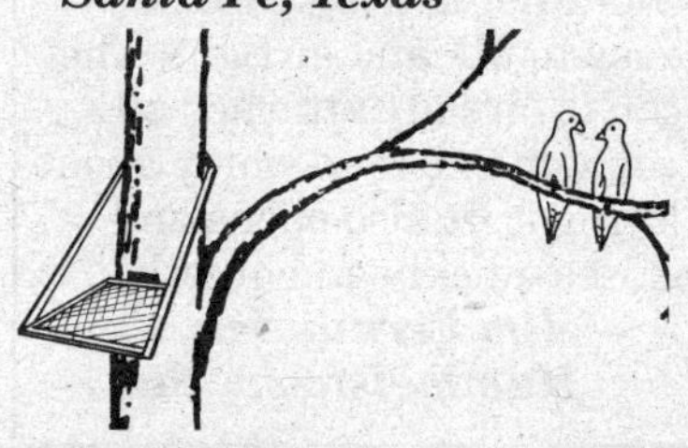

How Far Can a Wounded Deer Travel?

Every fall around the evening fires in the deer camps the old question has come up as to how it is possible for a deer to run from fifty to 200 yards after his heart had been perforated by a bullet. We all know he does

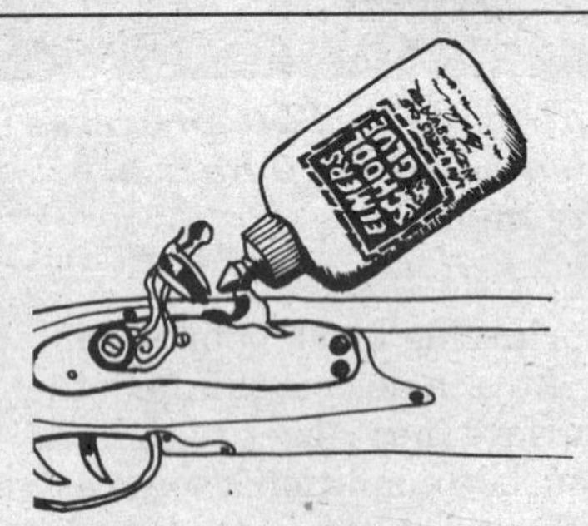

Cheap and Easy Powder Flask

In Pennsylvania, we are required to use flintlocks during the muzzleloading season. Often, the fine 4F powder leaks out into my coat pockets and makes a mess. It is also inconvenient to refill.

I found a glue bottle makes the job easy. I use a clean, dry school-glue bottle. The container is transparent, easy to fill, and airtight. The cap is already attached so you don't have to worry about losing it. It also opens and closes quickly and quietly.

— *Jim Fernandez,
Hummelstown, Pa.*

this but to date no answer has really explained how. We usually wound up the evening in agreement on but two points: 1) The deer should drop when circulation ceases and the brain ... "suffocates." This should happen almost immediately after the heart is perforated, for, of course, it is taken for granted the heart stops instantly. 2) As we know deer have run 200 yards after a heart shot, this explanation cannot be true and there is something phony about it somewhere. So the question has never been logically answered as far as the deer hunters are concerned.

Then, on October 31, 1928, murderer John W. Deering was placed before a stone wall in Utah State Prison with an electro cardiograph attached to his person. He was outwardly calm. The prison doctor placed a target over his heart. Five picked riflemen fired at that target at short range and four bullets simultaneously pierced his heart. Yet Deering's heart did not stop when pierced by four bullets but continued to beat for 15.6 seconds thereafter. The cardiograph record also showed that a few moments before the shots were fired, through fear, Deering's heart beats, normally 72 per minute, were increased to 180 per minute.

Now I cannot say that the

effect of a heart shot on a deer and a man are in any way similar. But let us see what would happen if we suppose this might have a bearing on the deer question.

If the deer is frightened before the shot, his heart beats would increase tremendously, also increasing circulation of blood to the brain and muscles. And how far would he run in the 15.6 seconds before his heart stopped? At Anticosti Island I timed a mature white-tailed deer over a measured course with a stopwatch. It was shot at but purposely missed. Its speed was 18 miles per hour.

The highest speed when another deer was fully extended and had to run, was about 30 miles per hour. At 18 miles per hour, the deer could travel 137 yards in 15.6 seconds. At 25 miles per hour the deer could travel about 152 yards. At 30 miles per hour the deer could travel about 229 yards.

Doesn't it sound to you a little bit as if John Deering may have solved the riddle and that the deer's heart does not stop when perforated?

— William Monypeny Newsom

How to, and Not to, Trail a Wounded Deer

More often than not, it's wise to trail a deer immediately. Three common myths on why a hunter should wait include:

1. The deer will lie down and "stiffen up."
2. The hunter needs a pipeful of tobacco.
3. The deer will get the "blind staggers."

In fact, there are several good reasons why a hunter should take up the trail immediately. Those reasons include:

1. It's snowing.
2. It's raining.
3. You're in an area of high

Positively Identify Deer Hair

Sometimes it's impossible to know exactly where your bullet or arrow strikes a deer. A great way to pinpoint a wound's location is by identifying hair cut off by the bullet or arrow. Be sure of your hits by making an identification book that contains actual deer hair. Use a tweezers to pluck hair from various locations of a hide, place them in small plastic bags and secure them in a notebook. Then, mark where the hairs came from. (i.e. heart area, brisket, back, etc.)

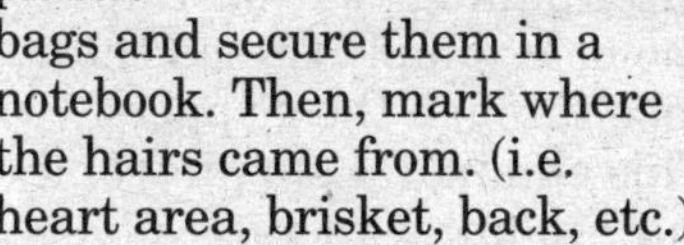

— Gary Huber
Hamburg, N.Y.

Hang Deer Fast, Easy

Hanging a deer can be a difficult one-person job because it's hard to tie off the rope at the desired hanging point. To make this job easier, I use the "grippers" that fishermen rely on to tie off anchors. I've found nylon grippers work better than steel ones.

Take two long screws and attach the grippers to the side post of your hang pole. After pulling your deer up the pole, simply thread the rope through the grippers. This eliminates slipping and hard-to-untie knots.

— Ronald Schiro, Lansing, Ill.

hunter density.

4. Darkness is approaching and you can't hunt in the morning.

5. Tracking takes place freely in warm weather.

6. Deer bleed freely in warm weather, which inhibits blood loss.

7. Trailing wounded deer with dogs is permitted in the area you hunt.

8. Rigor mortis does not occur until three to six hours after death.

9. A running deer has three times the heart rate of a bedded deer.

10. Movement creates greater and more rapid blood loss, thus inhibiting coagulation.

Wounded Deer Behavior

Total concentration and persistence are required to find wounded deer. Hunters must pay attention to details and treat every blood trail as the path to a dead deer.

While wounded deer can exhibit unusual behavior, hunters can study signs to determine where their bullet or arrow hit the animal. Use these descriptions to help unravel the trail of a wounded deer:

A. Broken Foreleg 

A deer with a broken fore- leg will leave

Attract Deer with Water

I use an antelope hunting tactic to attract deer to my hunting area. Deer need three things to survive: cover, food and water. Most places have adequate supplies of food and cover, but water is not always readily accessible.

Near my hunting stand, I installed a plastic swimming pool that's 5 feet wide and 12 inches deep. In just a few weeks, deer activity near my stand dramatically increased. Plastic 55-gallon drums cut in half also work well and are more durable.

It doesn't matter if a pond or river is located nearby. I live within a half-mile of a pond, but my pool is still a popular watering hole.

It's wise to add a small ramp on one side of the pool. You'll find that rodents and frogs will also use the pool as a watering hole. The ramp allows them a way out in case they fall into the pool.

— *Steve Strong, Mattawan, Mich.*

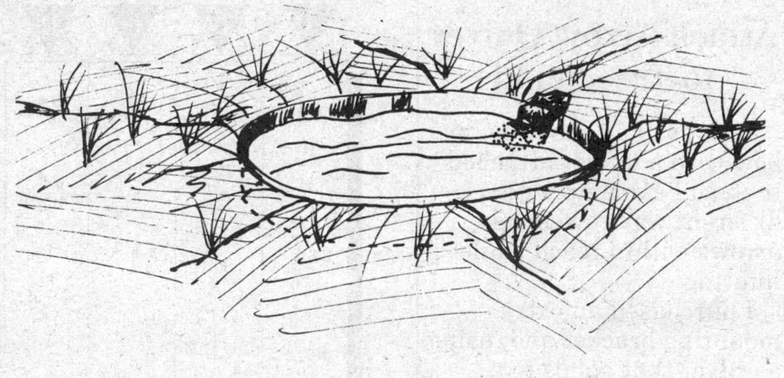

drag marks in the snow or dirt. A drag mark might not be evident at first. Another sign of a broken foreleg is the evidence of only three hoofprints in the tracks.

in the snow or dirt. Tracks from a deer with this wound will only include three hoof-prints: the two forelegs and one hind leg.

B. Broken Hind Leg

A deer with a broken hind leg will also leave drag marks

C. Bullet Through Lungs, Liver or Intestines

Deer shot through the intestines, liver or lungs often leave tracks that

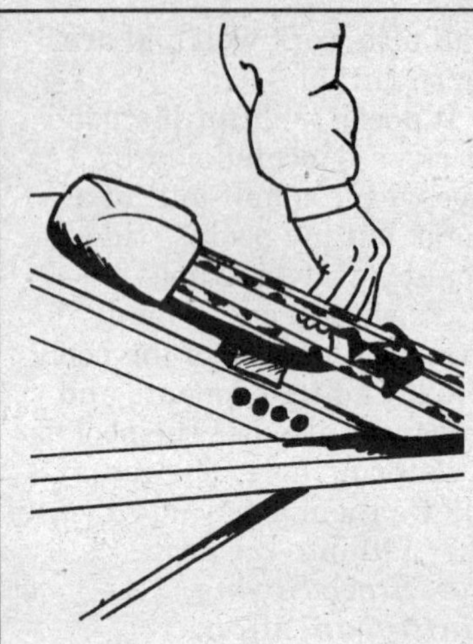

Attach Arrow Quiver to Tree Stand

I never liked shooting my bow with a quiver attached to it, so I came up with a different way to keep my arrows within reach while hunting.

I purchased an extra mounting bracket and, using a quiver that snaps to a bow's mounting bracket, attached it to the side of my climbing tree stand.

These brackets can be glued or screwed to the support arm of a stand. This trick makes it easier for me to get settled into my stand because the quiver snaps into place and keeps the arrows close, but out of the way.

— Charles Clark, Hales Corners, Wis.

are bunched in twos.

D. Bullet Through Intestines or Liver

A cross jump track results from a bullet through the intestines or liver with the animal standing broadside to the shooter.

Track patterns of these types of wounds resemble the following illustrations:

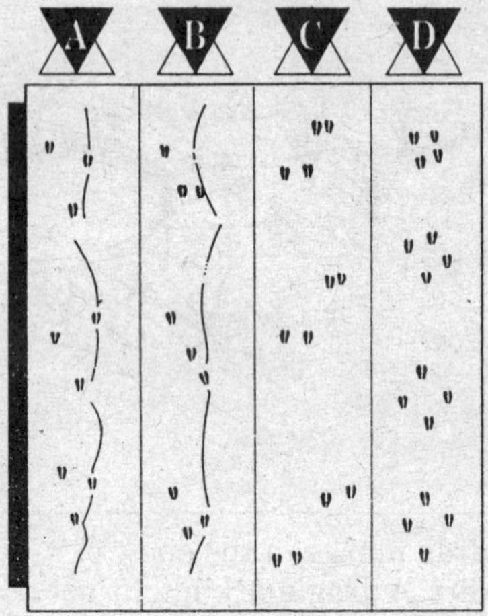

Make Wise Shooting Decisions

Making quick, certain kills should be the main goal of every gun- and bow-hunter. Keep these five facts in mind before taking a shot:

1. When shooting at deer with bow and arrow, aim for

the heart region.

If the deer "jumps the string" by dropping sharply before bounding away, the arrow will still hit the lungs.

2. The average white-tailed deer, weighing about 150 pounds, carries about eight pints of blood in its circulatory system. Massive hemorrhage is necessary to bring a deer down quickly.

3. A deer must lose at least 35 percent of its blood, or 2.75 pints in a 150-pound animal, before falling. The better the hit, the quicker blood loss.

4. Deer blood carries high levels of Vitamin K1 and K2 in early autumn. Vitamin K is an anti-hemorrhagic agent, which greatly aids blood clotting.

5. Frightened whitetails produce high levels of B-endorphin, which supports rapid wound healing.

Endorphins consist of morphine-like chemicals from the pituitary gland, allowing the animal to control pain.

6. Deer, particularly in northern areas, have thick layers of tallow along the back and below the brisket. This can plug wounds, preventing a good blood trail.

7. A string tracking device attached to a bow and arrow is sometimes useful in recovering game. However, the string does affect the arrow flight on long shots.

Attract Deer with Heated Scents

I've used scents successfully, but learned a trick that improves the effectiveness: heat. To use this trick, you'll need hot water, a thermos, plastic wrap, a rubber band, and deer lure.

Before leaving for the woods, pour a few cups of water into a pot and bring it to a boil. Pour the hot water into the thermos. Don't forget to take a rubber band and a sheet of plastic wrap.

When you get to your stand, make a small hole in the ground near a shooting lane. Place the thermos in the hole and remove the lid.

Using the rubber band, secure the plastic wrap over the top of the thermos. Finally, pour a few drops of your favorite lure onto the plastic.

The heat from the water makes the lure stronger and it lasts longer.

— *G. Duane Blanks, Spourt Springs, Va.*

Head-On Shot: For Guns Only

This shot presents gun-hunters with three vital targets. A shot in the chest will hit the heart or lungs. A bullet in the neck will usually break the neck or cause enough shock to drop the animal instantly. It could also destroy the esophagus and/or carotid artery or jugular vein.

The head-on shot is not good for bow-hunters. Unless the arrow hits the chest dead-center, which presents a very small target, it can easily deflect off bone.

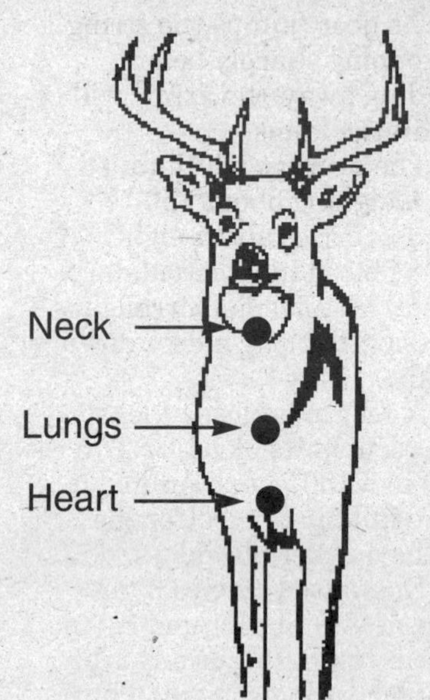

Broadside Shot: Bow & Gun

Gun-hunters can drop deer instantly with a broadside shot by putting a bullet through the shoulder blade. A well-constructed bullet will pass through the blade and hit the spine.

The broadside shot is also good for bow-hunters, but it doesn't leave much room for error as the quartering-away shot does. Arrows that pass through the vital organs produce quick, clean kills. Aim for the heart, knowing that a high shot will still hit the lungs. Archers must avoid the shoulder blade.

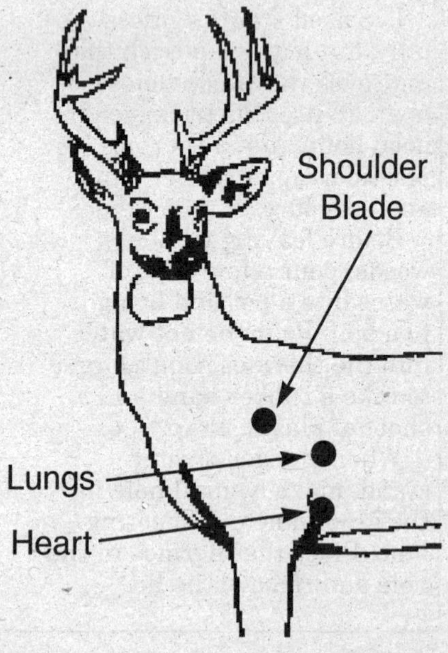

Quartering Away: Bow & Gun

For archers, the quar-
tering-away shot offers
the best chances for
success. Even if the
arrow hits a bit too far
back, it can angle forward
into the chest cavity for a
quick kill. When taking
this shot, the point of aim
should be through the
deer to the opposite
shoulder.

This is also a great shot
for gun-hunters. As with
the bow, the gun-hunter's
point of aim should be
through the deer to the
opposite shoulder.

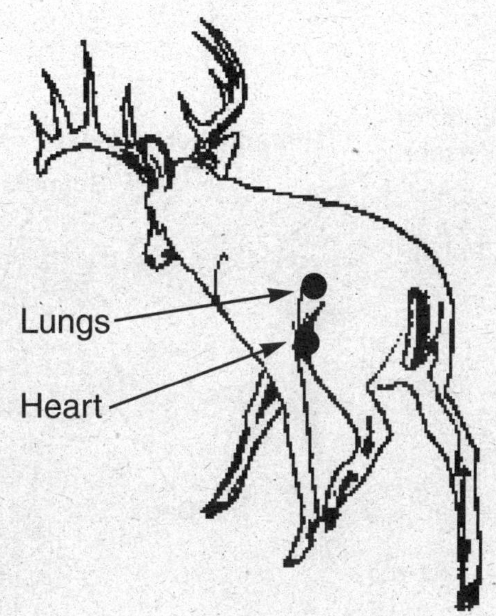

Quartering Toward

As with the head-on
shot, the quartering-
toward shot is good for
gun-hunters.

A shot high in the chest
will usually break the base
of the neck and travel
through the lungs. A lower
shot will hit the heart.

While this shot should be
avoided by bow-hunters, a
properly placed arrow can
hit the lungs or heart,
making for a clean kill.
However, the target again
is very small. If possible,
avoid this shot and wait for
a better opportunity.

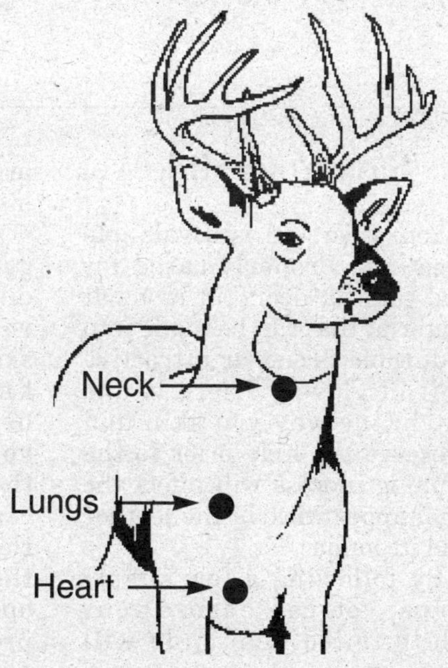

SKELETON

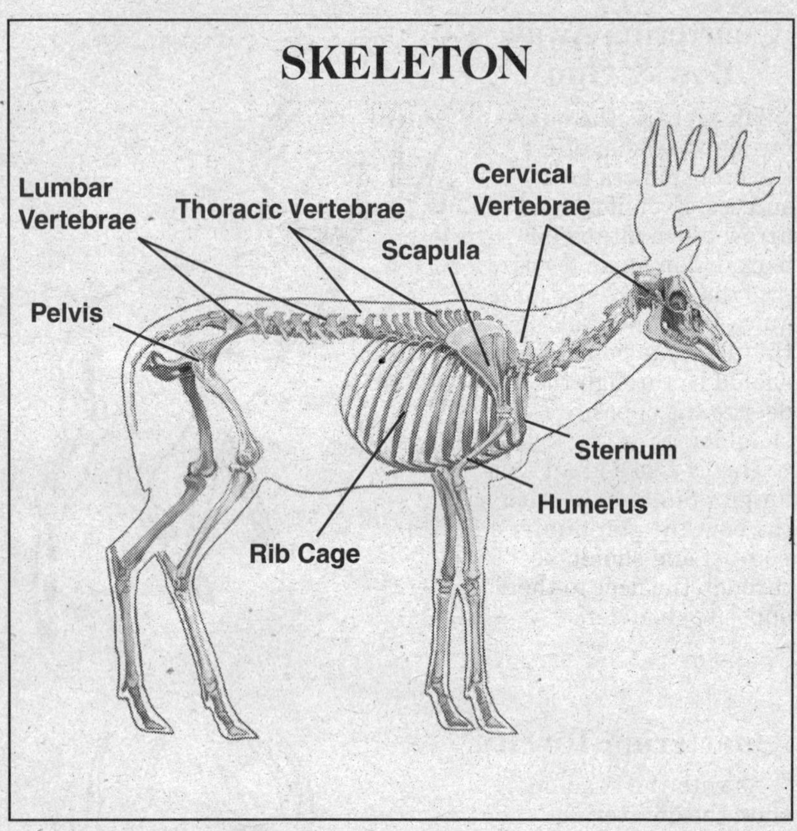

Save Your Hide

Your deerskin is a valuable resource. Properly cared for and tanned, deerskin is a soft material that can be made into a durable jacket or attractive pair of gloves. There is one catch: the way you skin and preserve the hide prior to the tanning process will affect the final appearance of the leather and its value.

By following a few simple steps, you can ensure your white-tailed deer hide will provide quality material to be made into quality garments.

Assuming the animal is in good condition, proper care during the skinning process is your first concern. Begin the skinning process with a sharp knife and then switch to using your hands. By using your hands to pry and pull the hide off the animal, you can avoid cutting holes into the hide. Knife cuts close to the surface of the hide can open up during the tanning process, ruining portions of

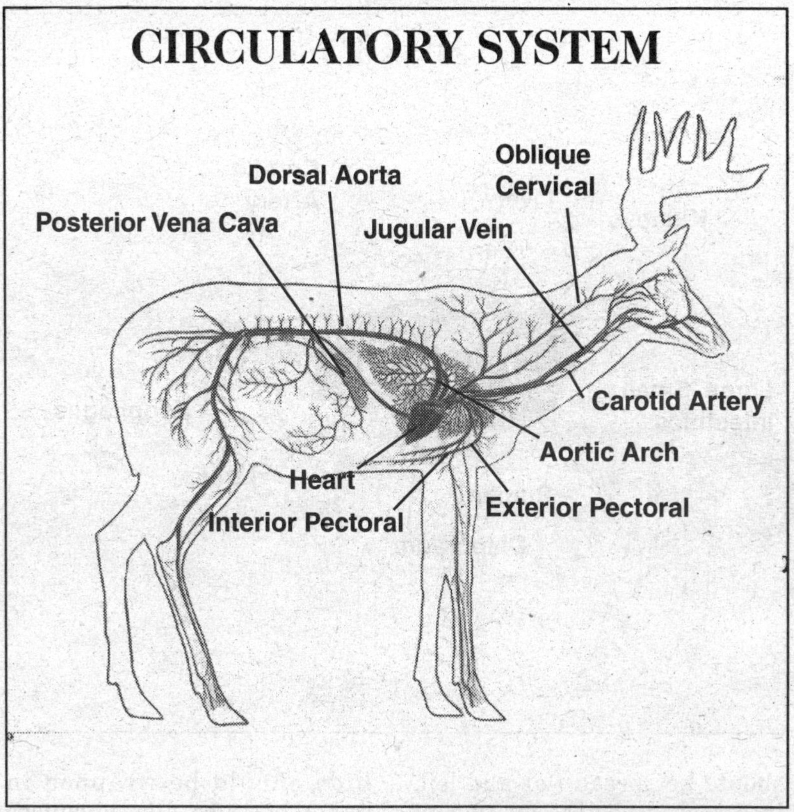

CIRCULATORY SYSTEM

the hide.

Another tip: Allow tallow to remain on the hide, but carefully remove all flesh.

Next, lay the hide flat, hair side down, and salt it. The average hide can be preserved with 3 to 5 pounds of canning or table salt. Spread the salt firmly onto the hide, taking care to cover it all the way to the edges. The salt draws moisture out of the hide, impeding the growth of bacteria.

After the hide is salted, it

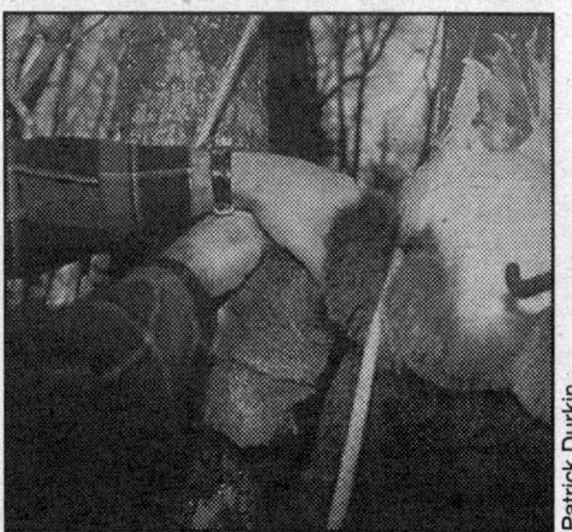

To avoid damaging a deer's hide, use your hands to pull it from the carcass.

ORGANS

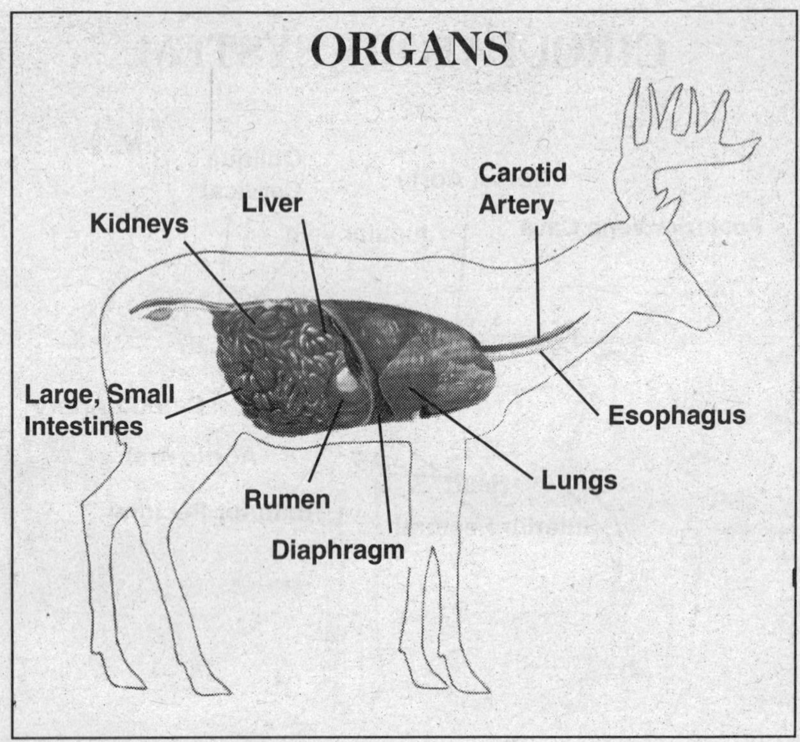

should be spread flat and left in a cool, dry place for two or three days until a crust forms. If your deer is frozen when skinned, allow the hide to thaw before salting it. Your hide is ready for tanning when the salt forms a crust.

If you plan to mail the hide to a tannery, fold the sides of the hide toward the center and roll up, hair side out. The hide should be wrapped in paper because plastic causes the hide to "sweat," which breeds bacteria. Wrap extra paper around the package to absorb any additional fluid, place the contents in a cardboard box, and ship immediately.

— Contributed by W.B. Place, Box 160, Dept. DDH, Hartford, WI 53027.

Three Things That Can Ruin Your Venison

The breakdown or ruin of frozen meat is caused mainly by three things: oxidation, poor packaging, and enlarging ice crystals that rupture the walls of muscle cells.

To Age or Not to Age?

The question of whether one should age deer meat or not remains a point of endless discussion among deer hunters, meat processors and scientists alike.

Some animal scientists view aging as impractical because so many people lack the proper facilities. Further, so much deer meat unfortunately winds up in sausage anyway, so why age it? Aging skinned deer meat all too frequently results in excessive weight loss, dehydration and discoloration of the lean tissue because of the lack of fat cover.

Under improper conditions, the meat becomes susceptible to deterioration by bacteria and mold growth. Further, because hunters shoot a large number of young animals with naturally tender meat (a majority of all deer shot today average only 1½ to 2½ years old), aging seems unnecessary in the opinion of some animal scientists and meat processors.

Most meat processors agree upon the difficulty of properly aging venison without a refrigerated cooler. Without a cooler, one has to rely on weather for the aging process. The obvious problem then is the constant fluctuation of temperatures, from below 30 degrees Fahrenheit (which freezes meat and prevents aging) to over 40 degrees Farhenheit (which dehydrates and spoils meat.)

It's nearly impossible to properly age venison without the use of a temperature-controlled facility. Hunters who try to age their deer by hanging them outside run the risk of cyclic freezing, which can ruin the meat. It's best to skin and process your deer as soon as possible.

Cyclic freezing and thawing, meat processors generally agree, produces poor-quality vension.

Processed meat should be frozen rapidly. Use the coldest setting on your freezer to achieve this result.

Aging Deer by Their Teeth

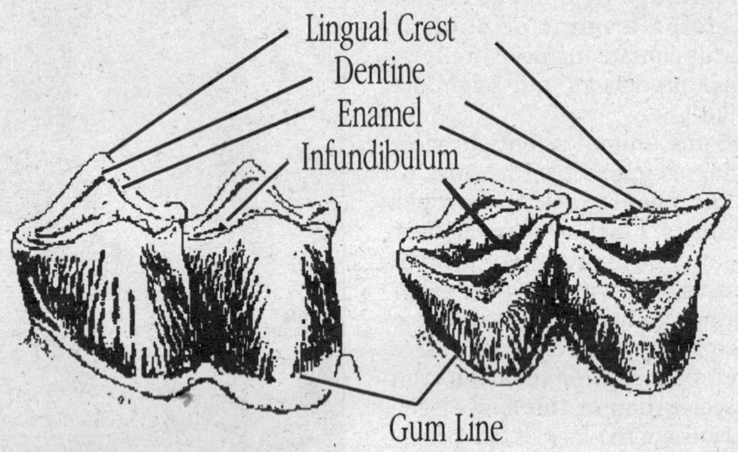

Wildlife biologists and deer researchers agree that analysis of tooth replacement and wear is perhaps the most reliable method for aging white-tailed deer.

Regardless of where they live, whitetails lose their baby teeth and wear-out their permanent teeth on a fairly predictable schedule.

At birth, white-tailed fawns have four teeth. Adult deer have 32 teeth — 12 premolars, 12 molars, six incisors and two canines.

Aging analysis often is based on the wear of the molars, which lose about 1 millimeter of height per year. It takes a deer about 10½ years to wear its teeth down to the gum line. Therefore, it's difficult to determine the age of a deer that's older than 10½ years.

Most importantly, the ability to predict a deer's age based on the wear of its teeth is something any hunter can learn easily with just a little studying.

The illustrations that follow help determine the age of deer by the lower jaw teeth of deer taken in November.

— Reprinted from Field Techniques for Sexing and Aging Game Animals, Special Wildlife Report No. 1, Wisconsin Conservation Department, 1957.

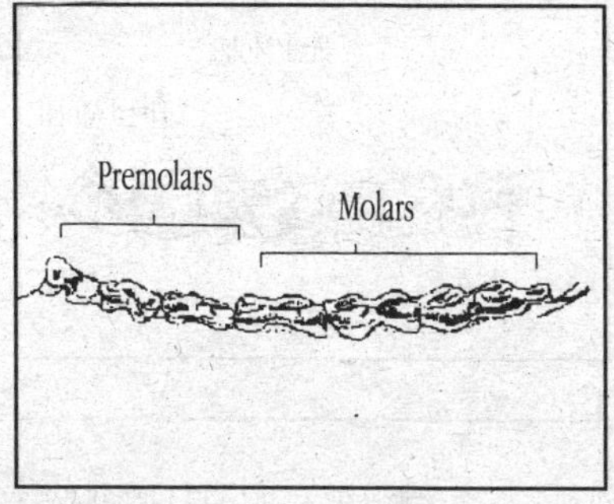

Yearling

Fawns are deer 1 year and 5 months or less — all milk teeth are firmly in place. Third premolar has three cusps. Yearlings are 1 year and 6 months or more. Milk premolars are loose or shed, with permanent premolars partially erupted.

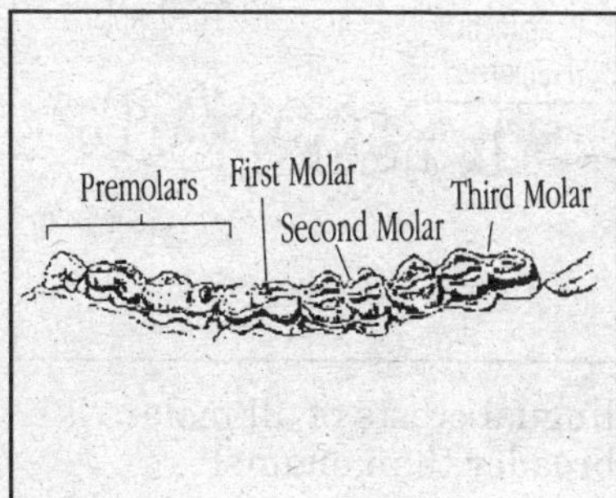

1 Year, 7 Months

1 year and 7 months or more. Permanent premolars fully erupted; they are white in contrast to pigmented older teeth. Third permanent premolars. Third molar partially erupted.

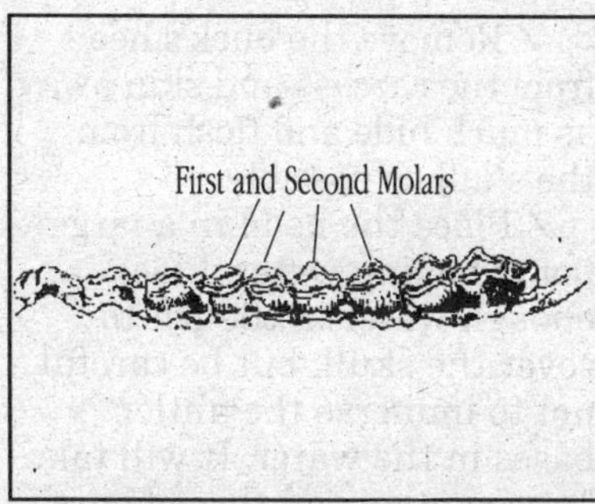

2½ Years

The lingual crests of the first molar are sharp, with the enamel well above the narrow dentine (the layer below the enamel) of the crest. Crests are fully as sharp as those of the second and third molar. Wear on the posterior cusp of the third molar is slight.

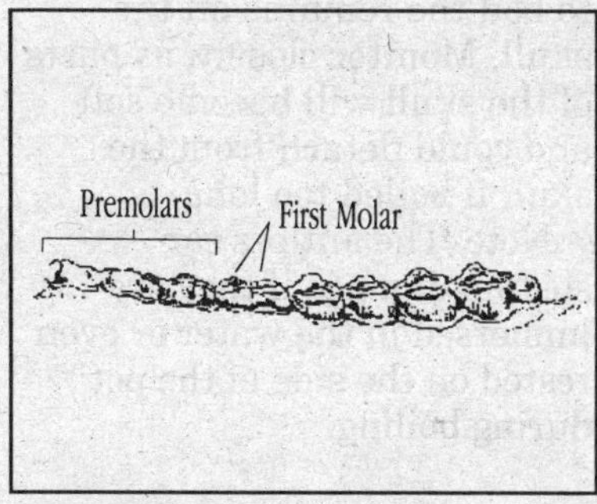

3½ Years

The lingual (next to tongue) crests of the first molar are blunt, and the dentine of the crests is as wide or wider than the enamel. The posterior cusp of the third molar is flattened by wear, forming a definite concavity on the biting surface of the teeth.

4½ Years

The lingual crests of the first molar are almost worn away. The posterior cusp of the third molar is worn at the edge of the cusp so that the biting surface slopes laterally downward.

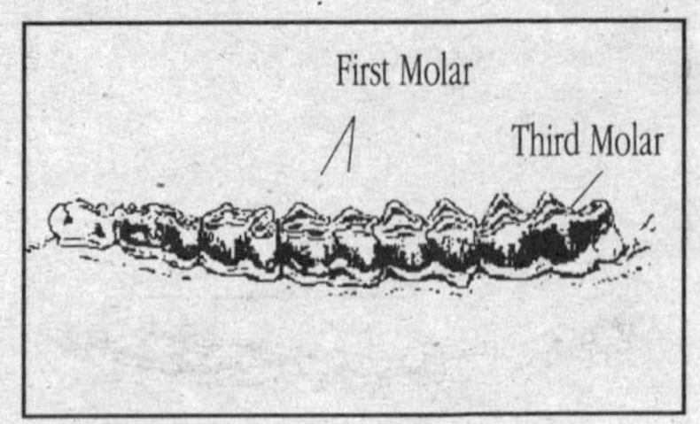

5½ Years

No lingual crests on the first and second molar, although rounded edges might appear like crests. An imaginary line drawn from lingual to outside edges of first and second molars would generally touch the enamel on both sides of the infundibulum (the depression between outside and lingual crests). Dentine of the

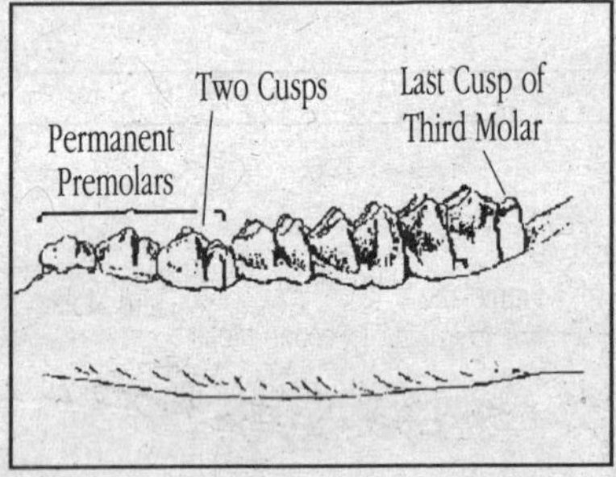

lingual crests of all molars is broader than enamel.

How to Bleach a Deer's Skull

Nothing comes close to capturing the memory of a great whitetail hunt like a head-and-shoulder mount of a dandy buck. However, you can inexpensively preserve your trophy by boiling and bleaching the skull rather than merely nailing the antlers to the outside of your garage or hunting camp.

European-style antler/skull preservation is easy, and it doesn't take a lot of time.

Follow these simple instructions to enhance the appeal of the antlers from your next better-than-average buck.

✓ Remove the buck's head from the carcass and skin away as much hide and flesh from the skull as possible.

✓ Place the head in a large pot of boiling water. Place enough water in the pot to cover the skull, but be careful not to immerse the antler bases in the water. It will take between two and three hours to boil the remains off the skull. Monitor closely, as parts of the skull will become soft and could detach from the skull if boiled too long.

Note: The antlers can sustain damage if they are immersed in the water or even rested on the side of the pot during boiling.

6½ Years

Wear is moderate on first premolar, heavy on second and third premolars. Infundibulum appears as fine line or chevron on first molar or might be absent. On third premolar infundibulum might appear as small triangular hole.

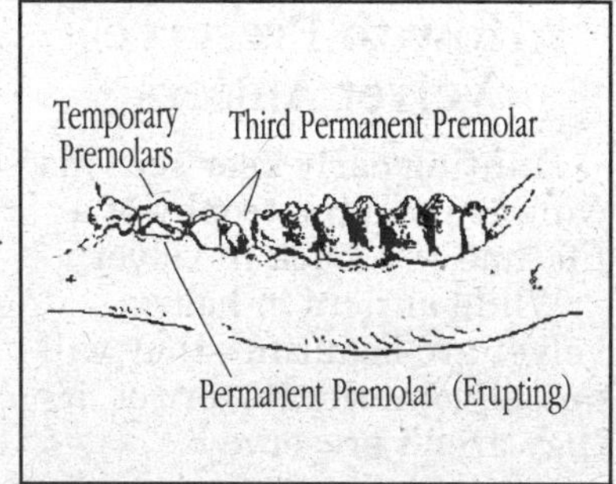

7½ Years

First molar worn within 2 or 3 mm of gum line on outside and 4 or 5 mm on lingual side. Second molar almost smooth and third molar worn down until lingual crests are completely gone. Infundibulum almost gone from the third premolar.

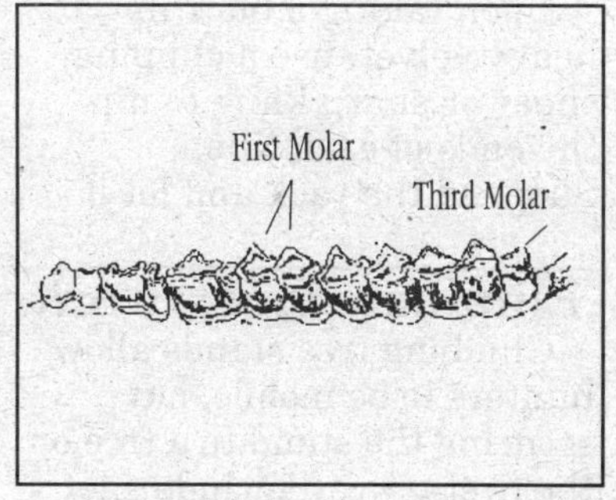

To help keep grease from sticking to the skull, add a small amount of baking soda to the water.

✓ Remove the skull from the water after most of the remains have fallen off. Use a needle-nose pliers or tweezers to remove small bones and gristle from inside the brain and nasal cavities.

You can use a small brush to remove other debris from the skull.

✓ There are several ways to bleach skulls. Bleach and alcohol can permanently discolor antlers, so be sure to proceed with caution.

One method of bleaching skulls is to place 1 part bleach and 3 parts water in a pan. Dip the skull into the solution and let stand for a few minutes. Next, remove the skull and let it dry.

It might be necessary to repeat this procedure several times to acquire the desired color.

Another bleaching method involves hydrogen peroxide. First, soak a cheesecloth in hydrogen peroxide and wrap it around the deer's skull. Set the wrapped skull in direct sunlight and let it dry for several hours.

Bleached skulls can be mounted to wood plaques, or they can be displayed "as is" for reminders of a special hunt.

How to Preserve Velvet Antlers

Hunting early deer seasons can result in the trophy of a lifetime — a buck in velvet.

While antlers in heavy velvet are beautiful, they will quickly deteriorate, or rot, if they aren't preserved promptly.

Upon taking a buck in heavy velvet, use a clipping shear or sharp knife to nip the ends of each tine. Suspend the rack and let it hang for a day or two to let the blood drain from the antlers.

To preserve the antlers, dip them in formaldehyde and hang to dry. Repeat this process two or three times. Some hunters prefer to use a syringe to inject formaldehyde directly into the antlers.

Of course, it's wise to allow a taxidermist to perform the preserving work on velvet antlers if you plan to mount the head and cape.

Eliminate Guesswork

Climbing tree stands allow hunters to be mobile, but securing the stand to a tree on the first try can include a lot of guesswork.

To make the job easy, take notes on the trees you usually hunt from. Remember the holes you use to secure the support bar, or any other pertinent mounting information. When you get home, write the information on a small sticker and place it next to the hole on the bar. For example, write "RO" to remind you of the holes you used for the red oak on your favorite ridge. "LP" could indicate the

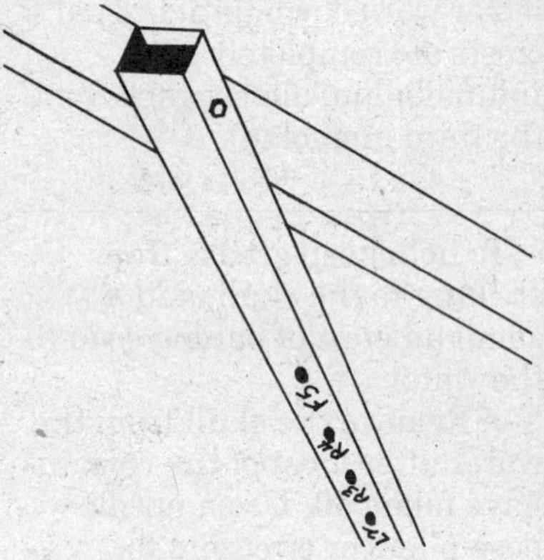

hole positions used for a lone poplar, and so on.

This method ensures proper stand placement on the first climb.

— Bob Korlewitz, Johnstown, Pa.

Tune Your Bow in a Jiffy

Paper tuning is a helpful method that indicates problems with bows and arrows. Make an inexpensive and portable paper-tuner by building an extended saw horse. On one end, mount a square foam target. On the other end, mount a frame that can tautly hold a sheet of paper.

To test for problems with arrow speed, stand about 5 feet from the setup, and shoot an arrow through the paper. To test for energy loss, shoot through the

paper from a hunting distance. Then, use a paper-tear chart to match your paper holes and identify problems with arrow flight.

— Jim Fernandez, Hummelstown, Pa.

Build Backyard Deer Feeders

To keep deer on your property or attract them to your back yard, build several portable "time-release" feeders.

Cut 6-foot sections of 3-inch plastic pipe, and cap them with 1-pound coffee cans. Strap the pipe to a tree in an area where you want to attract deer, making sure the bottom of the pipe is no more than 2 or 3 inches off the ground. Finally, place a tray, or dig a small hole, below the pipe so the feed will congregate in one spot. Fill the pipe with feed, such as corn, and cap the coffee can to keep out squirrels and birds.

Through gravity, the feeder

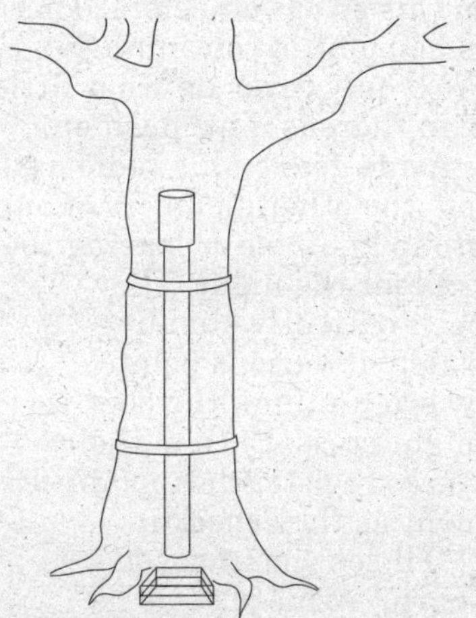

will empty itself as deer eat from the tray.

Some states have strict laws on baiting, so be sure to check the hunting regulations before using this type of feeder.

— Rob Somerville, Kenton, Tenn.

Book Learning

■ *Joel M. Spring*

I know by the hand on my shoulder that it's time to quit for the day. I strain my eyes in the fading orange daylight to make out just one more blood drop in the snow. Deer tracks are everywhere, and one of these sets is from the doe we've been following the past two hours.

"We'll pick it up first thing in the morning," Arnie says. "We'll do more harm than good if we keep going."

I know he's right. I've been in this situation before. There is no point in continuing. We'll only cover up what little sign there is if we push on.

Arnie gets on his radio and lets the other members of our group know we're leaving the trail for the night. They've been patiently standing watch at various points where we think the deer might cross. Each of their voices register disappointment as they check in.

"I'll see you at seven sharp," Arnie says as he drops me off at my house. "Tomorrow is Monday, and the other guys will be back to work. There will just be the two of us to take up the track in the morning."

Selfishly, I wish we could have found the deer while everyone was still around to see it. This area was new to me, and this was my first year hunting with this hard-core bunch of deer hunters. I was really beginning to feel like I fit in. We had spent this last week of the season driving some of the most miserable thickets I had ever seen. And, after eating my share of brush and briars for the past few days, I'd earned the right to "sit."

The Shot

At about 3 p.m., Arnie's friends pushed two does out of a dense thicket and into my sights. Squaring my shotgun's cross-hairs across the chest of the larger doe, I followed her steady trot broadside at 40 yards. Patience paid off as she slowed and stopped, turning to look for the drivers. I squeezed the trigger and the 12-gauge jumped. The doe might have staggered, but I couldn't be sure. Before I knew it, she dashed into another thicket and disappeared.

I called for Arnie and we began tracking her in the 12 inches of snow that carpeted the woods and fields. We debated waiting, but because the shot seemed good, we decided to go after her imme-

Dan Schmidt

diately.

We quickly found a grape-fruit-sized clump of hair, but no blood at the spot where the doe was standing. We followed her tracks as she weaved around the fringes of the thicket. Still no blood. Could the shot have gone low or high and just cut some hair? No. I should be dead-on at 40 yards. Could the shot have been across the brisket? No. The hair was too short.

At 80 yards we found blood, only one drop, but blood. By the time darkness arrived, we had found maybe 40 or 50 small drops of blood in the snow. By dark, the doe's tracks had mixed in with other deer tracks, and the trail was little more than a troll's tunnel through the thick briars.

Searching for Answers

The hot shower feels good, but I emerge unrefreshed. Supper is tasty, but I don't enjoy the meal. And the evening TV shows can't take my mind off the doe. I go downstairs to my bookcase and take out a book on blood trailing to see if it might shed light on my situation.

After three hours of studying the pages, I decide I might have a liver hit on my hands. Although I try to relive the shot in my mind,

Learn How to Store Your Firearms Correctly

It's a no-brainer that your firearm's bore should be cleaned before long storage, but what else should you do to protect it while it isn't being used? Several things, including:

✓ The action should be cleaned with a liberal dose of bore solvent and scrubbed with a toothbrush, then wiped clean. Follow up with a secondary bore cleaner, and then apply a light coating of high-quality lubricant.

✓ Just before storing the firearm, spray the action and all metal surfaces with a water displacer. This will help prevent rusting.

These simple procedures will help keep your gun in top working order.

— For more information on gun storage and cleaning supplies, contact Venco Industries, 16770 Hilltop Park Place, Dept. DDH, Chagrin Falls, OH 44023-4500.

the only image I see is with the scope's cross-hairs settling across the doe's shoulder.

Holding the tracking book in my hand, I look at a picture of the smiling author. Although I'm sure he's knowledgeable, I doubt his advice. If my shot hit the doe's liver, she would have died within three hours. If that's the case, the doe shouldn't be far from where we stopped trailing. However, I have a strong feeling it won't be that easy.

At 2 a.m., I find myself still awake, staring out the window watching snow fall gently in the backyard.

Things couldn't be much worse. I consider getting a lantern and going out before the snow completely obscures the blood sign, but common sense tells me a lantern won't do much to illuminate the sparse trail.

At 3 a.m., I find myself in front of the TV, switching

Protect and Organize Your Arrows

Modifying a cardboard box is an inexpensive and easy way to organize and protect your hunting arrows during the off-season. For best results, use a box that is 18 to 20 inches long. Fruit boxes are ideal.

Use a field point to punch corresponding holes in each end of the box, dividing the box into sections for bent and straight arrows. Suspending arrows in this fashion also allows you to

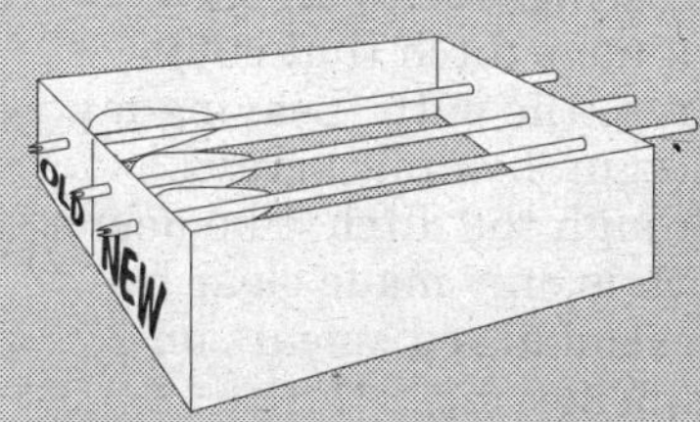

dry wet fletchings quickly.

This simple arrow holder makes it easy to load your quiver when it's time to hunt or practice.

*— John Yoder,
Millersburg, Ohio*

nervously between a bad
movie and an all-weather
channel.

At 4 a.m., 5 a.m. and 6
a.m., I lay wide awake staring up at my bedroom ceil-
ing.

Finally, 7 a.m. arrives. But
Arnie doesn't. I can't wait. I
head out.

Back on the Trail

I find our tracks easily in
the light dusting of snow, and
it takes only moments to find
the orange glove we hung on
a branch last night. A smat-
tering of blood drops jump
out at me from the branches
of a low blackberry bush.
Dragging my unloaded shotgun behind me like a sled, I
crawl through the brushy
tunnel. Although I see a few
drops of blood in the snow,
the trail is getting tougher.

Another 50 yards of crawling brings me to an old
drainage ditch that cuts
across the path. Leaving my
shotgun behind, I crawl
through the ditch. The deer's
path is only made clear by
occasional red smears on
branches.

My hopes are dashed when
the ditch becomes choked by
brush. I can't continue. I
can't tell which way the doe
might have gone, but she
didn't go straight. I've lost
her.

Soaked, frozen and not
altogether sure I can even
find my way back to my shotgun, I scramble out of the
water and try to gather my
thoughts. The doe had been
heading due west for the past
100 yards, and I know there's
a white pine stand due west
of here. Could she have
headed there?

After recovering my gun, I
bushwhack straight out of
the thicket. I find a clearing
and head north, and within
five minutes, I cross fresh
deer tracks coming out of the
ditch. Unbelievably, there's
blood in them.

I turn west and follow the
trail. The single set of tracks
winds around the thicket and
the pines. The trail circles
and crosses itself several
times. It looks as if the deer
was seeking a place to lie
down. The blood trail is
sparse, but the single set of
hoofprints is clear.

Lifting my focus from the
ground for a moment, I'm
suddenly facing her. She's
dead against the base of a
huge white pine, covered with
a light dusting of snow. As I
field dress her, I discover a
bullet wound in the liver's
forward lobe.

The grinning author was
right. Chalk one up for book
learning.

Chapter 4

Technical Tips for Gun- and Bow-Hunters

No doubt, deer hunting equipment has come a long way in the past decade. Bows are faster and easier to shoot. Guns and cartridges are more efficient and powerful. Camouflage clothing allows hunters to virtually disappear in the woods. And advancements in accessories have provided hunters with endless opportunities to make their hunting experiences more enjoyable.

Of course, all the gear in the world won't do the hunting for you. That's the way it should be. However, hunters can experience more success if they hone their woodsmanship skills and learn how their gear can work for them.

This chapter is packed with hundreds of tips and tactics that will make you a better hunter. Learn how to estimate distances, determine proper arrow flight, and mount a riflescope.

Also included are tips for muzzle-loading hunters, tactics for tree stand placement and much more!

Learn to Estimate Distances

The best archery equipment is only as good as the person who uses it. To be successful, a bow-hunter needs to be a woodsman and a good shooter. Above all, the bow-hunter must be a master in yardage estimation.

To get started, follow these six steps:

✓ Begin by choosing a distance that you can spot easily. The most common reference distance used by bow-hunters is 20 yards.

✓ Use this distance as your starting point for shorter or farther shots.

✓ Using only the 20-yard reference, estimate the distance of the shot.

✓ Fine-tune your estimation. Count toward the target in 10-yard increments. For example, if the target is 15 yards away, glance at your 20-yard reference point, estimate the halfway point, then count toward the target in 1-yard increments.

✓ Compare the fine-tuned yardage estimation with your first estimation. Split the difference if you're within 3 yards. For example: Using the 20 yards as a reference, you estimate the target to be 25 yards away. However, when fine-tuning the estimation, you count 29 yards.

Splitting the 4-yard difference in half, you estimate the target to be 27 yards away. Start over if the figures are off by more than 3 yards.

✓ Use the same method for farther shots.

The more you practice this method, the less time it takes to complete the process. Seasoned bow-hunters use this method to estimate the distances of trees, logs, rocks or other objects near shooting lanes.

No matter what method you use, never take a shot until you are satisfied with your yardage estimation. A lack of confidence is one of the biggest reasons why bow-hunters miss.

— For more information on archery techniques, contact Bear Archery, 4600 SW 41st Blvd., Dept. DDH, Gainesville, FL 32608-4999.

To be successful, a bow-hunter needs to master yardage estimation. This practice can be fun, especially when shooting with friends.

Become a Better Bow-Hunter

The first step to becoming a better bow-hunter is honing your shooting skills and gaining the confidence that you can place an arrow with pinpoint accuracy at a given distance.

Rather than plunking shot after shot into a straw bale, systemize your practice routines. This will not only improve your accuracy, but it will make you more disciplined when a deer walks into shooting range when you're in your tree stand or ground blind. Here are 14 ways to further improve your archery skills:

✓ Place your archery target in a wooded area when possible.

✓ Practice with the same size arrows and broadheads that you intend to hunt with.

✓ Always use an *unmarked* outline of a deer as your target. If you want to see if your shots are in the vital area, lightly sketch that area on the target, but make the outline light enough so you cannot focus on it while shooting.

✓ Shoot for a specific spot on the deer, never shoot "at" a deer.

✓ Once you can hit the target at 30 yards and less, make it a rule not to take more than one practice shot from each spot. It is the first shot that counts. You probably won't get a second chance.

Although straw bales serve a purpose, 3-D archery targets allow bow-hunters to practice real-life shots.

✓ Shoot from behind trees and shrubs, down on one knee and both knees, with your bow angled left and right, and standing on your tiptoes to shoot over a limb.

✓ When practicing, wear the clothes and equipment you'll be hunting in.

✓ Practice shooting from a tree stand. Take shots in every direction and angle possible to simulate realistic hunting situations.

✓ Practice year-round, if you can, by bow-fishing, varmint hunting and stump shooting.

✓ Set up an action archery course using plastic jugs and rubber blunts. This is easily done in a limited space and gives you a variety of shooting opportunities.

✓ If you use a sight, zero it in at a given distance (20 yards is common). When you get proficient, you can figure out how much lower or higher you can hold the sight to shoot at 12 yards or at 30 yards.

*— For more information on bow-hunting, contact the **National Bowhunter Education Foundation**, 249B E. 29th St., Box 503, Dept. DDH, Loveland, CO 80538.*

Ten Strategies for Concealment

Innovations in camouflage clothing allow deer hunters to literally blend in with any surrounding or terrain. White-tailed deer rely on their keen eyesight to avoid danger. Hunters, however, can escape detection by wearing a quality camouflage outfit and by following these 10 tips:

1. Match your camouflage pattern to the background of the area that you will be hunting. For maximum break-up, consider wearing different patterns on your jacket and pants.

2. Always use camouflage on your hands and face. Many hunters dress in full camouflage and fail to cover these important areas.

3. Cover anything that is shiny, such as your watch, buttons, snaps and zippers.

4. Purchase pants that are 2 inches to 3 inches longer than needed. This will keep light-colored socks and boots from standing out.

5. Wear boots with dark soles. A hunter's boots are sometimes the first things a deer will see if the hunter is sitting at ground level.

6. Avoid direct sunlight. If possible, face west in the morning and east in the afternoon.

7. Think about your intentions when you pick a spot. Your outline should blend in with the surroundings from at least 40 yards out.

8. Set up on edges and avoid hunting in the middle of thick cover. Hunting in thick cover

Camouflage on your face and hands is important. Notice how this hunter stays completely hidden with the addition of a face mask and gloves.

Haas Outdoors

hampers your vision.

9. Keep your outline as low as possible, but avoid setting up at a deer's eye level.

10. Use face paint to touch up glare areas around your eyes, even if you're wearing a face net.

*— For more information on camouflage strategies, contact **Haas Outdoors (Mossy Oak Camouflage)**, Box 757, Dept. DDH, West Point, MS 39773.*

How to Select Camouflage

With so many patterns to choose from, it isn't difficult to find camouflage clothing that perfectly meets your needs. However, maintaining hunting apparel isn't easy. Without proper care camouflage patterns can fade quickly.

Follow these tips for selecting and maintaining your outfits:

Selecting

✓ *Buy name brands.*

You'll build your camo wardrobe over time, so buy from a company that has a reputation for quality and longevity.

✓ *Read product reviews.*

Most hunting magazines print product reviews. These reviews highlight product features and innovations.

✓ *Match your camo with the terrain.*

Before choosing a pattern, think carefully about the

This photo shows how well camouflage can work in blending a hunter's outline with his surrounding's. Can you see the hunter? We've placed a black arrow showing the location of his head.

terrain and seasons you hunt. Match camo accordingly. You might choose to have a wardrobe for each situation.

✓ *Details make the garment.*

Pay attention to details. Look for extra pockets, comfortable linings, quiet cloth and form-fitted hoods.

✓ *Purchase larger sizes.*

Remember, you'll wear extra clothing in cold temperatures. If you dress in layers, you'll need bigger camo garments.

✓ *Make sure it's quiet.*

Select a material that doesn't make noise when scratched.

Maintaining

✓ *Wash new garments.*

Always wash garments in unscented soap in cold water. A tablespoon of vinegar should be added to help set the dye.

✓ *Keep garments scent-free.*

Store clean garments in an air-proof bag to keep them scent free. Sprinkle baking soda in odor areas — armpits, crotch and footwear — and keep clothes in the bag until you're in the field.

✓ *Dry your clothes on a cool dryer setting, or hang them outside to dry.*

Heat will break down inks and make your camo clothing fade. Properly cared for, camo clothing will last up to five years. Clothing not cared for can break down in one year.

*— For more information on camouflage selection, contact **Skyline Camouflage**, 184 Ellicott Road, Dept. DDH, West Falls, NY 14170.*

Tuning Tips for Broadheads

Broadheads should be checked for flight after shafts have been paper tuned. It's not uncommon for the impact point of a broadhead to be different than a field point. Follow these steps to tune your broadheads:

1. Set up a broadhead target 20 to 30 yards away. Using the same arrow (with field point) that you used for paper tuning, shoot at the target. This will give you a reference point. If the shot is off, make the necessary adjustments to your sights.

2. Remove the field point and install a broadhead to the shaft. Use the same aiming point, and shoot again. If the broadhead hits close to where the field point did, shoot the same arrow several times to be sure you are within a respectable group size.

3. The shot group is the key. If you are shooting good groups, but the impact is off from your aiming point, simply make your sight adjustments.

Solutions to Problems

Small adjustments often help correct problems if your broadheads don't group well after tuning.

The following tips will only work if your arrows are properly spined or slightly over-spined. If your arrows are underspined, broadheads become extremely difficult, if not impossible, to tune.

1. Move the nock down if the broadhead hits below the field point.

2. Move the nock up if the broadhead hits above the field point.

3. Move the rest right or soften the cushion button spring tension if the broadhead hits left of the field point.

4. Move the rest left or stiffen the cushion button

spring tension if the broadhead hits right of the field point.

If you experience problems, ask your local archery pro shop to check:

✓ Shaft spine/tip weight
✓ Tiller
✓ Center shot
✓ Wheel timing
✓ Shaft straightness and broadhead alignment/wobble.

— For more information on broadheads, contact New Archery Products, 7500 Industrial Drive, Dept. DDH,

Which Nocks are the Best for Your Arrows?

Serious bow-hunters know little things — like arrow nocks — make the difference between success and failure. Though often overlooked, nocks play a major role in arrow accuracy.

This guide to Bohning nocks will help you choose the right style of nocks for your arrows.

Apex CA Nock: A lightweight nock designed for the radical bowstring angles of short compound bows and carbon arrows. Apex-CA Nocks are available for AFC, Beman, Windsport, and Easton PC shafts.

Throat diameter is .118 inch.

Note: Apex nocks should be glued on carbon shafts.

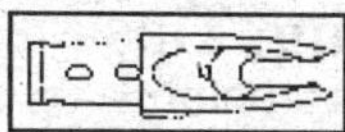

Signature Nock: A tuneable insert nock made of a high-impact plastic material. It provides correct nock/arrow alignment in a streamlined design. The nock throat is designed to help the arrow remain on the bowstring during draw or let down. This press-fit nock requires no adhesive. An installation tool is available for precise nock alignment.

Throat diameter is .111 inch.

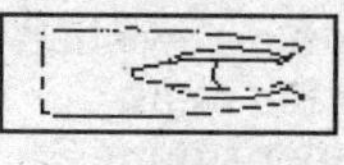

"T" Nock: An all-purpose nock that incorporates a tighter fit and a slightly deeper throat. Safety nodes are built into the inside rear of the nock throat to keep the arrow on the bowstring during let down. Available sizes $\frac{11}{32}$T, $8\frac{1}{2}$ mmT ($\frac{21}{64}$ inch), $\frac{5}{16}$T, $\frac{9}{32}$T, and $\frac{1}{4}$T.

Throat diameter is .115 inch.

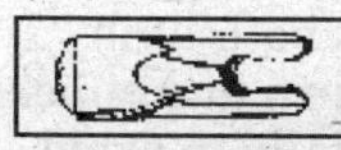

Legend II Nock: Designed for shooters who use short compounds and/or releases.

Available sizes $\frac{11}{32}$ inch, $\frac{5}{16}$ inch, $\frac{9}{32}$ inch, and $\frac{1}{4}$ inch.

Throat diameter is .115 inch.

*— Courtesy of **The Bohning Co.**, 6361 N. Seven Mile Road, Dept. DDH, Lake City, MI 49651.*

Bow-Tuning Tips

Paper tuning is a helpful method that helps determine problems with bows and arrows. To paper-test your arrows, place a sheet of paper in a frame, and position the frame vertically in front of a backstop. Next, stand about four feet away from the frame and shoot two or three arrows through different areas of the paper.

The paper tears can be examined to determine incorrect arrow flight. Before paper tuning, make sure you are using the correct arrows for your bow. Using an arrow shaft that is too stiff or too weak might prevent paper tuning from being effective. Refer to the arrow charts in this book, or visit an archery shop for information on shaft sizes.

The best arrow performance coincides with a tear that shows the fletching hitting ¼ inch to ¾ inch higher than the point between 11 and 1 o'clock. Start with the nocking point set ⅟₁₆ inch above the top of an arrow that is squared to the bowstring. It's also important that the arrow is set to insure the fletching does not make contact.

The following instructions are for a right-handed archer. Left-handed archers should use the reverse solutions. High and low tear solutions are identical for right- and left-handed archers.

— *Courtesy of **New Archery Products**, 7500 Industrial Drive, Dept. DDH, Forest Park, IL 60130.*

1. Left Tear

(This indicates a weak-spined arrow)

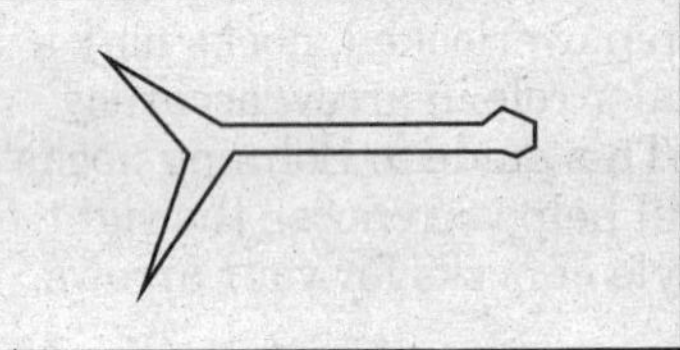

Solutions

a) Decrease the draw weight. Back out both limb bolts a quarter turn at a time. Adjust limbs equally to avoid changing the tiller and nock point. To avoid injury and bow damage, be careful not to back the limb bolts out too far.

b) Decrease the point weight. A lighter point will have some effect on increasing shaft stiffness. Too light of a point, however, might result in unstable arrow flight.

c) If these solutions don't reduce the length of the tear, change to a stiffer shaft.

d) Small tears can sometimes be improved by moving the arrow rest away from the riser or by increasing the tension on the cushion plunger or "berger button" if one is used.

2. Right Tear

(Indicates an arrow that is too stiff)

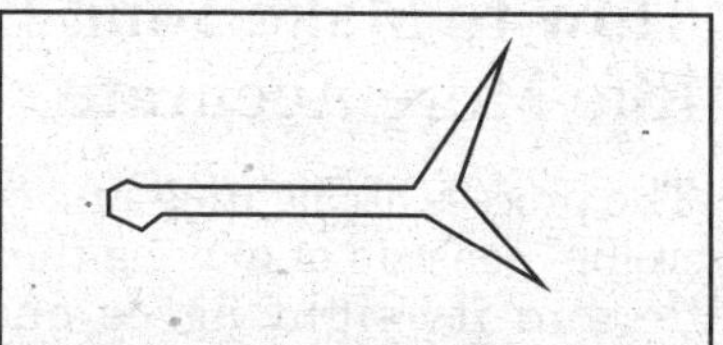

Solutions

a) Increase the draw weight. Tighten both limb bolts a quarter turn at a time. Adjust both limbs equally to avoid changing the tiller and nock point.

b) Increase the point weight. A heavier point will have some effect on decreasing shaft stiffness. However, arrow speed might be reduced.

c) If these solutions don't reduce the length of the tear, change to a weaker shaft.

d) Small tears can sometimes be improved by moving the arrow rest away from the riser or by increasing the tension on the cushion plunger or "berger button" if one is used.

3. High Tear

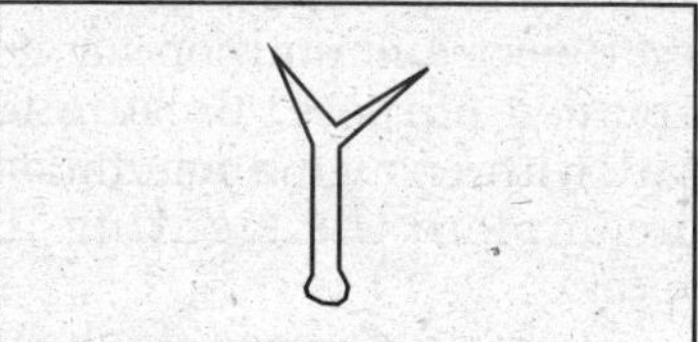

Solutions

a) Move the nocking point down in small increments.

b) If using a launcher or shoot-through rest, move the arrow support arm up. Increasing spring tension can also help.

c) Check for fletching interference and adjust rest position as needed.

4. Low Tear

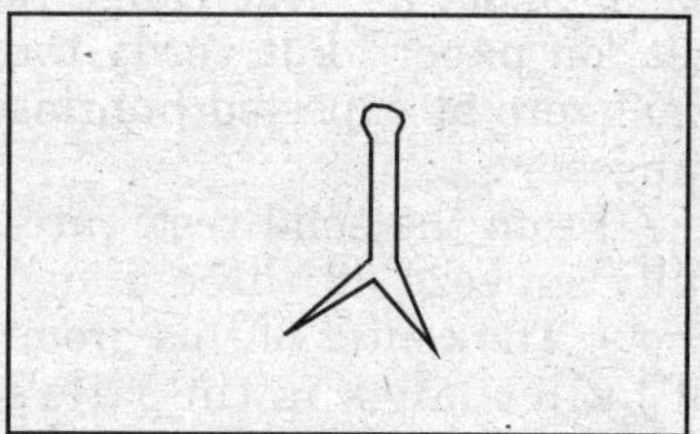

Solutions

a) Move the nocking point up in small increments.

b) If using a launcher or shoot-through rest, move the arrow support arm down. Increasing spring tension can also help.

c) Check for fletching interference and adjust rest position as needed.

How to Make Your Rifle More Accurate

The process of "sighting in" or "zeroing" consists of making the rifle and its sight agree on where the bullets strike. With proper procedures, sighting in a rifle is neither mysterious nor difficult.

To sight in your rifle properly, follow these steps:

✓ The rifle and its sight should be in good condition and properly assembled. Check action screws and scope mounts. Bore sighting, or the use of a collimator, is not a substitute for actually sighting in by shooting on a range.

✓ Select ammunition for its intended purpose. Be sure to start with enough ammunition to complete the sighting-in process.

✓ Pick a safe area to shoot with an adequate backstop to stop your bullets. Wear shooting glasses and hearing protection.

✓ Shoot from a solid rest, such as a bench rest and sand bags. Shoot at close range to get "on paper," but verify the final zero at expected hunting ranges.

✓ From the solid rest, carefully squeeze off three aimed shots. The center of this group of bullet holes is the rifle's point of impact. Adjusting the sight moves this point of impact to your desired zero. Move open rear sights in the same direction you want the

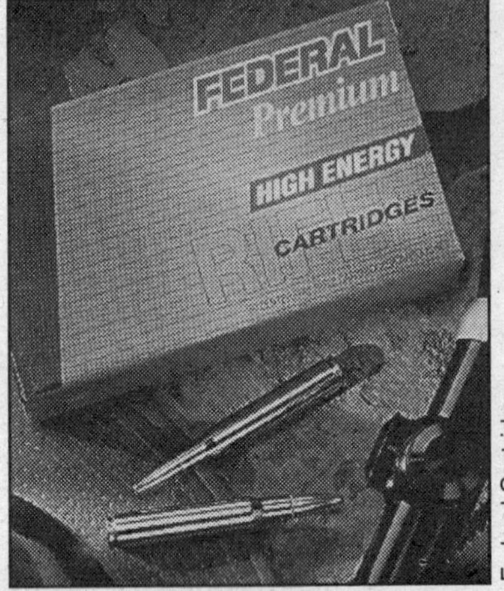

Federal Cartridge

Select ammunition for its intended purpose. Be sure to start with enough ammunition to complete the sighting-in process.

group to move. Adjust scopes following directions on the dials. Continue this process until the group is where you want it.

Do not adjust sights on the basis of single shots. An odd shot can lead to sight adjustment errors and ultimately wastes ammunition.

✓ Different brands and bullet weights may change the point of impact and necessitate re-sighting. If your rifle gets bumped or dropped, be sure to reverify your zero so you can bag your game with one shot.

*— Courtesy of **Federal Cartridge Co.**, 900 Ehlen Drive, Dept. DDH, Anoka, MN 55303.*

How to Mount a Riflescope

Although the process takes time and requires attention to details, mounting a riflescope properly can mean the difference between success and failure in the deer woods.

Use this guide when mounting a scope to your favorite deer rifle.

Tools required
- ✓ Hex wrench set (English)
- ✓ Gunsmith screwdrivers
- ✓ Scope-mounting adhesive
- ✓ Gun oil
- ✓ Long cotton swabs
- ✓ Soft cotton cloth
- ✓ Acetone, ether, or other cleaning/degreasing agent
- ✓ Riflescope bore-sighting device and arbors
- ✓ Scope alignment rods
- ✓ Shims
- ✓ Rubber hammer
- ✓ Rifle vise
- ✓ Short steel ruler
- ✓ Lapping kit
- ✓ Reticle leveler

Instructions

1. Place gun's safety in "on" position. Unload firearm and remove bolt, cylinder, clip, etc. Make sure the chamber is empty.

2. Remove old bases or rings. If the gun is new, you might have to remove the factory screws from the receiver. These screws protect the scope's mounting holes until needed.

3. Degrease the base screws and the receiver's mounting holes.

4. Temporarily install the bases. Shimming might be required under part of the base if the top of the receiver is not parallel to the axis of the bore. Mismatches might require a different set of bases and/or the help of a gunsmith.

5. Install the scope alignment rods into the rings and place on the firearm. If there is a misalignment, some shimming might be required. Very small adjustments can be made later by tapping the base with a rubber hammer.

6. Remove the rings when the rods indicate the system is aligned. Apply a light coating of gun oil to the underside of the base and the top of the receiver.

Also install the base and screws, using adhesive. Be sure the adhesive does not drip into the action. Use cotton swabs to check clean spillage.

7. Re-install the rings with the alignment rods. Again, if there is a small alignment problem, tapping with the rubber hammer might correct it. If there's gross misalignment, shimming might be required.

8. Once you are satisfied the rings and the base are aligned, install the riflescope in the rings. Degrease the inner surface of the rings and the area of contact on the scope.

Inspect the fit of the rings to the riflescope. Some inexpensive rings are not perfectly round, making for a poor fit between the ring and the scope's body tube.

If you're using Weaver-style rings, install them loosely on the scope, then attach them to the base. For Redfield-style rings, attach the twist-lock front ring by using a metal or wooden dowel that's 1 inch in diameter.

Do not use the riflescope to twist the ring in place.

When the scope is mounted on the gun, make sure there is at least ⅛ inch clearance between the bell of the scope and the gun. Also, make sure the action isn't touching the scope during cycling or power change.

9. Set up the bore-sighting system on the firearm. Adjust the ring screws so the scope can rotate but not wobble. Adjust the distance the scope is from the eye to prevent injury during recoil — about 3 inches.

10. Turn the scope to high power and adjust the windage and elevation controls so the image of the bore-sighting grid and the scope reticle do not move with each other as the scope is rotated. This step can also be performed by placing the scope in a cardboard V-block and sighting it in at a distant object.

11. Gently rotate the scope in the rings so the horizontal portion of the reticle is level when the gun is held in the shooting position. To aid this adjustment, use a bubble level or reticle leveler. Next, tighten all rings and base screws. Use adhesive on the screws, and let

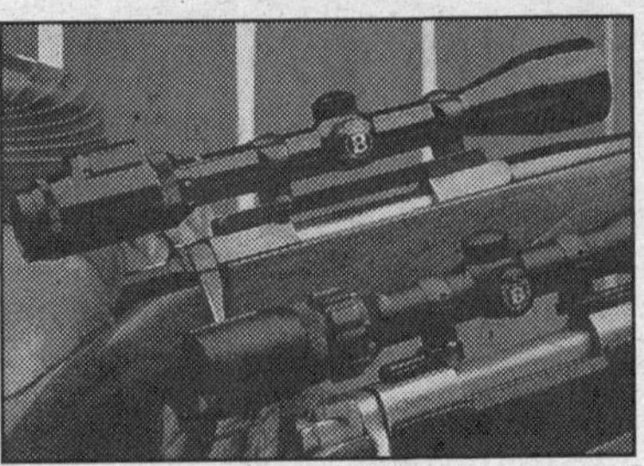

When the scope is mounted on the gun, make sure there is at least ⅛-inch clearance between the bell of the scope and the gun.

set over night.

12. Adjust the windage and elevation controls to place the center of the reticle on the center of the bore-sighting grid. Shimming might be required to bring it in alignment with the bore. If so, consider using a scope-mount system with windage control.

13. With everything secure, the riflescope is now ready for the range. The shooter should pick a common distance — 25, 50 or 100 yards — and adjust accordingly. Remember, ammunition, outside temperature, temperature of the barrel, and cleanliness of the barrel all affect a gun's accuracy.

14. Always make sure the scope's rings and the bases are tight. This will prevent movement during recoil.

*— For more information on scope mounting, contact **Bushnell Sport Optics**, 9200 Cody St., Dept. DDH, Shawnee Mission, KS 66214.*

Read Instructions Carefully Before Mounting Your Scope

Be sure the mounting system is compatible with your gun-scope combination. In some cases it may be necessary to use extra high rings or extension rings.

Ask your dealer to help you select a mounting system which will fit your needs.

Before beginning the mounting procedure, be sure the gun action is open, clip or magazine is removed and a round is not in the chamber. Do not attempt any work until the gun has been cleared and determined to be safe.

Maintaining Your Riflescope

Your Simmons scope is shockproof and waterproof. You should never try to take it apart or clean it internally. If your scope ever does need repair or adjustments, it should be returned to the Simmons Service Department.

Your Simmons scope will perform it's best if occasionally wiped clean with a lens cloth or an optical lens paper like that for eyeglasses and camera lenses. Keep protective lens covers in place when the scope is not being used.

Maintain the metal surfaces of your scope by removing any dirt or sand with a soft brush to avoid scratching the finish.

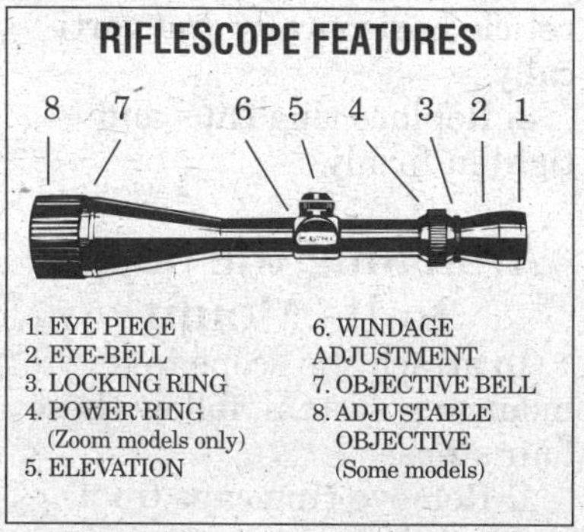

Wipe the scope with a damp cloth and follow with a dry cloth. Finally, wipe with a silicone treated cloth to restore luster and protect the scope against corrosion. Be careful not to touch the lenses with the silicone cloth.

Focusing the Eye Lens

1. Hold scope about 3 inches from your eye.

2. Quickly glance through the scope at a featureless area, such as a wall or open sky. *Caution:* Never use a scope to look directly into the sun.

3. If the reticle did not instantly appear in sharp focus, loosen the eye-bell locking ring, rotate the eye-bell in either direction until reticle is sharply focused.

1. Remove ring caps from mount, place scope in cradle formed by uncapped rings.

2. Slide scope fore or aft to position scope at the proper eye point. (Full field of view can be seen)

3. Rotate scope to align the

reticle horizontally and vertically.

4. Replace ring caps and tighten firmly.

Attaching the Scope to Its Mount

To attach the scope to its mounting system, follow these four steps:

1. Remove ring caps from mount, place scope in cradle formed by uncapped rings.

2. Slide scope fore or aft to position scope at the proper eye point. (Full field of view can be seen).

3. Rotate scope to align the reticle horizontally and vertically.

4. Replace ring caps and tighten firmly.

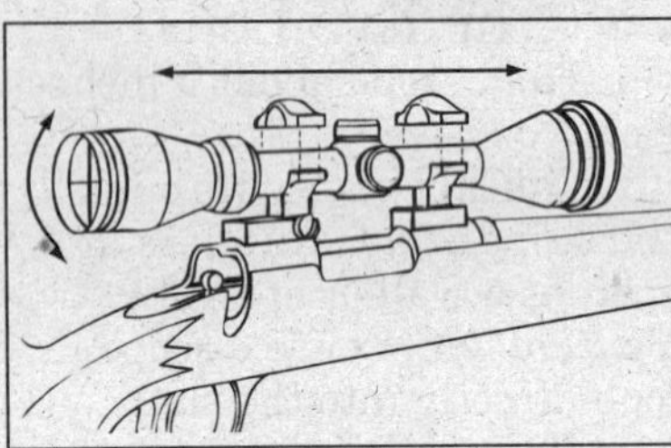

Pre-Zeroing

If available, use a bore sighter collimator to pre-zero your rifle.

At an approved range, or other safe area, bench rest the rifle. Remove the windage and elevation caps. If you have a bolt action rifle, remove bolt. If you have a lever, pump, or semi-auto loading rifle, use a mirror type bore sighting device, available from your gun retailer.

If you have a zoom power scope, turn the power change ring to the highest setting. If your scope model is equipped with an adjustable objective lens mount for a parallax correction, rotate the focusing ring to the appropriate setting.

Firearm Safety Depends on You

1. Always keep the muzzle pointed in a safe direction.
2. Firearms should be unloaded and cased when not in use.
3. Be sure of your target and what is beyond it.
4. Use correct ammunition.
5. Always wear eye and ear protection when shooting.
6. Be sure the barrel is clear.
7. Learn the mechanical and handling characteristics of the gun.

A. 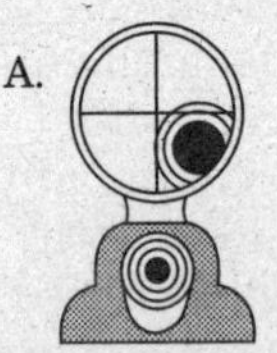

B. 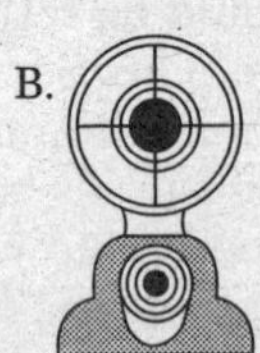

A.	B.
Sight through the bore at a target at 100 yards. Move the rifle to center the target in the bore.	Sight through the scope and adjust the windage and elevation screws to center on the reticle.

Final Zeroing

Since final zeroing involves live fire, check bore to be sure it is free of any obstructions before loading. Use eye and ear protection.

Fire three rounds at your target. Note impact on target. Measure the distance from group center to target center.

Adjust the windage and elevation screws accordingly. Each click adjustment will move the bullet impact by the amount shown on the dials (type C or D) at 100 yards.

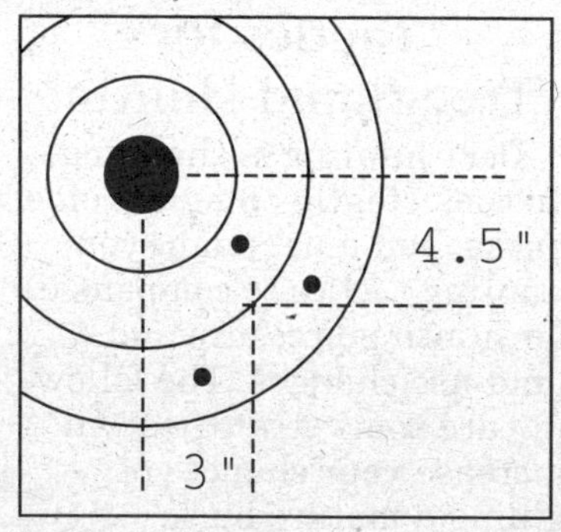

Replace windage and elevation caps when zeroing is completed.

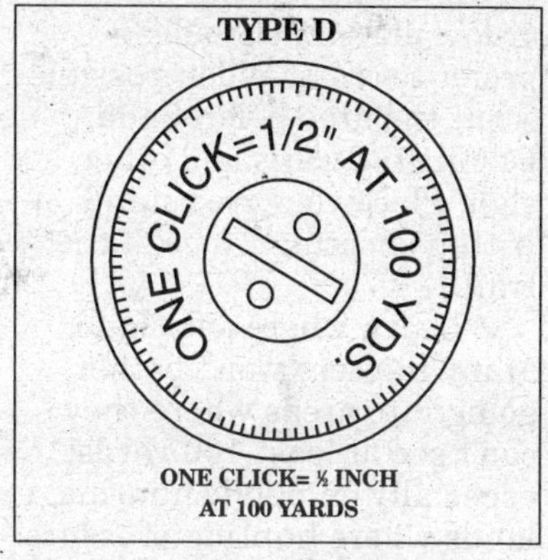

Each click of adjustment will move the bullet impact by the amount shown at the distance indicated.

	50 Yards	100 Yards	200 Yards
Type C	⅛ Inch	¼ Inch	½ Inch
Type D	¼ Inch	½ Inch	1 Inch

*— Information on scope maintenance, focussing and zeroing courtesy of **Simmons Outdoor Corp.** For more information on hunting scopes and optics, contact Simmons, 201 Plantation Oak Drive, Thomasville, GA 31792.*

Tactics for Tree-Stand Hunting

Deer hunting is changing. To consistently outsmart older bucks, you must adapt your hunting tactics to compensate for hunting pressure and land-use changes. The following are some strategies can increase your chances of killing a mature buck.

✓ Move away from hunting pressure by using topographical maps and a compass or global positioning system.

Enter the woods long before daylight and look for saddles or low places where deer prefer to cross. When possible, scout the area beforehand, looking for trails and other sign. Place your tree stand within shooting range of the trail.

✓ Learn where deer hide. Many hunters won't bother going into areas where they can't see at least 100 yards, especially on public hunting lands where hunting pressure is high. Be willing to hunt more exclusive spots and commit the whole day to that spot.

✓ Hunting pressure builds toward the end of hunting season and bigger bucks will hide deeper in thick cover. Try clearing small paths in the cover, and position yourself there well before daylight. Chances are you'll see these deer move into your lanes throughout the day as they

Install three or four tree stands in an area where you suspect a buck will appear. This will allow you to have several game plans if the wind shifts when you're ready to hunt.

are pressured back into the cover.

✓ Use free-standing tower stands in clearcuts and open fields. Deer rarely look up for danger when trees aren't present.

✓ All deer must eat. Study and learn the food sources used by deer at various times during the year. Learn to identify these foods, then scout until you find what the deer are feeding on during different periods.

Set up down wind of the

food source, and place your stand as high as possible to avoid spooking deer.

✓ Install three or four tree stands in an area where you suspect a buck will appear during the day. This will allow you to have several game plans if the wind shifts when you're ready to hunt.

✓ Let other hunters drive deer to you. Learn how to map hunting pressure and get ahead of it well before daylight. By staying put, you'll let the movement of other hunters push deer to you.

✓ Bucks often use funnels when traveling from bedding to feeding areas. Learn how to locate these terrain features, and set up your stands accordingly.

✓ Most hunters want to be able to hunt as easily as possible. Try expending more time and effort to find a more exclusive spot. For example, use waders or a small canoe to access flooded areas, and position yourself in a tree near a shoreline.

✓ "Buddy" hunting for bucks consistently pays off in more deer on the meat pole. Try placing your stands within 30 yards of each other near a food source. This will give you and your partner 120 yards of coverage when deer decide to feed.

✓ For two days before and three days after a full moon,

Judd Cooney

Bucks often use funnels when traveling from bedding to feeding areas. Learn how to locate these terrain features, and set up your stands accordingly.

don't bother to hunt early mornings. Sleep in and be on your stand by 10 a.m. Hunt through the afternoon, and you'll have better chances of seeing mature bucks.

— Ray McIntyre

*— For more information on tree stands and tree-stand hunting, contact **Warren & Sweat Mfg.**, Box 350440, Dept. DDH, Grand Island, FL 32735.*

Tactics for Muzzleloading Hunters

Unlike modern rifles, muzzleloaders require hunters to pay special attention to the gun to ensure safe and efficient shooting. Therefore, muzzle-loading hunters should always follow these 10 tips:

✓ Always wear safety glasses. Both flintlock and percussion guns can shower small bits of flint and cap when fired.

✓ Use only black powder in muzzle-loading guns. Smokeless powders create extremely high pressure. The barrel can explode and cause serious injury to the shooter.

✓ Do not exceed manufacturer's recommended maximum powder charge. Exceeding this limit will vastly increase barrel pressure without much change in muzzle velocity.

✓ Never load powder directly from a horn or flask into the barrel. A smoldering ember from the barrel can ignite the powder and explode the horn or flask. Use a separate powder measure.

✓ Keep face, body and hands clear — as far away as possible from the muzzle of the gun. Use only fingers to seat the ball. Never put the palm of your hand over the end of a ramrod.

✓ Never cap or prime the gun unless the muzzle is pointed in a safe direction.

✓ Always seat the ball firmly on the powder charge. Don't try to fire one that is not properly seated. Damage and injury to gun and shooter can result.

✓ When in doubt, pull it out. Never try to shoot a ball that is not firmly seated on the powder charge. Make sure the gun is not capped or primed, then, remove it with a ball puller.

✓ Never smoke while shooting, loading or handling black powder.

✓ Muzzleloaders deserve to be handled with the same respect accorded all firearms.

Remember, muzzleloaders require special cleaning needs, ones you won't have encountered with modern guns. Because the component chemicals of black powder are corrosive, your muzzleloader requires frequent and thorough cleaning. Above all, do not use a phosphor bronze brush to scrub the barrel. These brushes cannot be reversed in the bore without bending, snagging or breaking the bristles, which can damage the barrel.

*— For more information on gun care, contact **Hoppe's**, Airport Industrial Mall, Dept. DDH, Coatesville, PA 19320.*

Chapter 5

Weather Data, Moon Phases & Deer Behavior

This chapter will help you gauge a number of factors related to weather and the moon.

Traveling hunters will appreciate the quick-reference charts on temperatures, precipitation and the wind chill factor. The temperature and precipitation data allow you to predict weather trends for various regions across the United States. Best of all, the data is presented for the most productive hunting months: September, October, November and December.

Northern hunters will appreciate the wind chill factor chart. A quick scan of the morning newspaper will give you an idea of the temperature and wind speed ranges of the state you'll be hunting. With that information, you can calculate how cold it will feel when you're in the deer woods.

Also included in this chapter are handy guides to moon phases for all 12 months of 1998. This information is followed by full-page guides to key dates for all four moon phases. Plan ahead by circling the full moon dates on your hunting calendar!

You'll also learn how deer activity decreases as wind speed increases. Included are descriptions of how high-pressure systems affect deer behavior and how white-tails take advantage of thermal currents while bedding and feeding.

Average Normal Temperatures and Precipitation

City	September T	September P	October T	October P	November T	November P	December T	December P
Albany, N.Y.	61	3.0	50	2.8	40	3.2	27	2.9
Asheville, N.C.	66	3.9	56	3.6	48	3.6	40	3.5
Atlanta, Ga.	73	3.4	62	3.1	53	3.9	45	4.3
Birmingham, Ala.	73	3.9	63	2.8	53	4.3	45	5.1
Bismarck, N.D.	57	1.5	46	0.9	29	0.5	14	0.5
Caribou, Maine	54	3.5	43	3.1	31	3.6	15	3.2
Columbus, Ohio	66	3.0	54	2.2	43	3.2	32	2.9
Dallas, Texas	77	3.4	67	3.5	56	2.3	47	1.8
Denver, Colo.	62	1.2	51	1.0	39	0.9	31	0.6
Des Moines, Iowa	65	3.5	54	2.6	39	1.8	24	1.3
Duluth, Minn.	54	3.8	44	2.5	28	1.8	13	1.2
Fairbanks, Alaska	46	1.0	25	0.9	3	0.8	-7	0.9
Galveston, Texas	80	5.9	73	2.8	64	3.4	56	3.5
Grand Junct., Colo.	67	0.7	55	0.9	40	0.6	28	0.6
Helena, Mont.	55	1.2	45	0.6	32	0.5	21	0.6
Indianapolis, Ind.	67	2.9	55	2.6	43	3.2	31	3.3
Jackson, Miss.	76	3.6	65	3.3	56	4.8	48	5.9
Juneau, Alaska	49	6.4	42	7.7	33	5.2	27	4.7
Kansas City, Mo.	68	4.9	57	3.3	43	1.9	30	1.6
Lexington, Ky.	68	3.2	57	2.6	46	3.4	36	4.0
Little Rock, Ark.	74	7.4	63	6.3	52	5.2	43	4.3
Louisville, Ky.	70	3.2	58	2.7	47	3.7	37	3.6
Marquette, Mich.	54	4.1	44	3.6	30	2.9	17	2.6
Memphis, Tenn.	74	3.5	63	3.0	53	5.1	44	5.7
Milwaukee, Wis.	62	3.4	50	2.4	38	2.5	24	2.3
Minneapolis, Minn.	61	2.7	49	2.2	33	1.6	18	1.1
New Orleans, La.	78	5.5	69	3.1	61	4.4	55	5.8
Norfolk, Va.	72	3.9	61	3.2	53	2.9	44	3.2
Okla. City, Ok.	73	3.4	62	2.7	49	1.5	40	1.2
Omaha, Nebr.	65	3.7	53	2.3	39	1.5	25	1.0
Philadelphia, Pa.	68	3.4	56	2.6	46	3.3	35	3.4
Phoenix, Ariz.	86	0.9	75	0.7	62	0.7	54	1.0
Portland, Maine	59	3.1	49	3.9	39	5.2	27	4.6
Portland, Ore.	63	1.8	55	2.7	46	5.3	40	6.1
Rapid City, S.D.	60	1.2	49	1.1	35	0.6	24	0.5
Salt Lk. City, Utah	65	1.3	53	1.4	41	1.3	30	1.4
San Antonio, Texas	79	3.4	70	3.2	60	2.6	52	1.5
Seattle, Wash.	61	1.9	54	3.3	46	5.7	42	6.0
Syracuse, N.Y.	62	3.8	51	3.2	41	3.7	28	3.2

T = Temperature   **P = Precipitation**

The Wind Chill Factor

ACTUAL THERMOMETER READING (F°)

50	40	30	20	10	0	-10	-20	-30	-40

EQUIVALENT TEMPERATURE (F°)

Calm	50	40	30	20	10	0	-10	-20	-30	-40
5	48	37	27	16	6	-5	-15	-26	-36	-47
10	40	28	16	4	-9	-21	-33	-46	-58	-70
15	36	22	9	-5	-18	-36	-45	-58	-72	-85
20	32	18	4	-10	-25	-39	-53	-67	-82	-96
25	30	16	0	-15	-29	-44	-59	-74	-88	-104
30	28	13	-2	-18	-33	-44	-63	-79	-94	-109
35	27	11	-4	-20	-35	-49	-67	-82	-98	-113
40	26	10	-6	-21	-37	-53	-69	-85	-100	-116

Over 40 MPH (little added effect)	Little Danger (for properly clothed)	Increasing Danger	Great Danger

Deer Hunters' 1998

January 1998

First Quarter   Jan. 5
Full Moon   Jan. 12
Last Quarter   Jan. 20
New Moon   Jan. 28

February 1998

First Quarter   Feb. 3
Full Moon   Feb. 11
Last Quarter   Feb. 19
New Moon   Feb. 26

March 1998

First Qtr.   March 5
Full Moon   March 13
Last Qtr.   March 21
New Mn.   March 28

April 1998

First Quarter   April 3
Full Moon   April 11
Last Quarter   April 19
New Moon   April 26

May 1998

First Quarter   May 3
Full Moon   May 11
Last Quarter   May 19
New Moon   May 25

June 1998

First Quarter   June 2
Full Moon   June 10
Last Quarter   June 17
New Moon   June 24

Calendar of Moon Phases

July 1998

First Quarter   July 1
Full Moon   July 9
Last Quarter   July 16
New Moon   July 23

August 1998

First Quarter (July 31)
Full Moon   Aug. 8
Last Quarter Aug. 14
New Moon   Aug. 22

September 1998

First Qtr.   (Aug. 30)
Full Moon   Sept. 6
Last Qtr.   Sept. 13
New Mn.   Sept. 20

October 1998

First Quarter (Sept. 28)
Full Moon   Oct. 5
Last Quarter Oct. 12
New Moon   Oct. 20

November 1998

First Quarter (Oct. 28)
Full Moon   Nov. 4
Last Quarter Nov. 11
New Moon   Nov. 19

December 1998

First Quarter (Nov. 27)
Full Moon   Dec. 3
Last Quarter Dec. 10
New Moon   Dec. 18

First Quarter & Full Moon

**1998
FIRST QUARTER
MOON**

First Quarter Schedule

January 5
February 3
March 5
April 3
May 3
June 2
July 1
July 31
August 30
September 28
October 28
November 27

Full Moon Schedule

January 12
February 11
March 13
April 11
May 11
June 10
July 9
August 8
September 6
October 5
November 4
December 3

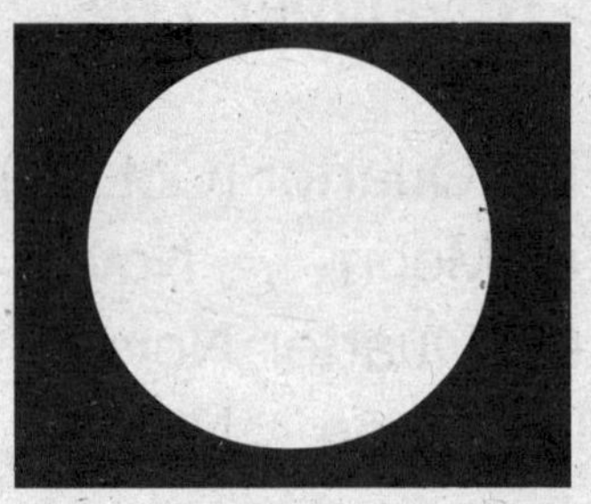

**1998
FULL MOON**

A Rut-Hunter's Guide to Full-Moon Dates

Throughout much of the whitetail's range, the rut usually peaks in late October or early November.

Charles J. Alsheimer, Northern field editor for *Deer & Deer Hunting*, and Vermont biologist Wayne Laroche, believe it's possible to accurately predict the peak times for deer activity. Their research, published in the August, September and October 1997 issues of *Deer & Deer Hunting*, reveals a new theory on the moon's influence on deer activity.

The following chart, provided by Alsheimer, lists the full-moon dates for the next several years. Use this guide to help plan future rut-time hunts.

Year	Full Moon
1998	Nov. 4
1999	Oct. 24
2000	Nov. 11
2001	Oct. 31
2002	Oct. 21
2003	Nov. 8
2004	Oct. 28
2005	Oct. 17
2006	Nov. 5

Deer & the Wind

Generally speaking, deer activity decreases as wind speed increases. Calm and light winds produce more deer sightings, while moderate and gusty winds reduce them. The dividing line seems to be somewhere around 15 mph.

However, some researchers and hunters have documented an increase in buck activity during calm winds.

Deer tend to group up and become excitable in high winds. During cold months, high winds cause deer to seek shelter on the lee slopes of hills and in dense coniferous woodlands. Conifer stands reduce wind speed by up to 75 percent.

Research proves that even though deer will move in all directions in relation to the wind, they'll move directly into the wind whenever possible. Deer trails closely match the prevailing wind direction and traditional wind changes. Wind fits two basic patterns:

Pattern A — Occurs during stable, high-pressure weather systems with clear or partly cloudy skies. This pattern brings little or no wind at sunrise and sunset, and maximum wind speeds in mid to late afternoon.

Pattern B — Occurs during changing weather conditions. This pattern brings constant wind speeds throughout the day with frequent gusts reflecting atmospheric turbulence.

Thermal winds — Thermal currents move uphill as the air temperature increases in the morning. Thermals move downhill as air cools toward evening.

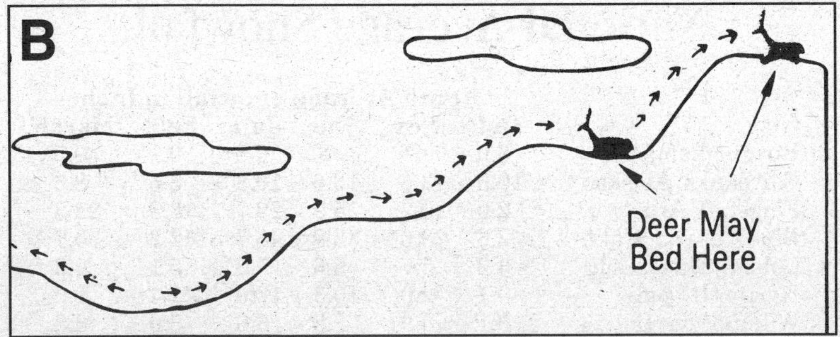

Whitetails prefer to bed on slightly higher ground when the terrain permits. Consequently, when they move down-slope toward their feeding area in the afternoon, they experience ideal wind coverage on their trails with the thermal air currents still moving up-slope.

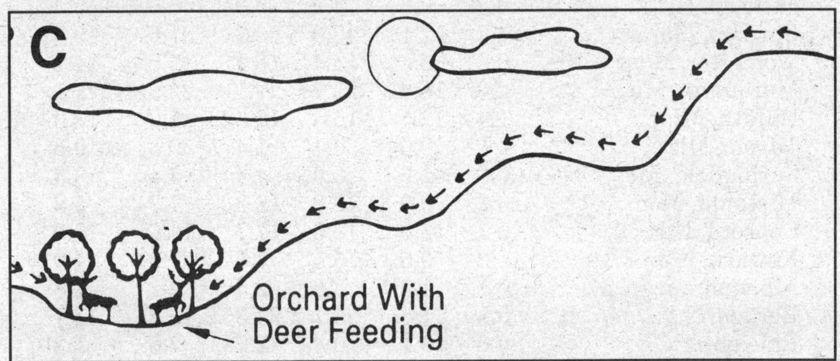

When returning to their bedding areas in the morning, whitetails take advantage of ideal wind coverage with the downwind thermal air currents still holding from the higher elevations to the lower ground.

Tips for Judging Wind Speeds

✓ Calm, less than 1 mph: Smoke rises vertically, leaves on tree s remain motionless.
✓ 1 to 3 mph: Smoke drifts, but wind vanes stay motionless.
✓ 7 to 10 mph: Flags extend and leaves are in constant motion.
✓ 11 to 16 mph: Small branches move, dust blows and loose paper flies.
✓ 17 to 21 mph: Noticeable motion in tall tree tops; small trees sway.
✓ 22 to 27 mph: Large branches in motion, whistling in wire.

National Average Snowfall

City	Oct.	Nov.	Dec.	Jan.	Feb.	March
Birmingham, Ala.	0.0	T	T	0.8	0.1	0.5
Fairbanks, Alaska	10.9	13.6	13.8	10.8	8.6	8.6
Flagstaff, Ariz.	2.0	10.2	15.9	20.7	18.3	22.3
Blue Canyon, Calif.	2.6	23.6	33.8	46.7	42.2	50.7
Colo. Springs, Colo.	3.2	5.7	5.6	5.0	5.1	9.3
Hartford, Conn.	0.1	2.0	10.3	12.0	11.4	9.9
Wilmington, Del.	0.1	0.9	8.9	6.6	6.0	3.3
Athens, Ga.	0.0	0.1	0.2	0.9	0.7	0.5
Pocatello, Idaho	1.9	5.3	8.9	10.0	6.2	5.9
Chicago, Ill.	0.4	1.9	8.3	10.7	8.1	7.0
Rockford, Ill.	0.1	2.6	9.3	8.6	6.7	6.6
South Bend, Ind.	0.7	8.0	17.7	18.9	14.9	9.1
Des Moines, Iowa	0.2	3.0	5.6	8.1	7.2	6.2
Topeka, Kan.	0.0	1.3	4.9	6.1	4.7	3.7
Jackson, Ky.	0.2	0.3	3.9	5.0	6.6	3.3
Caribou, Maine	1.7	12.1	23.0	23.3	21.6	19.2
Worcester, Mass.	0.5	3.6	13.4	16.1	15.9	14.1
Marquette, Mich.	4.0	16.8	25.7	27.1	22.9	21.1
Duluth, Minn.	1.4	12.5	15.4	16.8	11.2	13.3
Tupelo, Miss.	T	0.0	0.4	1.4	0.8	0.3
Springfield, Mo.	0.0	1.6	3.0	4.4	4.4	3.3
Missoula, Mont.	0.9	6.0	10.8	12.3	7.7	5.9
Concord, N.H.	0.1	3.8	18.6	17.7	14.6	10.9
Newark, N.J.	0.0	0.5	5.5	7.5	7.9	4.9
Albuquerque, N.M.	0.1	1.3	2.6	2.5	2.2	1.8
Buffalo, N.Y.	0.3	11.5	22.7	23.3	18.2	11.7
Raleigh, N.C.	0.0	0.1	0.8	2.2	2.6	1.3
Bismarck, N.D.	1.7	6.3	5.9	7.2	6.7	8.1
Cleveland, Ohio	0.6	5.0	11.9	12.6	12.3	10.6
Tulsa, Okla.	0.0	0.4	1.6	3.3	2.4	1.4
Burns, Ore.	0.7	6.4	12.4	8.3	8.8	4.7
Erie, Pa.	0.3	10.3	22.9	22.8	16.1	10.4
Sioux Falls, S.D.	0.7	5.4	7.2	6.4	8.1	9.6
Chattanooga, Tenn.	T	0.0	0.6	1.8	1.2	0.7
Amarillo, Texas	0.3	1.8	2.7	3.9	3.6	2.5
Salt Lake City, Utah	1.3	6.6	12.0	13.5	9.4	9.4
Burlington, Vt.	0.2	6.6	13.1	18.8	16.8	12.4
Roanoke, Va.	0.0	1.5	3.8	6.2	7.0	3.8
Charleston, W. Va.	0.2	2.2	5.1	10.1	8.7	5.1
Green Bay, Wis.	0.2	4.7	11.0	10.5	8.2	8.9
Cheyenne, Wyo.	3.7	7.4	5.2	6.4	5.9	12.1

The column group header reads: **Month/Average Snowfall in Inches**

T = Trace

To Hunt the Snow

Dan Schmidt

■ *Michael L. Duarte*

The man stood at the tent's door, his gaze fixed on the thin flashlight beam that probed the darkness. Specks of ice crowded the air around the light. A small smile crossed his face.

For 20 years he had dreamed of this hunt, imagining its look and feel, its smell and taste. To hunt the snow. He closed the door flap and huddled next to the gas lantern, watching tiny, half-frozen beads of condensation sparkle across the white

To Hunt the Snow

canvas roof. He was a long way from Louisiana — 1,500 miles across the middle of America — far from the cypress and Spanish moss, and the sweet and sour odor of methane rising from swampy bogs.

Closing his eyes, he again pictured the 12-pointer moving slowly below his stand, its swollen neck bent to the ground as it drew strong drafts of pheromone from the doe's fresh track. How had he missed? Fifteen-hundred miles to hunt the North's huge bucks, and he had cleanly missed a 20-yard shot — not a branch or leaf to share the blame.

At least he would have tomorrow; in fact, three more tomorrows, before having to pack it in. In the end, it would matter little whether he killed a good buck. He had already spent four magnificent days in the land of his boyhood dreams; four days bathing in the crimson and scarlet hue of maple, and the rich, golden glow of popple; four frosted nights around the campfire, and the pungent aroma of birch smoke clouding the Northern airlike incense. And now the snow.

Private Dreams

The man was glad to be alone. It was his private dream, spawned by the hunting stories he had read as a boy. In those magazines of the '60s and '70s, the great hunts, spectacular whitetails and precious moments were always the grand moments shared in the ancient Pennsylvania deer camps or deep forests of northern Minnesota. He had promised himself that one day, while blood still pulsed strongly in his veins, he would also sit in a blind surrounded by the autumnal explosion of the North Woods. And when he wasn't doing that, he would start out a morning by silently tracking a buck — its heavy hoof and dew-points crushed into the fresh snow.

"Why the hell would you drive 2,000 miles to hunt deer?" his friends asked. "Got plenty-enough whitetails sneaking right behind Old Man Colter's store down the road."

There was no way to explain the dream, no way to explain the alluring intangibles of sights and scents. To a Southern lad weaned on North Woods deer stories, only one lifelong desire burned brightly.

"Now if you was heading to Alaska to hunt grizzly, or up to Colorado for elk, hell, we could understand," friends said. "But to go that dang far for a whitetail, hoo boy, that's twisted."

Again, the man opened the tent flap, this time reaching down to scoop a small pile of the sparkling white into his hands. The snow was letting up. A small sliver of moonlight escaped from between dark, rolling clouds, casting a soft glow on the darkened forest. Good. He had always read that deer moved willingly on the tail-end of a snowstorm. Tomorrow might be the day.

The man squinted into the night, shaking his head in child-like wonder. Just five hours earlier, this very forest was alive in spectacular colors that defied description or name — brilliant shades of autumn intensity he had only

glimpsed in pictures. Now, a strange and alien landscape returned his stare. Strange and white, but quietly inviting.

Awaiting Dawn

He thought morning would never come. The anticipation of knowing he would finally hunt the snow robbed the man of deep sleep. Though he was tired, anxiety's adrenaline rush fueled his morning ritual. With stoic, practiced patience, he forced himself to eat a small breakfast, supply his day pack and give his bow a thorough, last-minute check.

Soon, he was outside in the pre-dawn darkness, moving toward the stand he had placed in a grove of hardwoods by the spring. As his feet bit into 4 inches of November's first snow, he was glad he had decided on the luxury of felt-pac boots. They were expensive and would serve little purpose back home, but they were worth their weight in gold these past few frozen mornings. Today, they were priceless.

The storm was not quite over. Little flakes fell and spotted his camo. Shortly after getting into the stand, he was watching the antics of two squirrels when he spotted a doe picking her way through the grove. Though he had seen several deer over the past few days, he was still astounded by the size of Northern deer. This lone doe was easily the largest he had ever seen. He watched her nervous twitch; head turned to watch her back track, the white flag of her tail bent to the side in a hormonal-spurred invitation.

The man knew what was coming next and, within minutes, he spotted the buck. The grace of hunting luck was smiling down upon the man. It was the same huge 12-pointer. With a pounding heart and little chills of excitement crawling across his neck, he drew the bow and sighted on the 30-yard pin. A tumbling veil of white, silent flakes blinked past his eyes.

No, the boys back home would never understand; never feel the vibration of

thrill the man knew; never know the rare, sweet gift of a dream fulfilled.

It was his chance to hunt the snow.

Chapter 6

White-Tailed Deer Harvest Records

The facts are clear: Sound deer management by state wildlife officials combined with conservation dollars generated by sportsmen have produced the largest deer populations in modern times.

With 88 percent of all hunters actively hunting whitetails, the estimated 12 million deer hunters dominate the American hunting scene.

Record-keeping systems vary among states. For example, some Western states only keep track of combined deer harvest, which includes whitetails and mule deer. In addition, some states estimate their annual whitetail harvest based on mail-in surveys, while other states account for every deer killed through mandatory registration procedures. We've made every attempt to present data uniformly for accurate comparisons among states.

This chapter not only gives you a numerical look at deer hunting history, it boldly shows that white-tailed deer hunting is increasing in popularity.

Alabama

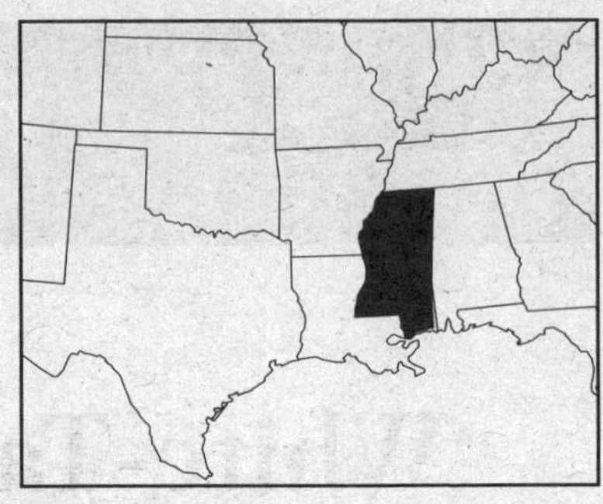

Year	Firearm	Bow	Total
1963-64	NA	NA	31,123
1964-65	NA	NA	59,230
1965-66	NA	NA	37,819
1966-67	NA	NA	47,842
1967-68	NA	NA	68,406
1968-69	NA	NA	63,674
1969-70	NA	NA	74,239
1970-71	NA	NA	63,502
1971-72	NA	NA	80,184
1972-73	NA	NA	82,555
1973-74	NA	NA	121,953
1974-75	NA	NA	120,727
1975-76	NA	NA	125,625
1976-77	NA	NA	144,155
1977-78	NA	NA	147,113
1978-79	NA	NA	152,733
1979-80	NA	NA	140,685
1980-81	NA	NA	130,532
1981-82	NA	NA	202,449
1982-83	NA	NA	141,281

Year	Firearm	Bow	Total
1983-84	NA	NA	192,231
1984-85	NA	NA	237,378
1985-86	NA	NA	280,436
1986-87	288,487	17,653	306,140
1987-88	309,517	15,683	325,200
1988-89	257,734	18,854	276,588
1990-91	263,100	31,300	294,400
1991-92	269,500	25,500	295,000
1992-93	261,500	31,600	293,100
1993-94	305,300	45,200	350,500
1994-95	290,600	40,400	331,000

Arizona

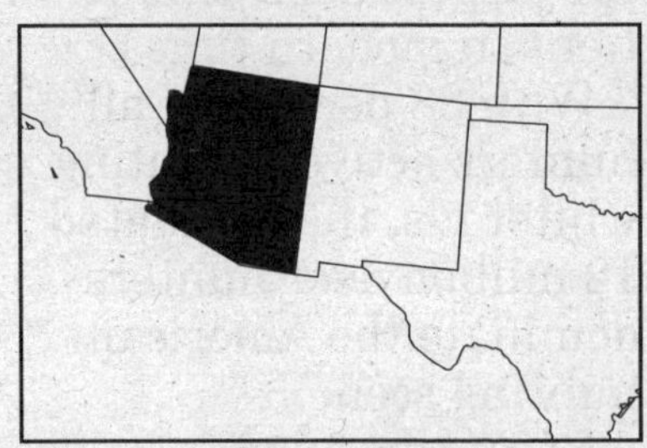

Year	Firearm	Bow	Total
1958	5,096	NA	5,096
1959	5,421	NA	5,421
1960	4,982	NA	4,982
1961	4,734	NA	4,734
1962	4,194	NA	4,194
1963	4,343	NA	4,343
1964	4,339	NA	4,339
1965	3,612	NA	3,612
1966	2,993	NA	2,993
1967	2,662	NA	2,662
1968	2,927	NA	2,927
1969	2,202	NA	2,202
1970	2,232	NA	2,232
1971	1,535	NA	1,535

Year	Firearm	Bow	Total
1972	1,673	NA	1,673
1973	2,097	NA	2,097
1974	3,248	NA	3,248
1975	2,870	NA	2,870
1976	2,662	NA	2,662
1977	2,319	NA	2,319
1978	2,287	NA	2,287
1979	3,264	NA	3,264
1980	3,523	NA	3,523

Arizona White-Tailed Deer Harvest Totals, Continued

Year	Firearm	Bow	Total	Year	Firearm	Bow	Total
1981	3,504	NA	3,504	1989	4,387	189	4,576
1982	4,002	60	4,062	1990	4,449	100	4,549
1983	4,221	71	4,292	1991	5,375	129	5,504
1984	7,116	65	7,181	1992	5,737	95	5,832
1985	6,902	138	7,040	1993	5,556	152	5,772
1986	5,934	94	6,028	1994	5,363	1,315	6,678
1987	4,895	115	5,010	1995	4,899	239	5,138
1988	4,600	108	4,708	1996	4,126	NA	4,126

Arkansas

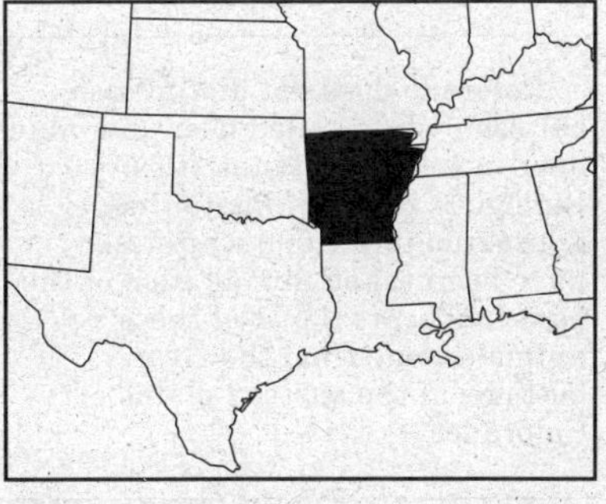

Year	Firearm	Bow	Total	Year	Firearm	Bow	Total
1938	203	NA	203				
1939	540	NA	540				
1940	408	NA	408				
1941	433	NA	433				
1942	1,000	NA	1,000				
1943	1,723	NA	1,723				
1944	1,606	NA	1,606	Year	Firearm	Bow	Total
1945	1,687	NA	1,687	1965	17,138	NA	17,138
1946	1,661	NA	1,661	1966	20,028	NA	20,028
1947	2,016	NA	2,016	1967	21,751	NA	21,751
1948	2,779	NA	2,779	1968	20,063	NA	20,063
1949	3,075	NA	3,075	1969	24,018	1,678	25,696
1950	4,122	NA	4,122	1970	24,784	1,233	26,017
1951	4,600	NA	4,600	1971	23,375	1,345	24,720
1952	6,090	NA	6,090	1972	31,415	672	32,087
1953	6,245	NA	6,245	1973	32,292	1,502	33,794
1954	7,343	NA	7,343	1974	32,168	1,595	33,763
1955	6,856	NA	6,856	1975	32,210	1,112	33,322
1956	8,249	NA	8,249	1976	27,249	540	27,789
1957	9,438	NA	9,438	1977	27,862	1,247	29,109
1958	9,993	NA	9,993	1978	41,018	2,434	43,452
1959	12,280	NA	12,280	1979	32,841	3,233	36,074
1960	15,000	NA	15,000	1980	41,693	3,509	45,202
1961	19,359	NA	19,359	1981	41,567	3,024	44,591
1962	27,772	NA	27,772	1982	35,051	7,822	42,873
1963	25,148	NA	25,148	1983	42,709	17,539	60,248
1964	16,637	NA	16,637	1984	53,679	12,360	66,039

Arkansas White-Tailed Deer Harvest Totals, Continued

Year	Firearm	Bow	Total	Year	Firearm	Bow	Total
1985	48,027	12,049	60,076	1991	NA	NA	110,896
1986	67,941	11,939	79,880	1992	NA	NA	110,401
1987	89,422	16,970	106,392	1993	106,119	15,944	122,063
1988	94,193	16,014	110,207	1994	104,061	16,433	120,494
1989	97,031	16,048	113,079	1995	144,932	18,992	163,924
1990	70,498	20,412	90,910	1996	133,180	17,981	151,161

Colorado

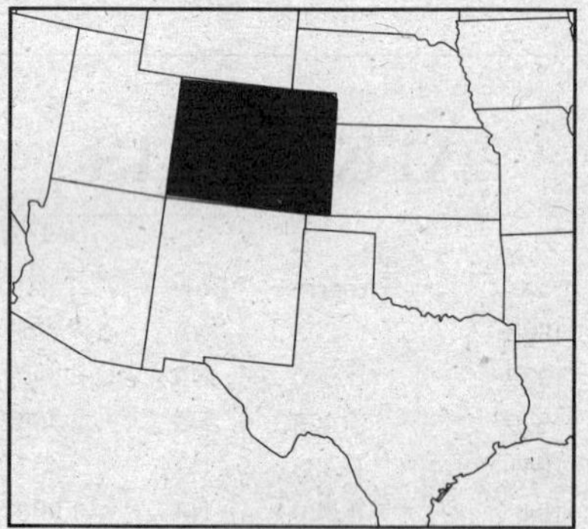

Colorado does not distinguish between white-tailed deer and mule deer in its harvest statistics. Biologists there estimate that approximately 1,000 whitetails have been taken during each of the past five years. Most of these animals come from the river bottoms of the eastern plains of Colorado.

Connecticut

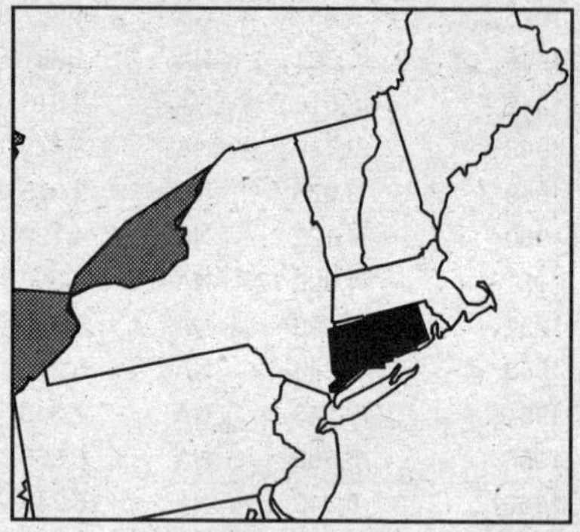

Year	Firearm	Bow	Total
1975	475	75	550
1976	530	100	630
1977	780	125	905
1978	805	125	930
1979	870	140	1,010
1980	2,189	376	2,565
1981	2,463	393	2,856
1982	2,233	391	2,624
1983	3,152	639	3,791
1984	3,742	596	4,338
1985	3,817	722	4,539
1986	4,575	819	5,394
1987	5,618	854	6,472
1988	6,843	799	7,642
1989	7,837	926	8,763

Year	Firearm	Bow	Total
1990	NA	NA	9,896
1991	NA	NA	11,311
1992	NA	NA	12,486
1993	NA	NA	10,360
1994	NA	NA	10,438
1995	10,140	2,606	12,746
1996	9,372	2,604	11,976

Delaware

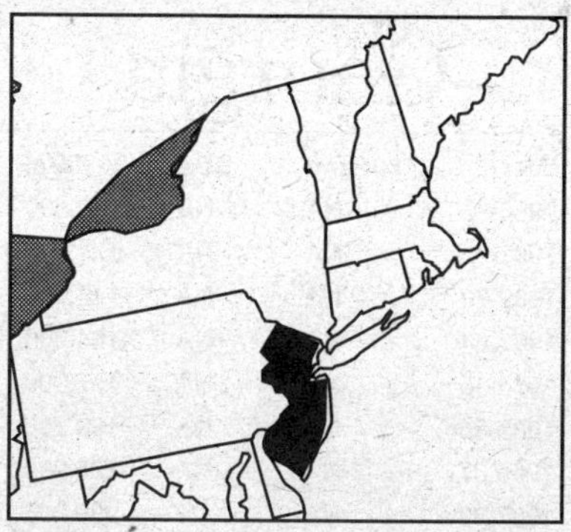

Year	Firearm	Bow	Total
1976-77	1,475	19	1,494
1977-78	1,630	22	1,652
1978-79	1,679	20	1,699
1979-80	1,783	20	1,803
1980-81	1,737	17	1,754
1981-82	2,080	31	2,111
1982-83	2,046	48	2,094
1983-84	2,210	21	2,231
1984-85	2,473	41	2,514
1985-86	2,383	58	2,439
1986-87	2,772	78	2,850
1987-88	3,420	121	3,541
1988-89	3,844	154	3,998
1989-90	4,292	212	4,504
1990-91	4,814	252	5,066
1991-92	4,970	362	5,332
1992-93	6,721	524	7,245
1993-94	6,917	548	7,465
1994-95	7,151	673	7,824
1995-96	8,050	728	8,778

Florida

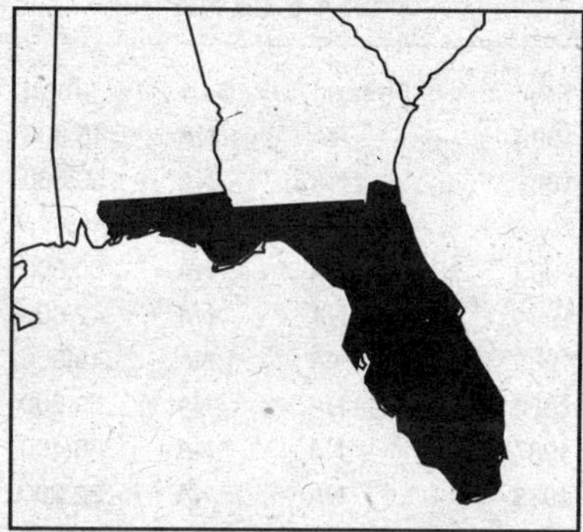

Year	Firearm	Bow	Total
1971	NA	NA	48,900
1972	NA	NA	58,500
1973	NA	NA	57,122
1974	NA	NA	54,102
1975	NA	NA	54,380
1976	NA	NA	60,805
1977	NA	NA	85,744
1978	NA	NA	NA
1979	NA	NA	54,765
1980	NA	NA	72,039
1981	NA	NA	66,489
1982	NA	NA	64,557
1983	NA	NA	77,146
1984	NA	NA	73,895
1985	NA	NA	80,947
1986	NA	NA	89,212
1987	NA	NA	105,917
1988	NA	NA	107,240
1989	NA	NA	85,753
1990	NA	NA	79,170
1991	NA	NA	81,255
1992	NA	NA	81,942
1993	NA	NA	104,178
1994	NA	NA	84,408
1995	NA	NA	81,891

Georgia

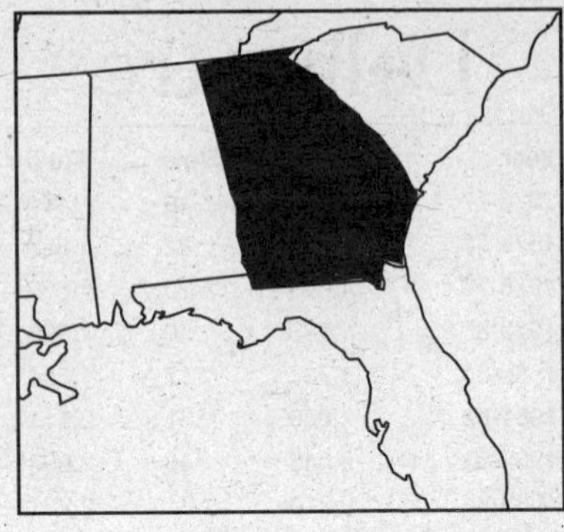

Year	Firearm	Bow	Total
1980-81	NA	NA	135,500
1981-82	NA	NA	134,000
1982-83	NA	NA	144,000
1983-84	NA	NA	164,000
1984-85	NA	NA	177,000
1985-86	NA	NA	189,600
1986-87	NA	NA	226,000
1987-88	NA	NA	280,536
1988-89	NA	NA	300,624
1989-90	NA	NA	293,167
1990-91	NA	NA	351,652
1991-92	265,352	15,708	281,060
1992-93	284,412	21,841	306,253
1993-94	309,522	37,331	346,853
1994-95	345,869	35,687	381,556
1995-96	355,267	36,328	391,595

Idaho

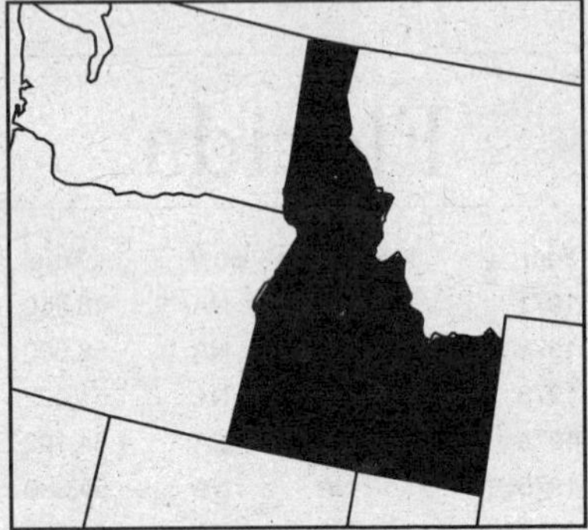

Year	Firearm	Bow	Total
1980	NA	NA	45,988
1981	NA	NA	50,580
1982	NA	NA	48,670
1983	NA	NA	50,600
1984	NA	NA	42,600
1985	NA	NA	48,950
1986	NA	NA	59,800
1987	NA	NA	66,400
1988	NA	NA	82,200
1989	NA	NA	95,200
1990	NA	NA	72,100
1991	16,721	364	17,085
1992	NA	NA	23,633
1993	23,251	303	23,554
1994	29,760	595	30,355
1995	28,180	320	28,500

NOTE — The figures before 1991 include white-tailed deer and mule deer.

Almanac Insights

Fatally Wounded Deer Can Travel Far

A white-tailed deer, if it lives for just 15 seconds after being shot through the heart, could travel more than 220 yards. Research indicates wounded whitetails can run as fast as 30 mph.

Illinois

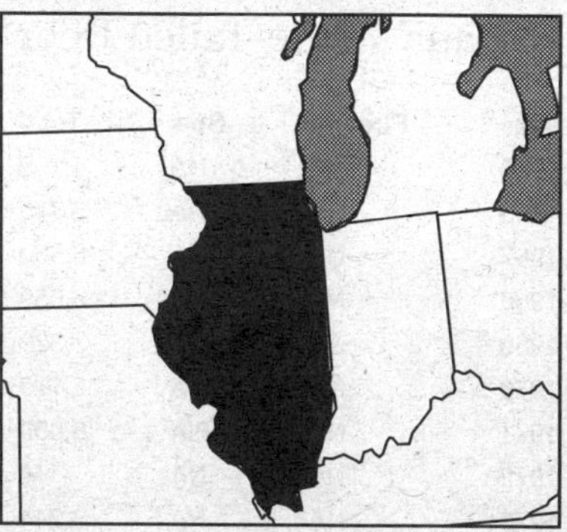

Year	Firearm	Bow	Total
1957	1,709	NA	1,709
1958	2,493	NA	2,493
1959	2,604	NA	2,604
1960	2,438	NA	2,438
1961	4,313	NA	4,313
1962	6,289	NA	6,289
1963	6,785	NA	6,785
1964	9,975	NA	9,975
1965	7,651	NA	7,651
1966	7,357	NA	7,357
1967	6,588	NA	6,588
1968	8,202	NA	8,202
1969	8,345	NA	8,345
1970	8,889	590	9,479
1971	10,359	566	10,925
1972	10,100	552	10,652
1973	12,902	960	13,862
1974	12,853	1,425	14,278
1975	15,614	1,608	17,222
1976	15,308	1,600	16,908
1977	16,231	2,810	19,041
1979	20,058	1,074	21,132
1980	20,825	1,463	22,288
1981	20,800	1,766	22,566

Year	Firearm	Bow	Total
1982	22,657	2,205	24,862
1983	26,112	2,554	28,666
1984	29,212	3,023	32,235
1985	31,769	3,746	35,515
1986	36,056	4,357	40,413
1987	42,932	6,646	49,578
1988	47,786	7,820	55,606
1989	56,143	10,000	66,143
1990	NA	NA	81,000
1991	83,191	18,099	101,290
1992	84,537	19,564	104,101
1993	92,276	23,215	115,491
1994	97,723	25,607	123,330
1995	107,742	34,491	142,233
1996	96,693	35,245	131,938

Indiana

Year	Firearm	Bow	Total
1951	NA	NA	1,590
1952	NA	NA	1,112
1953	NA	NA	83
1954	NA	NA	68
1955	NA	NA	149
1956	NA	NA	198
1957	NA	NA	NA
1958	NA	NA	592
1959	NA	Bow	800
1960	NA	NA	1,523
1961	NA	NA	2,293

Year	Firearm	Bow	Total
1962	NA	NA	3,212
1963	NA	NA	4,634
1964	NA	NA	6,001

Indiana White-Tailed Deer Harvest Totals, Continued

Year	Firearm	Bow	Total	Year	Firearm	Bow	Total
1965	NA	NA	4,155	1981	12,600	5,527	18,127
1966	NA	NA	5,775	1982	16,267	4,651	20,918
1967	NA	NA	6,560	1983	21,244	3,988	25,232
1968	NA	NA	6,659	1984	21,944	5,640	27,584
1969	NA	NA	7,323	1985	25,768	6,371	32,139
1970	NA	NA	5,175	1986	33,837	9,621	43,458
1971	NA	NA	5,099	1987	38,937	12,841	51,778
1972	NA	NA	NA	1988	46567	13,667	60,234
1973	NA	NA	8,244	1989	62,901	16,417	79,318
1974	NA	NA	9,461	1990	70,928	17,775	88,703
1975	NA	NA	8,758	1991	77,102	21,581	98,683
1976	NA	NA	11,344	1992	73,396	21,918	95,314
1977	NA	NA	12,476	1993	77,226	23,988	101,214
1978	NA	NA	9,896	1994	89,037	23,379	112,416
1979	NA	NA	13,718	1995	92,496	25,233	117,729
1980	NA	NA	19,780	1996	99,886	23,200	123,086

Iowa

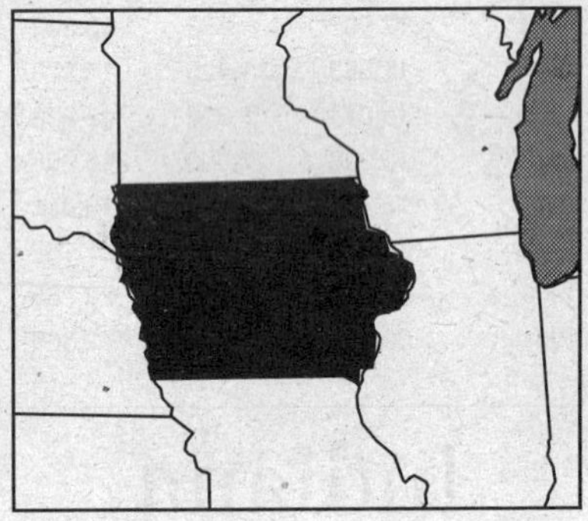

Year	Firearm	Bow	Total	Year	Firearm	Bow	Total
1953	4,007	1	4,008				
1954	2,413	10	2,423				
1955	3,006	58	3,064				
1956	2,561	117	2,678				
1957	2,667	138	2,805				
1958	2,729	162	2,891				
1959	2,476	255	2,731				
1960	3,992	277	4,269				
1961	4,997	367	5,364	1974	15,817	2,173	17,990
1962	5,299	404	5,703	1975	18,948	2,219	21,167
1963	6,612	538	7,151	1976	14,257	2,350	16,607
1964	9,024	670	9,694	1977	12,788	2,400	15,188
1965	7,910	710	8,620	1978	15,168	2,957	18,125
1966	10,742	579	11,321	1979	16,149	3,305	19,454
1967	10,392	791	11,183	1980	18,857	3,803	22,660
1968	12,941	830	13,771	1981	21,578	4,368	25,946
1969	10,731	851	11,582	1982	21,741	4,720	26,461
1970	12,743	1,037	13,780	1983	30,375	5,244	35,619
1971	10,459	1,232	11,691	1984	33,756	5,599	39,355
1972	10,485	1,328	11,813	1985	38,414	5,805	44,219
1973	12,208	1,822	14,030				

Iowa White-Tailed Deer Harvest Totals, Continued

Year	Firearm	Bow	Total	Year	Firearm	Bow	Total
1986	52,807	9,895	62,702	1992	68,227	8,814	77,684
1987	66,036	9,722	75,758	1993	67,139	9,291	76,430
1988	83,184	9,897	93,756	1994	75,191	12,040	87,231
1989	87,300	11,857	99,712	1995	83,884	13,372	97,256
1990	87,856	10,146	98,002	1996	90,000	16,000	106,000
1991	74,828	8,807	83,635	*The 1996 totals are estimates.			

Kansas

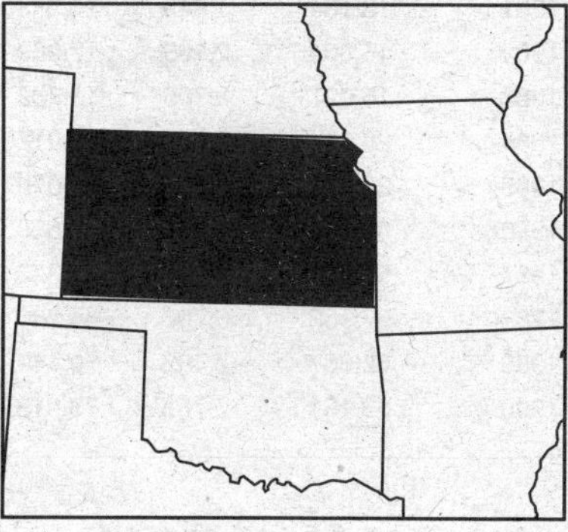

Year	Firearm	Bow	Total
1965	1,340	164	1,504
1966	2,139	376	2,515
1967	1,542	434	1,976
1968	1,648	614	2,262
1969	1,668	583	2,251
1970	2,418	793	3,211
1971	2,569	578	3,147
1972	2,318	664	2,982
1973	3,220	892	4,112
1974	4,347	1,130	5,477
1975	4,352	1,136	5,488
1976	3,955	1,114	5,069
1977	3,766	1,174	4,940
1978	4,942	1,738	6,680
1979	5,810	2,259	8,069
1980	7,296	3,007	10,303
1981	9,413	2,939	12,352
1982	11,446	3,441	14,887
1983	13,640	3,918	17,558
1984	19,446	4,167	23,613

Year	Firearm	Bow	Total
1985	21,296	4,230	25,526
1986	24,123	4,358	28,481
1987	31,664	4,329	35,993
1988	35,236	5,118	40,354
1989	34,000	5,550	39,550
1990	40,800	5,000	45,800
1991	34,770	4,500	39,270
1992	26,400	4,500	30,900
1993	NA	NA	NA
1994	NA	NA	NA

Almanac Insights

Not While You're Sleeping

Contrary to what many people believe, only a small percentage of hunters fall from tree stands because they were asleep. According to a 1993 *Deer & Deer Hunting* survey, only 4 percent of falls from tree stands were attributed to drowsiness.

Kentucky

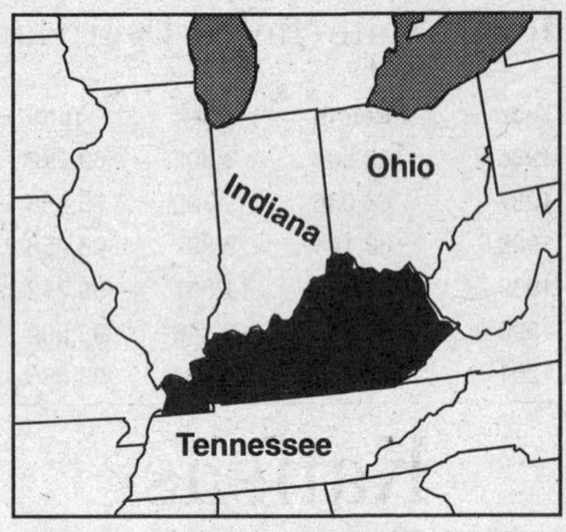

Year	Firearm	Bow	Total
1976	3,476	NA	3,476
1977	5,682	NA	5,682
1978	6,012	421	6,433
1979	7,442	620	8,062
1980	7,988	1,714	9,702
1981	13,134	1,849	14,983
1982	15,804	2,165	17,969
1983	16,027	2,705	18,732
1984	20,344	2,668	23,012
1985	26,024	4,051	30,075
1986	34,657	4,863	39,520
1987	54,372	6,000	60,372
1988	57,553	6,707	64,260
1989	62,667	7,482	70,149
1990	66,151	7,767	73,918

Year	Firearm	Bow	Total
1991	84,918	8,016	92,934
1992	73,664	8,274	81,938
1993	64,598	8,680	73,278
1994	93,444	12,672	106,116
1995	98.033	12,900	110,933
1996	98,430	13,010	111,440

Louisiana

Year	Firearm	Bow	Total
1960-61	16,500	NA	16,500
1961-62	NA	NA	NA
1962-63	NA	NA	NA
1963-64	24,000	NA	24,000
1964-65	23,000	NA	23,000
1965-66	26,000	NA	26,000
1966-67	32,500	NA	32,500
1967-68	36,000	NA	36,000
1968-69	50,000	NA	50,000
1969-70	53,000	NA	53,000
1970-71	53,500	NA	53,500
1971-72	61,000	NA	61,000
1972-73	65,000	NA	65,000
1973-74	74,500	NA	74,500
1974-75	82,000	NA	82,000
1975-76	77,000	NA	77,000
1976-77	84,500	NA	84,500
1977-78	82,500	NA	82,500
1978-79	85,000	BOA	85,000
1979-80	90,000	5,000	95,000
1980-81	105,500	5,000	110,500

Year	Firearm	Bow	Total
1981-82	115,000	5,500	120,500
1982-83	132,000	5,500	137,500
1983-84	131,000	6,000	137,000
1984-85	128,000	6,500	134,500
1985-86	139,000	7,500	146,500
1986-87	149,000	8,750	157,750
1987-88	164,000	9,500	173,500
1988-89	161,000	10,500	171,500
1989-90	162,000	11,000	173,000
1990-91	176,200	18,200	194,300
1991-92	186,400	17,700	204,100
1992-93	192,300	22,600	214,900
1993-94	193,000	20,100	213,100
1994-95	193,700	24,000	217,700
1995-96	212,400	25,000	237,400

DEER HUNTERS' 1998 ALMANAC

Maine

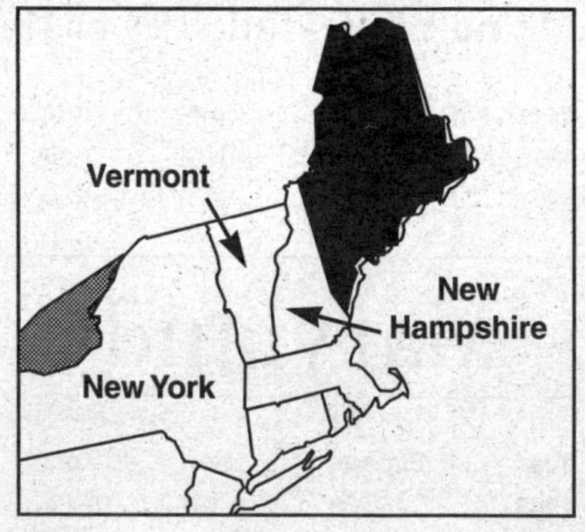

Year	Firearm	Bow	Total
1919	5,784	NA	5,784
1920	5,829	NA	5,829
1921	8,861	NA	8,861
1922	7,628	NA	7,628
1925	8,379	NA	8,379
1927	8,112	NA	8,112
1928	9,051	NA	9,051
1929	11,708	NA	11,708
1930	13,098	NA	13,098
1931	14,694	NA	14,694
1932	15,465	NA	15,465
1933	18,935	NA	18,935
1934	13,284	NA	13,284
1935	19,726	NA	19,726
1936	19,134	NA	19,134
1937	19,197	NA	19,197
1938	19,363	NA	19,363
1939	19,187	NA	19,187
1940	22,201	NA	22,201
1941	19,881	NA	19,881
1942	22,591	NA	22,591
1943	24,408	NA	24,408
1944	21,708	NA	21,708
1945	24,904	NA	24,904
1946	31,728	NA	31,728
1947	30,349	NA	30,349
1948	35,364	NA	35,364
1949	35,051	NA	35,051
1950	39,216	NA	39,216
1951	41,730	NA	41,730
1952	35,171	NA	35,171
1953	38,609	NA	38,609
1954	37,379	NA	37,379
1955	35,591	NA	35,591
1956	40,290	NA	40,290
1957	40,125	17	40,142
1958	39,375	18	39,393
1959	41,720	15	41,735
1960	37,752	22	37,774
1961	32,740	7	32,747
1962	38,795	12	38,807

Year	Firearm	Bow	Total
1963	29,816	23	29,839
1964	35,286	19	35,305
1965	37,266	16	37,282
1966	32,142	18	32,160
1967	34,693	14	34,707
1968	41,064	16	41,080
1969	30,388	21	30,409
1970	31,738	12	31,750
1971	18,873	30	18,903
1972	28,664	34	28,698
1973	24,681	39	24,720
1974	34,602	65	34,667
1975	34,625	50	34,675
1976	29,918	47	29,965
1977	31,354	76	31,430
1978	28,905	97	29,002
1979	26,720	101	26,821
1980	37,148	107	37,255
1981	32,027	140	32,167
1982	28,709	125	28,834
1983	23,699	100	23,799
1984	19,225	133	19,358
1985	21,242	182	21,424
1986	19,290	302	19,592
1987	23,435	294	23,729
1988	27,754	302	28,056
1989	29,844	416	30,260
1990	25,658	319	25,977
1991	26,236	500	26,736
1992	28,126	694	28,820
1993	26,608	682	27,402
1994	23,967	716	24,683

Maine White-Tailed Deer Harvest Totals, Continued

Year	Firearm	Bow	Total	Year	Firearm	Bow	Total
1995	NA	NA	NA	1996	NA	NA	NA

Maryland

Year	Firearm	Bow	Total
1983	16,239	2,181	18,420
1984	17,324	2,501	19,825
1985	17,241	2,549	19,790
1986	22,411	3,404	25,815
1987	24,846	4,216	29,062
1988	27,625	5,983	33,608
1989	38,305	7,988	46,293
1990	37,712	8,605	46,317
1991	36,169	10,454	46,623
1992	39,858	11,240	51,098
1993	39,429	11,251	51,234
1994	39,547	11,324	50,871

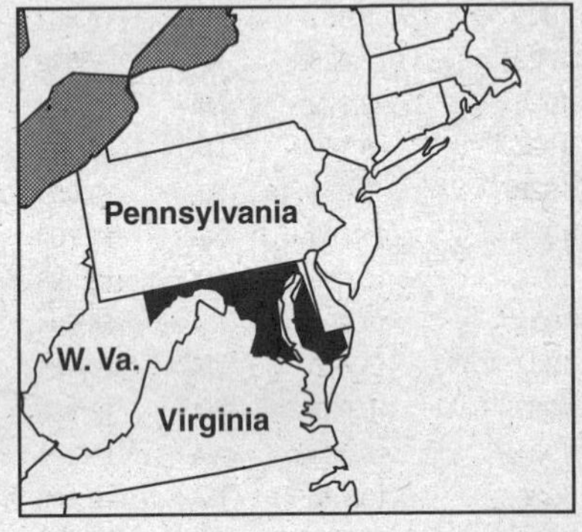

Year	Firearm	Bow	Total
1995	49,237	12,397	61,634
1996	39,048	13,588	52,636

Massachusetts

Year	Firearm	Bow	Total
1989	5,818	890	6,708
1990	5,829	1,061	6,890
1991	8,085	1,378	9,463
1992	8,470	1,570	10,040
1993	6,514	1,387	8,345
1994	7,545	1,587	9,132
1995	9,145	1,901	11,046
1996	7,156	1,687	8,843

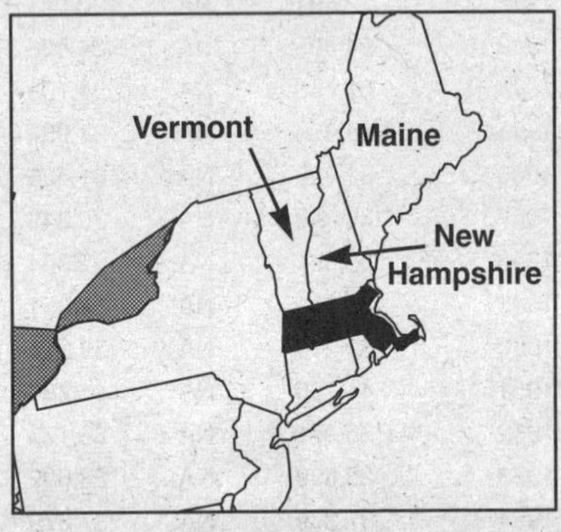

Almanac Insights

Why All the Spikes?

In overbrowsed habitat, more than 50 percent of yearling bucks will likely have spikes, as would a portion of the 2½-year-old bucks. This is typical of a deer herd that is at or above the habitat's carrying capacity.

Michigan

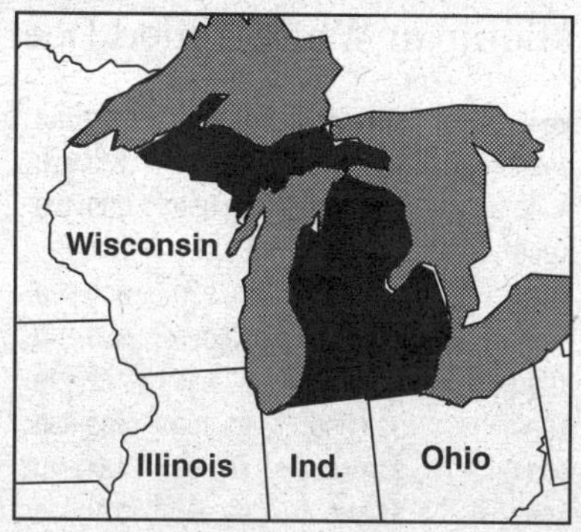

Year	Firearm	Bow	Total
1878	NA	NA	21,000
1879	NA	NA	80,000
1880	NA	NA	70,000
1881	NA	NA	80,000
1899	NA	NA	12,000
1900	NA	NA	12,000
1911	NA	NA	12,000
1916	NA	NA	8,000
1919	NA	NA	20,000
1920	NA	NA	25,000
1921	NA	NA	11,520
1922	NA	NA	11,700
1923	NA	NA	13,270
1924	NA	NA	15,190
1925	NA	NA	18,120
1926	NA	NA	20,200
1927	NA	NA	22,810
1928	NA	NA	24,810
1929	NA	NA	28,710
1930	NA	NA	32,150
1931	NA	NA	23,500
1932	NA	NA	20,500
1933	NA	NA	25,500
1934	NA	NA	27,000
1935	NA	NA	30,000
1936	NA	NA	42,000
1937	39,760	4	39,764
1938	44,390	8	44,398
1939	44,770	6	44,776
1940	51,380	10	51,390
1941	73,430	24	73,454
1942	62,190	22	62,212
1943	51,610	37	51,647
1944	51,730	37	51,767
1945	85,080	68	85,148
1946	90,510	170	90,680
1947	82,360	390	82,750
1948	64,540	580	65,120
1949	77,750	780	78,530
1950	84,410	1,340	85,750
1951	82,240	1,320	83,560

Year	Firearm	Bow	Total
1952	162,630	1,840	164,470
1953	97,650	1,820	99,470
1954	67,740	1,820	69,560
1955	74,160	2,310	76,470
1956	74,050	2,430	76,480
1957	77,300	1,760	79,060
1958	100,010	2,570	102,580
1959	115,400	1,840	117,240
1960	75,490	1,230	76,720
1961	58,090	1,980	60,070
1962	95,917	1,643	97,560
1963	124,217	2,143	126,360
1964	141,466	2,814	144,280
1965	112,347	2,173	114,520
1966	94,327	1,933	96,260
1967	104,170	2,650	106,820
1968	101,669	2,681	104,350
1969	106,698	2,582	109,280
1970	68,843	3,187	72,030
1971	62,076	3,354	65,430
1972	55,796	3,694	59,490
1973	66,359	4,631	70,990
1974	92,111	7,969	100,080
1975	106,800	8,790	115,590
1976	107,625	10,365	117,990
1977	137,110	21,250	158,360
1978	145,710	25,140	170,850
1979	119,790	25,640	145,430
1980	137,380	28,110	165,490
1981	175,090	33,320	208,410
1982	163,520	38,420	201,940
1983	127,770	30,640	158,410

Michigan White-Tailed Deer Harvest Totals, Continued

Year	Firearm	Bow	Total	Year	Firearm	Bow	Total
1984	131,280	32,630	163,910	1995	346,830	132,130	478,960
1985	197,370	42,050	239,420	1996	300,000	100,000	400,000
1986	219,260	57,960	277,220				
1987	265,860	72,820	338,680				
1988	311,770	72,020	383,790				
1989	355,410	97,080	452,490				
1990	338,890	93,800	432,690				
1991	318,460	115,880	434,340				
1992	274,650	99,990	374,640				
1993	232,820	98,160	330,980				
1994	251,420	112,490	363,910				

NOTE: Michigan's harvest totals are estimates. Firearm harvest totals prior to 1975 did not include muzzleloader harvest. Also, harvest totals since 1978 do not include deer taken with camp deer permits. In addition, prior to 1961, camp deer harvests were not separated by firearm and bow.

Minnesota

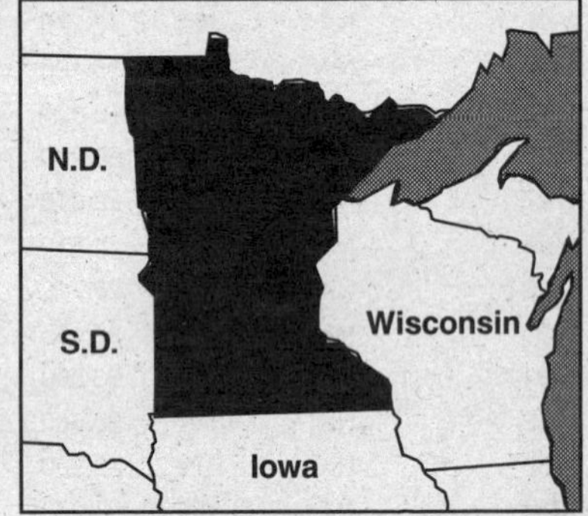

Year	Firearm	Bow	Total	Year	Firearm	Bow	Total
1918	9,000		9,000				
1919	18,300		18,300				
1920	18,600		18,600				
1921	13,600		13,600				
1922	11,200		11,200				
1923			closed				
1924	15,600		15,600				
1925			closed				
1926	28,000		28,000	Year	Firearm	Bow	Total
1927			closed	1943	67,700		67,700
1928	27,300		27,300	1944	62,800		62,800
1929			closed	1945	67,100		67,100
1930	27,800		27,800	1946	93,400		93,400
1931			closed	1947	74,400		74,400
1932	42,300		42,300	1948	61,600		61,600
1933	26,200		26,200	1949	49,900		49,900
1934	39,100		39,100	1950			closed
1935			closed	1951	72,700	43	72,743
1936	50,100		50,100	1952	57,300	34	57,334
1937	33,600		33,600	1953	61,000	66	61,066
1938	44,500		44,500	1954	56,000	182	56,182
1939			closed	1955	79,000	214	79,214
1940	56,000		56,000	1956	69,000	325	69,325
1941			closed	1957	67,000	392	67,392
1942	77,000		77,000	1958	75,000	403	75,403

Minnesota White-Tailed Deer Harvest Totals, Continued

Year	Firearm	Bow	Total	Year	Firearm	Bow	Total
1959	104,000	390	104,390	1979	55,400	2,578	57,978
1960	95,000	445	95,445	1980	77,100	3,641	80,741
1961	107,000	490	107,490	1981	108,100	5,535	113,635
1962	96,000	519	96,519	1982	107,000	5,566	112,566
1963	113,000	713	113,713	1983	NA	5,977	NA
1964	122,000	780	122,780	1984	132,000	6,390	138,390
1965	127,000	871	127,871	1985	138,000	7,575	145,575
1966	115,000	604	115,604	1986	129,800	7,610	137,410
1967	107,000	598	107,598	1987	135,000	7,535	142,535
1968	103,000	819	103,819	1988	138,900	8,262	147,162
1969	68,000	776	68,776	1989	129,600	9,307	138,907
1970	50,000	453	50,453	1990	166,600	11,106	177,706
1971	closed	1,279	1,279	1991	206,300	12,964	219,264
1972	73,400	1,601	75,001	1992	230,064	13,004	243,068
1973	67,100	1,935	69,035	1993	188,109	13,722	202,928
1974	65,000	2,176	67,176	1994	180,008	13,818	193,826
1975	63,600	2,265	65,865	1995	200,638	14,180	214,818
1976	36,200	1,167	37,367	1996	138,100	13,000	151,100
1977	58,100	2,609	60,709				
1978	57,800	2,608	60,408				

Mississippi

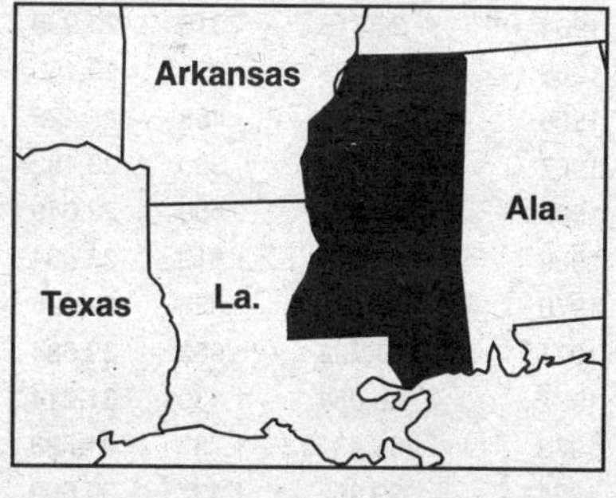

Year	Firearm	Bow	Total	Year	Firearm	Bow	Total
1971-72	580	39	619				
1972-73	816	53	869				
1973-74	919	57	976				
1974-75	NA	NA	NA				
1975-76	NA	NA	NA				
1976-77	2,529	975	3,504				
1977-78	NA	NA	NA				
1978-79	NA	NA	NA	1988-89	236,012	28,744	264,756
1979-80	NA	NA	NA	1989-90	236,012	28,744	262,386
1980-81	184,163	17,437	201,600	1990-91	218,347	29,982	249,572
1981-82	196,856	14,860	211,716	1991-92	243,175	33,940	277,714
1982-83	227,432	16,222	243,654	1992-93	260,093	40,886	300,980
1983-84	176,400	19,747	196,147	1993-94	229,425	32,971	262,409
1984-85	209,574	17,815	227,389	1994-95	262,342	47,345	309,687
1985-86	216,959	18,120	235,079	1995-96	286,293	48,669	334,962
1986-87	237,075	19,209	256,284				
1987-88	240,337	24,662	264,999				

Missouri

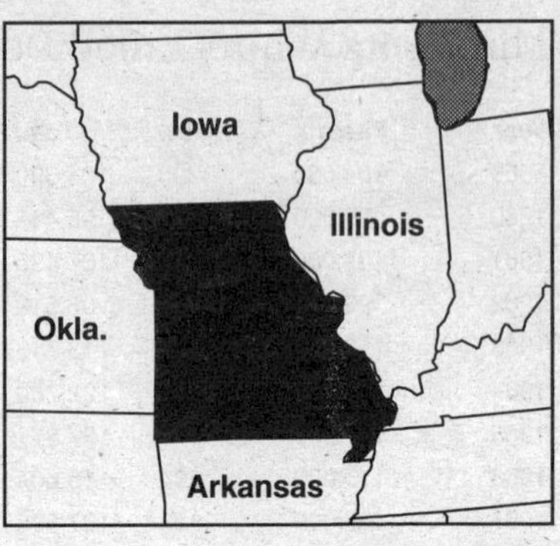

Year	Firearm	Bow	Total
1944	583	NA	583
1945	882	NA	882
1946	743	NA	743
1947	1,387	NA	1,387
1948	1,432	NA	1,432
1949	1,353	NA	1,353
1950	1,623	1	1,624
1951	5,519	NA	5,519
1952	7,466	2	7,468
1953	7,864	5	7,869
1954	7,648	22	7,670
1955	7,988	37	8,025
1956	7,864	33	7,897
1957	9,986	58	10,044
1958	13,610	71	13,681
1959	16,306	90	16,396
1960	17,418	263	17,681
1961	15,967	116	16,083
1962	16,516	231	16,747
1963	17,304	268	17,572
1964	20,619	316	20,935
1965	18,785	371	19,156
1966	27,965	458	28,423
1967	22,802	380	23,182
1968	22,090	559	22,649
1969	23,265	619	23,884
1970	28,400	828	29,228
1971	31,722	962	32,684
1972	30,084	1,130	31,214
1973	33,438	1,285	34,723
1974	29,262	1,437	30,699

Year	Firearm	Bow	Total
1975	51,823	1,850	53,673
1976	40,683	1,973	42,656
1977	36,562	2,199	38,761
1978	40,261	2,781	43,042
1979	53,164	3,327	56,491
1980	49,426	3,661	53,087
1981	50,183	3,495	53,678
1982	55,852	4,191	60,043
1983	57,801	4,626	62,427
1984	71,569	5,134	76,703
1985	80,792	5,621	86,413
1986	102,879	5,832	108,711
1987	132,500	8,077	140,577
1988	139,726	10,183	149,909
1989	157,506	10,970	168,476
1990	161,857	11,118	172,975
1991	149,112	14,096	164,384
1992	150,873	15,029	166,929
1993	156,704	14,696	172,120
1994	164,624	17,136	181,760
1995	187,406	20,077	207,483
1996	189,578	23,395	212,973

Almanac Insights

Missouri Hunters Fear Poachers

In a mail survey of 10,000 Missouri firearms deer hunters, researcher Lonnie Hansen concluded deer hunters considered poaching, anti-hunters and poor hunter behavior as the main threats to deer hunting.

Missouri Brings White-Tailed Deer Back From Brink of Extinction

The restoration of Missouri's white-tailed deer population is one of the state's greatest wildlife success stories.

Careful managment by the Missouri Department of Conservation has brought deer back from the brink of extinction in the 1920s to a current population of about 800,000.

The comeback of whitetails has provided Missourians with hours of aesthetic enjoyment, economic benefit and hunting opportunities. When bow-hunters went afield Oct. 1, 1996, the state celebrated 50 years of bow-hunting.

The state not only celebrates the growing popularity of bow-hunting, it recognizes the importance of bow-hunting as a deer-management tool.

Important years in Missouri bow-hunting history include:

✓1946: State's first archery season. Three-day season, restricted to one county, attracts 73 hunters. No deer were killed.

✓1950: Hugh Collins bags state's first deer with bow and arow during modern era.

✓1952: Five counties open to bow-hunting. Two deer harvested.

✓1963: Bow-hunting opens statewide.

✓1972: Deer harvest exceeds 1,000 for the first time.

✓1977: More than 33,000 bow-hunters take part in archery season.

✓1992: Number of bow-hunters rises to 94,809.

✓1996: State celebrates 50 years of bow-hunting.

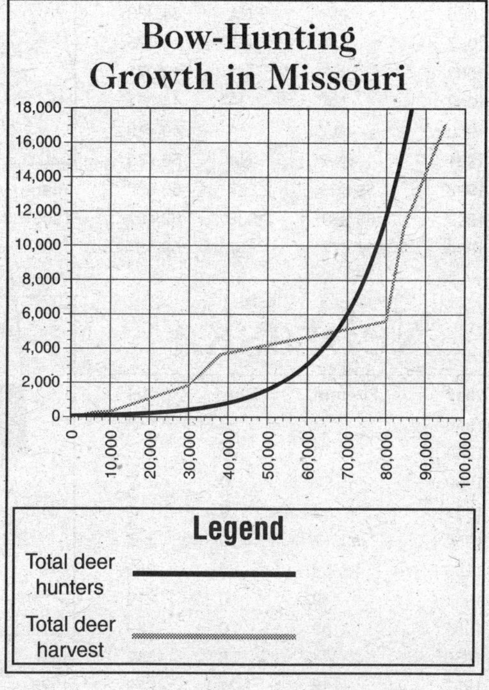

Montana

Year	Firearm	Bow	Total
1984	NA	NA	56,760
1985	NA	NA	43,019
1986	NA	NA	44,733
1987	NA	NA	40,675
1988	NA	NA	43,971
1989	NA	NA	44,261
1990	NA	NA	49,419
1991	NA	NA	56,789
1992	58,565	2,067	60,632
1993	60,369	2,038	62,407
1994	67,577	1,857	69,434

Year	Firearm	Bow	Total
1995	60,907	1,636	62,543
1996	NA	NA	NA

Nebraska

Year	Firearm	Bow	Total
1945	2	0	2
1949	0	0	0
1950	7	0	7
1951	2	0	2
1952	7	0	7
1953	353	0	353
1954	219	0	219
1955	189	0	189
1956	344	8	352
1957	258	21	279
1958	340	103	443
1959	975	111	1,086
1960	1,355	108	1,463
1961	1,443	198	1,641
1962	3,280	194	3,474
1963	3,710	246	3,956
1964	5,138	326	5,464
1965	6,853	338	7,191
1966	6,920	375	7,295
1967	4,773	546	5,319
1968	5,067	399	5,466
1969	5,440	524	5,964
1970	6,460	654	7,114
1971	6,343	662	7,005
1972	5,635	624	6,259

Year	Firearm	Bow	Total
1973	7,090	865	7,955
1974	7,894	1,032	8,926
1975	8,404	1,155	9,559
1976	7,595	831	8,426
1977	5,921	769	6,690
1978	6,164	958	7,122
1979	7,899	1,151	9,050
1980	9,939	1,639	11,578
1981	11,364	2,025	13,389
1982	12,957	2,049	15,006
1983	15,980	2,781	18,761
1984	19,679	2,471	22,150
1985	20,930	2,593	23,523
1986	22,859	2,291	25,150
1987	24,266	2,812	27,078
1988	24,938	2,951	27,889

Nebraska White-Tailed Deer Harvest Totals, Continued

Year	Firearm	Bow	Total	Year	Firearm	Bow	Total
1989	24,359	2,847	27,206	1994	26,050	3,830	29,880
1990	21,973	2,716	24,689	1995	26,000	4,000	30,000
1991	20,820	2,931	23,751	1996	30,400	4,500	34,900
1992	20,125	3,141	23,266				
1993	23,377	3,282	26,683				

New Hampshire

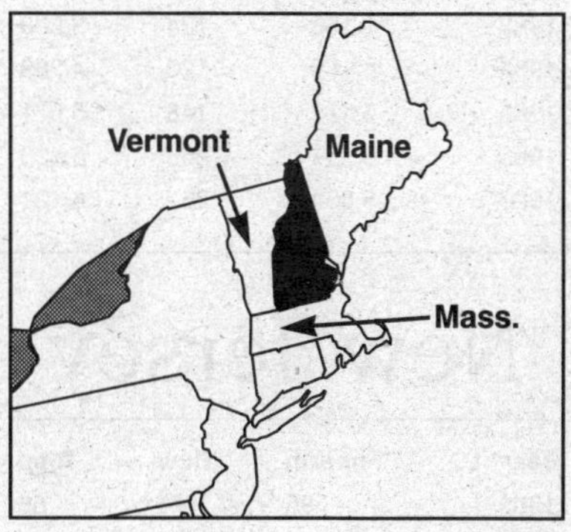

Year	Firearm	Bow	Total	Year	Firearm	Bow	Total
1922	1,896	NA	1,896				
1923	1,402	NA	1,402				
1924	1,537	NA	1,537				
1925	1,493	NA	1,493				
1926	1,665	NA	1,665				
1927	1,481	NA	1,481				
1928	1,474	NA	1,474				
1929	1,598	NA	1,598				
1930	1,735	NA	1,735	1954	9,328	NA	9,328
1931	1,498	NA	1,498	1955	10,275	NA	10,275
1932	1,687	NA	1,687	1956	10,917	NA	10,917
1933	2,064	NA	2,064	1957	9,901	NA	9,901
1934	1,526	NA	1,526	1958	10,221	NA	10,221
1935	1,845	NA	1,845	1959	8,435	NA	8,435
1936	2,751	NA	2,751	1960	7,560	9	7,569
1937	3,216	NA	3,216	1961	7,763	12	7,775
1938	3,363	NA	3,363	1962	7,917	5	7,922
1939	3,820	NA	3,820	1963	8,626	2	8,628
1940	5,699	NA	5,699	1964	7,559	9	7,568
1941	3,897	NA	3,897	1965	9,676	3	9,679
1942	4,844	NA	4,844	1966	9,105	16	9,121
1943	5,029	NA	5,029	1967	14,153	33	14,186
1944	5,029	NA	5,029	1968	12,712	36	12,748
1945	6,449	NA	6,449	1969	8,778	13	8,791
1946	6,356	NA	6,356	1970	7,214	17	7,231
1947	10,172	NA	10,172	1971	7,263	12	7,275
1948	6,767	NA	6,767	1972	6,923	20	6,943
1949	9,852	NA	9,852	1973	5,440	22	5,462
1950	10,051	NA	10,051	1974	6,875	20	6,895
1951	11,462	NA	11,462	1975	8,308	24	8,332
1952	6,932	NA	6,932	1976	9,076	14	9,090
1953	9,517	NA	9,517				

New Hampshire White-Tailed Deer Harvest Totals, Cont.

Year	Firearm	Bow	Total	Year	Firearm	Bow	Total
1977	6,877	62	6,939	1988	5,900	225	6,125
1978	5,545	57	5,602	1989	6,749	489	7,238
1979	4,939	42	4,981	1990	6,466	482	7,872
1980	5,353	31	5,384	1991	8,060	732	8,792
1981	6,028	125	6,153	1992	9,013	1,202	10,215
1982	4,577	97	4,674	1993	9,012	877	9,889
1983	3,156	124	3,280	1994	7,478	901	8,379
1984	4,169	120	4,289	1995	9,627	1,580	11,207
1985	5,523	148	5,671	1996	8,901	1,462	10,363
1986	6,557	263	6,820				
1987	5,864	257	6,121				

New Jersey

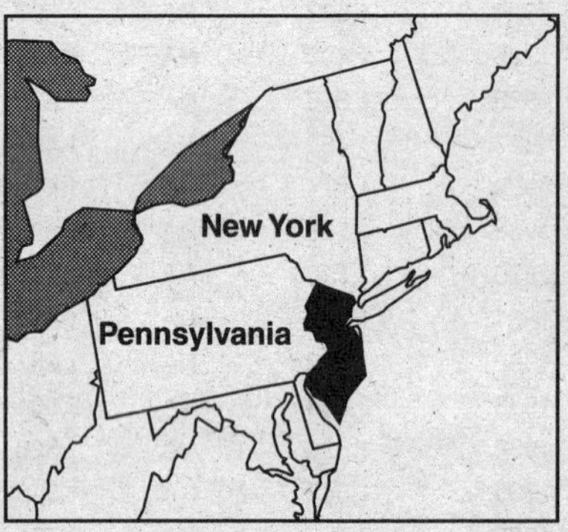

Year	Firearm	Bow	Total	Year	Firearm	Bow	Total
1909	86	NA	86				
1910	127	NA	127				
1911	141	NA	141				
1912	109	NA	109				
1913	149	NA	149				
1914	149	NA	149				
1915	180	NA	180				
1916	481	NA	481				
1917	255	NA	255	1934	2,466	NA	2,466
1918	327	NA	327	1935	2,387	NA	2,387
1919	353	NA	353	1936	2,034	NA	2,034
1920	522	NA	522	1937	2,173	NA	2,173
1921	834	NA	834	1938	2,339	NA	2,339
1922	771	NA	771	1939	2,336	NA	2,336
1923	890	NA	890	1940	2,622	NA	2,622
1924	1,216	NA	1,216	1941	2,182	NA	2,182
1925	1,063	NA	1,063	1942	2,532	NA	2,532
1926	1,249	NA	1,249	1943	2,458	NA	2,458
1927	1,790	NA	1,790	1944	2,633	NA	2,633
1928	1,415	NA	1,415	1945	2,704	NA	2,704
1929	1,331	NA	1,331	1946	3,043	NA	3,043
1930	1,484	NA	1,484	1947	3,938	NA	3,938
1931	1,702	NA	1,702	1948	3,249	NA	3,249
1932	1,575	NA	1,575	1949	3,618	9	3,627
1933	1,875	NA	1,875				

New Jersey White-Tailed Deer Harvest Totals, Continued

Year	Firearm	Bow	Total	Year	Firearm	Bow	Total
1950	3,796	12	3,808	1974	11,429	1,717	13,146
1951	5,005	14	5,019	1975	10,675	2,013	12,688
1952	4,514	141	4,655	1976	10,908	2,110	13,018
1953	4,824	287	5,111	1977	11,828	2,591	14,419
1954	4,767	319	5,086	1978	13,177	2,641	15,818
1955	6,114	368	6,482	1979	13,843	2,263	16,106
1956	6,070	690	6,760	1980	16,030	5,161	21,191
1957	6,643	1,104	7,747	1981	16,291	5,846	22,137
1958	6,115	1,252	7,367	1982	16,817	6,928	23,745
1959	9,612	1,230	10,842	1983	16,403	6,902	23,305
1960	6,072	1,298	7,370	1984	17,920	7,699	25,619
1961	11,325	1,081	12,406	1985	21,480	7,971	29,451
1962	7,219	978	8,197	1986	23,590	10,187	33,777
1963	7,868	952	8,820	1987	27,415	11,813	39,228
1964	6,933	1,116	8,049	1988	33,140	12,760	45,900
1965	5,136	1,109	6,245	1989	34,812	13,714	48,526
1966	8,517	1,329	9,846	1990	34,372	13,850	48,222
1967	8,467	1,456	9,923	1991	29,936	15,480	45,416
1968	7,100	1,501	8,601	1992	31,257	16,418	47,675
1969	7,121	1,356	8,477	1993	32,936	17,006	49,942
1970	6,866	1,387	8,253	1994	32,602	18,840	51,442
1971	6,111	1,434	7,545	1995	39,176	20,593	59,769
1972	9,557	1,464	11,021	1996	36,709	19,995	56,704
1973	9,629	1,689	11,318				

New York

Year	Firearm	Bow	Total
1941	18,566	NA	18,566
1942	19,217	NA	19,217
1943	31,510	NA	31,510
1944	38,808	NA	38,808
1945	15,136	NA	15,136
1946	22,296	NA	22,296
1947	24,194	NA	24,194
1948	54,896	8	54,906
1949	27,584	13	27,597
1950	38,924	47	38,971
1951	31,049	75	31,124
1952	59,986	341	60,327

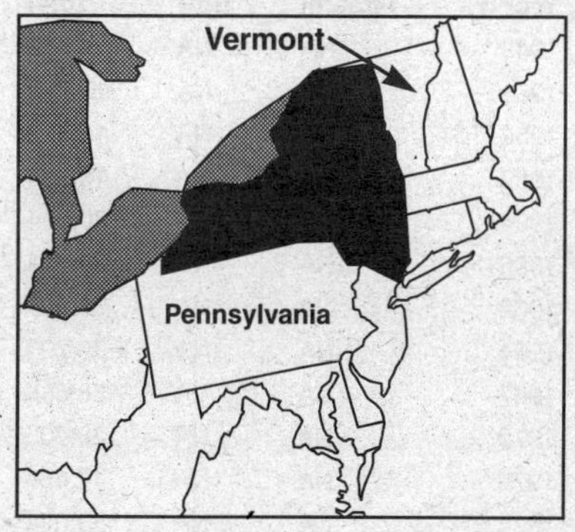

Year	Firearm	Bow	Total
1953	29,273	529	29,802
1954	37,879	670	38,549
1955	58,593	939	59,532

New York White-Tailed Deer Harvest Totals, Continued

Year	Firearm	Bow	Total	Year	Firearm	Bow	Total
1956	71,208	1,107	72,315	1977	79,035	4,169	83,204
1957	71,478	1,199	72,677	1978	81,749	3,810	85,559
1958	65,439	1,030	66,469	1979	90,691	3,368	94,059
1959	41,345	961	42,306	1980	131,606	4,649	136,255
1960	44,913	842	45,755	1981	161,593	3,792	165,385
1961	57,723	731	58,454	1982	178,825	6,175	185,000
1962	62,042	739	62,781	1983	161,640	5,466	167,106
1963	63,244	623	63,867	1984	124,244	5,400	129,644
1964	60,174	582	60,756	1985	142,802	9,705	152,507
1965	66,577	843	67,420	1986	168,366	9,705	178,071
1966	73,092	1,065	74,157	1987	192,867	11,325	204,192
1967	77,834	821	78,655	1988	181,186	11,644	192,830
1968	90,758	1,407	92,165	1989	167,558	12,770	180,328
1969	86,888	1,241	88,129	1990	175,544	14,664	190,208
1970	63,865	1,148	65,013	1991	192,812	19,008	211,820
1971	47,039	1,243	48,282	1992	212,988	18,947	231,935
1972	54,041	1,596	55,637	1993	200,240	20,048	220,288
1973	73,191	2,002	75,193	1994	146,255	19,428	165,683
1974	100,097	3,206	103,303	1995	166,430	21,854	188,284
1975	99,835	3,288	103,323	1996	176,093	21,573	197,666
1976	86,421	3,794	90,215				

North Carolina

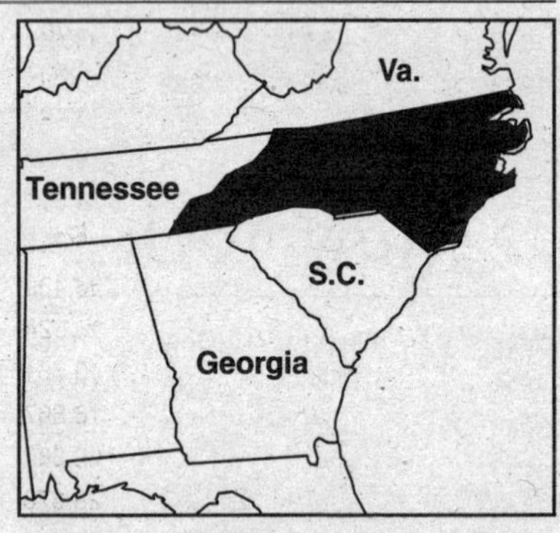

Year	Firearm	Bow	Total	Year	Firearm	Bow	Total
1949	NA	NA	14,616				
1951	NA	NA	17,739				
1952	NA	NA	15,572				
1953	NA	NA	18,598				
1954	NA	NA	20,084				
1955	NA	NA	20,114				
1962	NA	NA	28,808				
1964	NA	NA	39,793				
1967	NA	NA	38,688	1980	27,792	1,142	28,934
1970	NA	NA	38,405	1981	33,644	1,400	35,044
1972	NA	NA	47,469	1982	35,840	2,092	37,932
1974	NA	NA	53,079	1983	45,316	2,543	47,859
1976	22,645	539	23,184	1984	47,565	2,355	49,920
1977	28,182	679	28,861	1985	52,315	2,759	55,074
1978	29,193	781	29,974	1986	59,767	2,924	62,691
1979	29,246	841	30,087				

North Carolina White-Tailed Deer Harvest Totals, Continued

Year	Firearm	Bow	Total	Year	Firearm	Bow	Total
1987	74,767	3,498	78,265	1993	125,130	9,322	134,452
1988	79,694	3,405	83,099	1994	116,462	8,235	124,697
1989	85,030	4,660	89,690	1995	115,443	8,003	123,446
1990	98,978	5,978	104,956				
1991	98,121	6,655	104,776				
1992	109,911	8,727	118,638				

* — Harvest figures prior to 1976 are from mail survey estimates.

North Dakota

Year	Firearm	Bow	Total
1941	NA	NA	2,665
1943	NA	NA	2,765
1950	NA	NA	13,933
1952	NA	NA	27,024
1954	NA	NA	22,705
1955	NA	NA	17,123
1956	NA	NA	21,790
1957	NA	NA	19,714
1958	NA	NA	9,828
1959	NA	NA	23,812
1960	NA	NA	25,262
1961	NA	NA	26,324
1962	NA	NA	23,429
1963	NA	NA	9,929
1964	NA	NA	24,311
1965	NA	NA	25,837
1966	NA	NA	26,469
1967	NA	NA	26,524
1968	NA	NA	10,761
1969	NA	NA	18,367
1970	NA	NA	22,882
1971	NA	NA	28,673
1972	NA	NA	25,424
1973	NA	NA	27,780
1974	NA	NA	23,445
1975	NA	NA	20,666
1976	NA	NA	19,969
1977	NA	NA	17,201
1978	NA	NA	17,120
1979	NA	NA	18,118

Year	Firearm	Bow	Total
1980	NA	NA	24,179
1981	NA	NA	27,006
1982	NA	NA	31,210
1983	NA	NA	35,709
1984	NA	NA	41,582
1985	NA	NA	43,074
1986	NA	NA	60,122
1987	NA	NA	47,157
1988	NA	NA	41,190
1989	47,025	2,934	49,959
1990	42,347	2,862	45,209
1991	46,980	3,299	50,279
1992	54,144	3,996	58,142
1993	58,246	4,006	62,252
1994	56,462	3.946	60,408
1995	61,307	3,740	65,047

Ohio

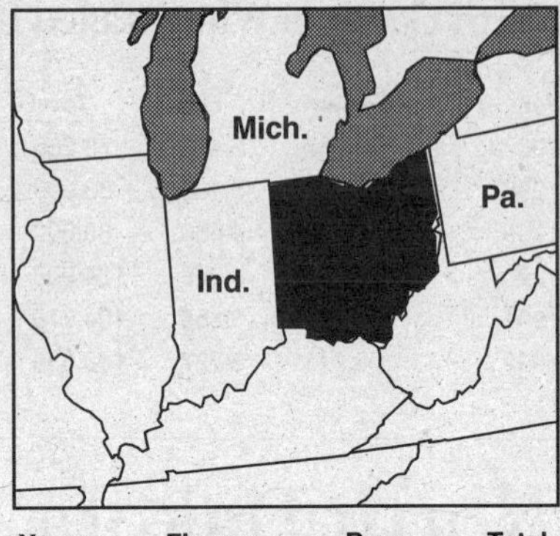

Year	Firearm	Bow	Total
1952	NA	NA	450
1953	NA	NA	4,000
1954	NA	NA	closed
1955	NA	NA	4,200
1956	NA	NA	3,911
1957	NA	NA	4,784
1958	NA	NA	4,415
1959	NA	NA	2,960
1960	NA	NA	2,584
1961	NA	NA	closed
1962	NA	NA	2,114
1963	NA	NA	2,074
1964	NA	NA	1,326
1965	NA	NA	406
1966	NA	NA	1,073
1967	NA	NA	1,437
1968	NA	NA	1,396
1969	NA	NA	2,105
1970	NA	NA	2,387
1971	NA	NA	3,831
1972	NA	NA	5,074
1973	NA	NA	7,594
1974	NA	NA	10,747
1975	NA	NA	14,972
1976	NA	NA	23,431
1977	NA	NA	22,319
1978	NA	NA	22,967
1979	NA	NA	34,874

Year	Firearm	Bow	Total
1980	NA	NA	40,499
1981	NA	NA	47,634
1982	NA	NA	52,885
1983	NA	NA	59,812
1984	NA	NA	66,860
1985	NA	NA	64,263
1986	NA	NA	67,626
1987	NA	NA	79,355
1988	NA	NA	100,674
1989	NA	NA	91,236
1990	80,109	12,087	92,196
1991	94,342	17,109	111,451
1992	97,676	19,577	117,253
1993	104,540	23,160	138,752
1994	141,137	29,390	170,527
1995	137,811	27,299	165,110
1996	131,221	21,250*	152,471

*Denotes harvest total for first six weeks of 1996 bow season.

Almanac Insights

That'll Cost You a Buck

The slang for a dollar bill has roots to the white-tailed deer. Before the American Revolution, deer hides were valuable trade items. In fact, settlers often received one dollar's worth of goods for every hide they brought to market. Traders eventually used the term "buck" interchangeably of "dollar" when bartering with storekeepers for goods.

Oklahoma

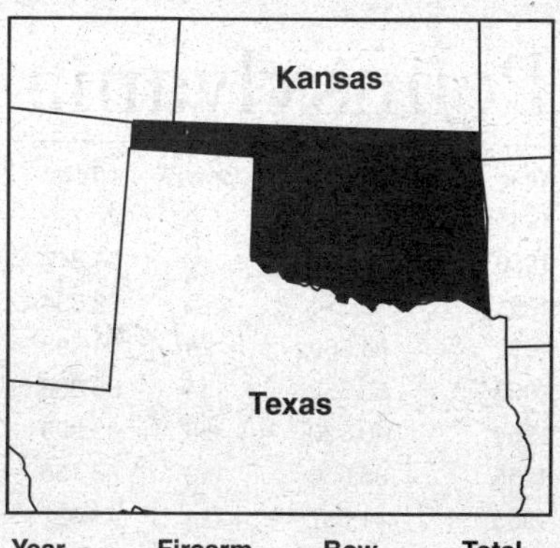

Year	Firearm	Bow	Total
1964	3,368	140	3,508
1965	4,090	213	4,303
1966	4,925	275	5,200
1967	4,976	259	5,235
1968	5,490	260	5,750
1969	6,069	304	6,373
1970	6,895	331	7,226
1971	6,587	465	7,052
1972	7,714	508	8,222
1973	7,140	427	7,567
1974	7,821	489	8,310
1975	9,028	649	9,677
1976	10,544	1,004	11,548
1977	10,192	680	10,872
1978	13,080	1,028	14,108
1979	13,023	1,185	14,208
1980	12,800	1,497	14,297
1981	11,446	1,964	13,410
1982	17,006	2,249	19,255
1983	19,222	2,698	21,920
1984	20,041	2,568	23,609

Year	Firearm	Bow	Total
1985	16,664	3,523	20,187
1986	25,096	3,320	28,416
1987	29,239	4,115	33,354
1988	34,436	4,414	38,850
1989	33,752	4,589	38,341
1990	38,545	5,525	44,070
1991	40,197	7,079	47,286
1992	42,620	7,792	50,412
1993	49,978	7,853	57,831
1994	51,145	9,054	60,199
1995	56,770	9,116	65,886
1996	54,444	9,692	64,136

Oregon

Year	Firearm	Bow	Total
1992	422	NA	422
1993	594	NA	594
1994	707	NA	707
1995	NA	NA	NA

NOTE: The 1992 season was the first time Oregon Department of Wildlife officials distinguished between mule deer and white-tailed deer in its harvest totals.

Fast Fact on Oregon

Oregon's 76-day muzzle-loading season is the longest in the United States.

Pennsylvania

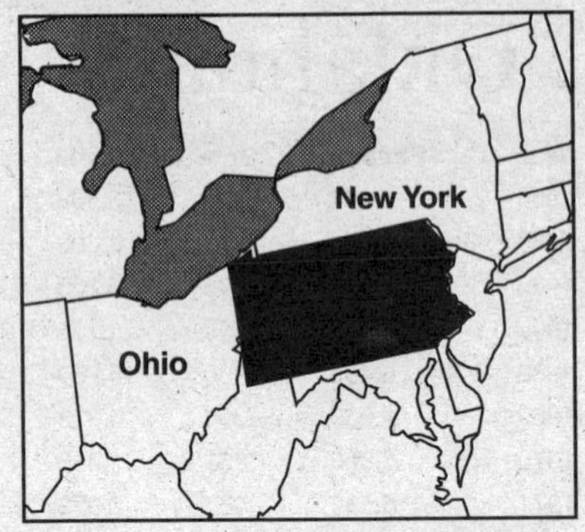

Year	Firearm	Bow	Total
1949	130,723	0	130,723
1950	54,817	0	54,817
1951	72,534	0	72,534
1952	64,969	24	64,993
1953	53,552	84	53,636
1954	40,870	55	40,925
1955	86,036	119	86,155
1956	41,697	224	41,921
1957	103,758	1,358	105,116
1958	110,567	1,358	111,925
1959	88,845	1,327	90,172
1960	67,489	1,174	68,663
1961	54,515	1,517	56,032
1962	71,603	1,310	72,913
1963	83,028	1,388	84,416
1964	89,534	1,600	91,134
1965	97,669	2,119	99,788
1966	116,416	2,337	118,753
1967	141,164	3,251	144,415
1968	139,127	2,747	141,874
1969	113,515	3,169	116,684
1970	96,688	2,998	99,686
1971	101,458	2,769	104,227
1972	104,270	2,945	107,215
1973	123,239	3,652	126,891
1974	121,743	3,909	125,652
1975	133,134	5,061	138,195
1976	118,385	3,648	122,033
1977	141,400	4,678	146,078

Year	Firearm	Bow	Total
1978	116,188	5,053	121,241
1979	110,562	4,232	114,794
1980	129,703	5,774	135,477
1981	142,592	5,938	148,530
1982	130,958	7,264	138,222
1983	130,071	6,222	136,293
1984	133,606	6,574	140,180
1985	154,060	7,368	161,428
1986	148,562	8,570	157,132
1987	164,055	8,901	172,956
1988	185,565	9,834	195,399
1989	184,856	10,951	195,807
1990	396,529	19,032	415,561
1991	365,267	22,748	388,015
1992	335,439	25,785	361,224
1993	359,224	49,409	408,557
1994	345,184	49,897	395,081
1995	375,961	54,622	430,583
1996	294,674	56,323	350,997

Rhode Island

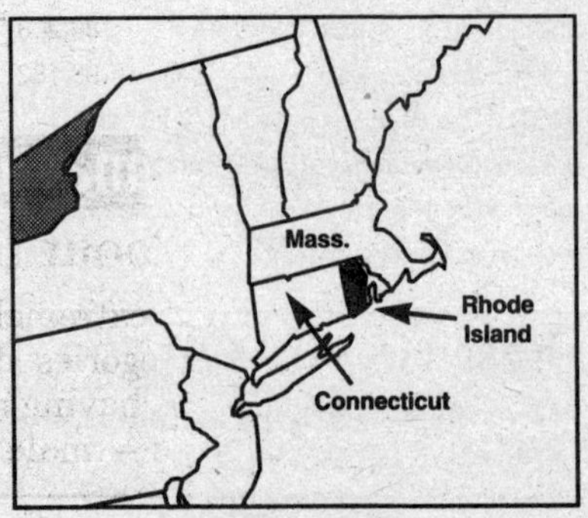

Year	Firearm	Bow	Total
1972	93	57	150
1973	46	56	102
1974	62	48	110
1975	57	54	111
1976	61	50	111
1977	95	62	157
1978	91	78	169

Rhode Island White-Tailed Deer Harvest Totals, Cont.

Year	Firearm	Bow	Total	Year	Firearm	Bow	Total
1979	103	93	196	1989	466	169	635
1980	145	72	217	1990	701	238	943
1981	155	88	243	1991	857	291	1,148
1982	112	104	216	1992	1,052	417	1,474
1983	123	99	222	1993	945	378	1,323
1984	139	109	248	1994	1,157	252	1,409
1985	144	112	256	1995	1,346	415	1,761
1986	299	126	425	1996	1,689	474	2,163
1987	252	179	431				
1988	323	125	448				

South Carolina

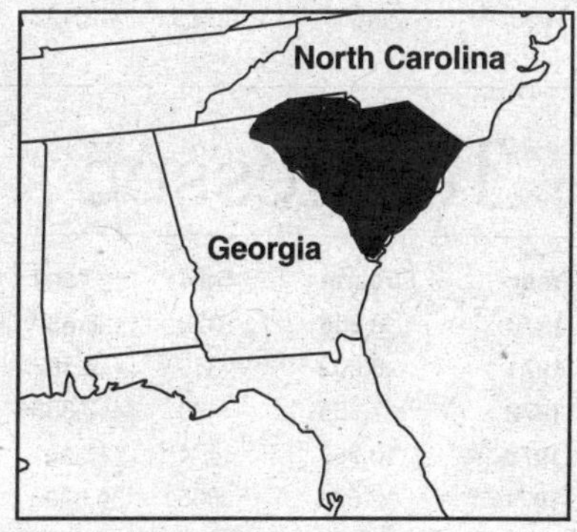

Year	Firearm	Bow	Total	Year	Firearm	Bow	Total
1972	NA	NA	18,894				
1973	NA	NA	23,703				
1974	NA	NA	26,727				
1975	NA	NA	29,133				
1976	NA	NA	33,749				
1977	NA	NA	36,363				
1978	NA	NA	39,721				
1979	NA	NA	43,569				
1980	NA	NA	44,698	1989	NA	NA	107,081
1981	NA	NA	56,410	1990	NA	NA	125,171
1982	NA	NA	54,321	1991	NA	NA	130,848
1983	NA	NA	57,927	1992	NA	NA	126,839
1984	NA	NA	60,182	1993	NA	NA	142,795
1985	NA	NA	62,699	1994	NA	NA	138,964
1986	NA	NA	69,289	1995	NA	NA	148,123
1987	NA	NA	86,208	1996	NA	NA	156,404
1988	NA	NA	98,182				

Almanac Insights

Did You Know About Does?

True antlered does are extremely rare. In most cases, these deer fall into one of four categories: diseased does; does that are very old; hermaphrodites — having both male and female organs; or pseudohermaphrodites — male animals with undeveloped testes.

South Dakota

Year	Firearm	Bow	Total
1985	43,989	2,738	46,727
1986	40,798	1,953	42,751
1987	32,018	2,456	34,474
1988	33,265	2,327	35,592
1989	42,947	3,081	46,028
1990	38,902	2,986	41,888
1991	39,915	2,686	42,601
1992	41,959	2,964	44,923
1993	45,431	2,963	48,394
1994	47,142	2,325	49,467
1995	39,868	2,625	42,493

Year	Firearm	Bow	Total
1996	39,936	3,107	43,043

Tennessee

Year	Firearm	Bow	Total
1970	8,258	372	8,630
1971	6,202	365	6,567
1972	7,354	499	7,853
1973	10,937	474	11,411
1974	12,624	685	13,309
1975	13,897	993	14,890
1976	16,374	1,739	18,113
1977	19,527	1,770	21,297
1978	22,819	2,465	25,284
1979	25,970	2,570	28,540
1980	27,196	3,457	30,653
1981	28,885	3,407	32,292
1982	35,726	4,644	40,370
1983	42,528	6,347	48,875
1984	49,493	5,883	55,376
1985	53,118	7,278	60,396
1986	69,044	8,578	77,622
1987	86,777	12,040	98,817

Year	Firearm	Bow	Total
1988	81,469	10,796	92,265
1989	95,475	13,287	108,762
1990	97,172	16,061	113,233
1991	105,832	15,764	121,596
1992	106,168	19,728	125,896
1993	118,946	19,596	138,542
1994	111,598	20,832	132,430
1995	124,179	20,953	145,132
1996	127,129	22,501	149,630

They're Proficient with the Smokepole

Tennessee has a success rate of about 32 percent among its muzzle-loading hunters — one of the highest in the United States.

Tennessee Improves Deer Hunting Opportunities, and Success Rates

When the Tennessee Wildlife Resources Agency began its effort to restore the state's white-tailed deer population in the 1950s, there were so few animals left in the state that it was forced to import deer from other states.

The success of the state's deer restoration program is now highly visible. Tennessee's deer herd is estimated at 850,000, and hunters routinely harvest more than 125,000 deer annually.

The state attracts about 140,000 deer hunters annually, including 5,000 non-residents.

The charts on this page represent some of the more interesting facts on Tennessee's deer hunting opportunities and success rates.

Figure 1 shows how the state offers quality hunting for bucks. About 26.6 percent of the bucks killed each year sport racks with eight or more points.

Figure 2 details the state's increasing annual harvest and hunter success rate. In 1991, 188,064 hunters killed 121,596 whitetails — a success rate of 40 percent. Four years later, 186,342 hunters killed 87,827 deer — a success rate of 47.1 percent.

Figure 3 breaks down

Antler Points of Tennessee Bucks

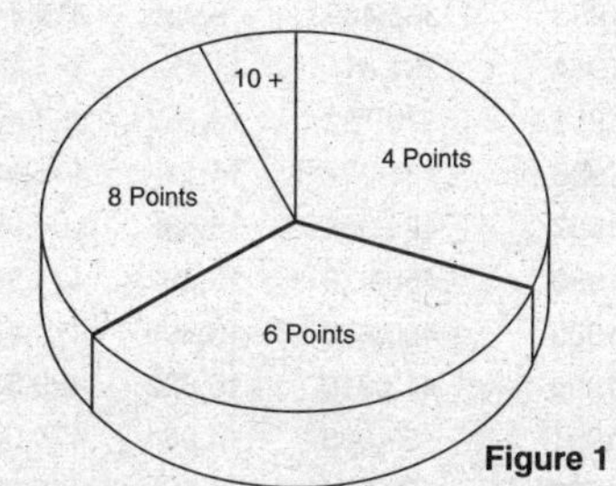

Tennessee Hunter Success Data

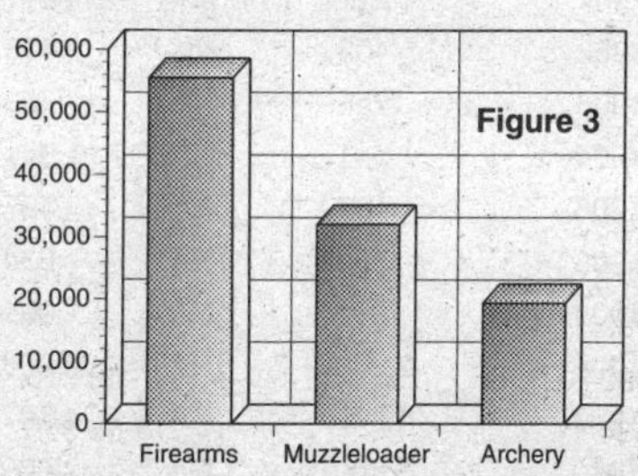

Tennessee Deer Harvest, 1995

Tennessee's overall deer harvest by season. Surprisingly, muzzle-loading hunters take more deer than bow-hunters. In 1995, muzzle-loading hunters took almost 25 percent more deer than bow-hunters did.

Texas

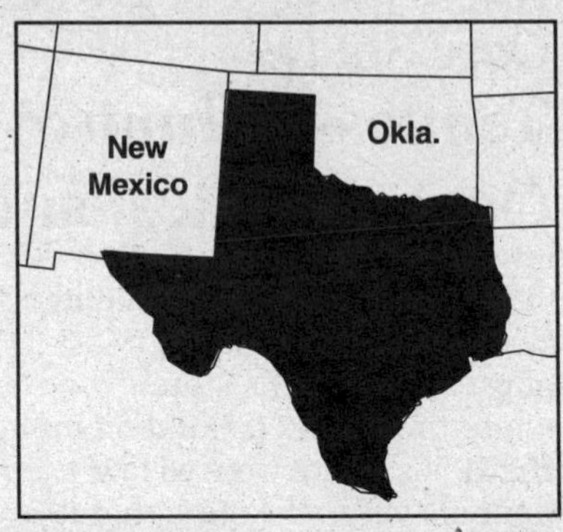

Year	Firearm	Bow	Total
1980	253,993	6,390	260,383
1981	292,525	7,527	300,052
1982	328,678	8,943	337,621
1983	309,409	8,935	318,344
1984	361,811	11,451	373,262
1985	370,732	12,767	383,499
1986	431,002	14,117	445,119
1987	489,368	15,585	504,953
1988	458,576	16,392	474,968
1989	460,896	16,595	477,491
1990	413,910	15,622	429,532
1991	459,083	14,964	474,047
1992	453,361	15,532	468,893

Year	Firearm	Bow	Total
1993	13,575	135,753	452,509
1994	12,643	126,427	421,423
1995	13,518	135,148	450,493

Vermont

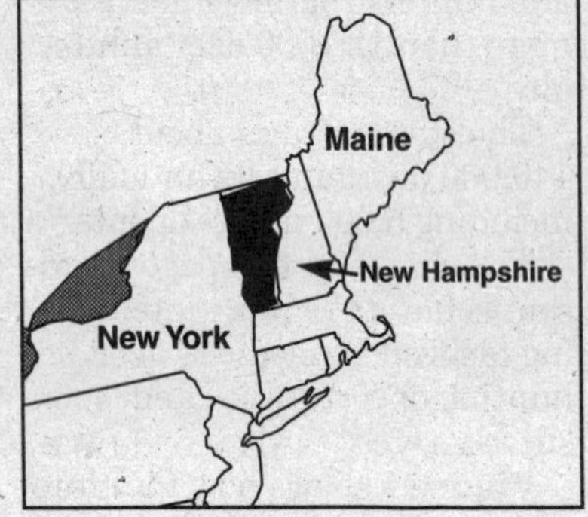

Year	Firearm	Bow	Total
1897	103	NA	103
1898	134	NA	134
1899	90	NA	90
1900	123	NA	123
1901	211	NA	211
1902	403	NA	403
1903	753	NA	753
1904	541	NA	541
1905	497	NA	497
1906	634	NA	634
1907	991	NA	991
1908	2,208	NA	2,208
1909	4,597	NA	4,597
1910	3,609	NA	3,609
1911	2,644	NA	2,644
1912	1,692	NA	1,692
1913	1,802	NA	1,802
1914	2,041	NA	2,041
1915	6,042	NA	6,042
1916	1,630	NA	1,630
1917	992	NA	992
1918	825	NA	825

Year	Firearm	Bow	Total
1919	4,092	NA	4,092
1920	4,477	NA	4,477
1921	1,507	NA	1,507
1922	787	NA	787
1923	686	NA	686
1924	1,537	NA	1,537
1925	952	NA	952
1926	882	NA	882
1927	869	NA	869
1928	1,063	NA	1,063
1929	1,438	NA	1,438
1930	1,481	NA	1,481
1931	1,758	NA	1,758

Vermont White-Tailed Deer Harvest Totals, Continued

Year	Firearm	Bow	Total	Year	Firearm	Bow	Total
1932	1,992	NA	1,992	1965	16,029	544	16,573
1933	2,397	NA	2,397	1966	20,616	704	21,320
1934	1,633	NA	1,633	1967	21,942	934	22,876
1935	2,039	NA	2,039	1968	12,934	1,432	14,366
1936	1,997	NA	1,997	1969	20,753	1,547	22,300
1937	2,446	NA	2,446	1970	17,592	1,197	18,789
1938	2,433	NA	2,433	1971	7,760	604	8,364
1939	2,589	NA	2,589	1972	8,980	1,073	10,053
1940	3,400	NA	3,400	1973	8,560	1,040	9,600
1941	3,111	NA	3,111	1974	11,254	1,580	12,834
1942	3,280	NA	3,280	1975	9,939	1,606	11,545
1943	2,871	NA	2,871	1976	10,278	1,200	11,478
1944	3,657	NA	3,657	1977	10,029	2,094	12,123
1945	3,510	NA	3,510	1978	7,087	1,688	8,775
1946	4,523	NA	4,523	1979	14,936	1,587	16,523
1947	5,635	NA	5,635	1980	24,675	1,257	25,932
1948	4,298	NA	4,298	1981	19,077	1,169	20,246
1949	5,983	NA	5,983	1982	9,148	798	9,946
1950	6,106	NA	6,106	1983	6,092	538	6,630
1951	6,940	NA	6,940	1984	12,418	630	13,048
1952	6,554	NA	6,554	1985	13,150	727	13,877
1953	7,475	7	7,482	1986	11,943	810	12,753
1954	8,402	8	84,10	1987	8,046	958	9,004
1955	9,936	42	9,978	1988	6,451	627	7,078
1956	9,645	62	9,707	1989	8,030	1,202	9,232
1957	11,293	142	11,435	1990	7,930	1,053	8,983
1958	10,510	150	10,660	1991	9,993	1,591	11,584
1959	11,268	232	11,500	1992	11,215	3,245	14,460
1960	11,164	261	11,425	1993	10,043	2,999	13,333
1961	15,526	297	15,823	1994	9,177	3,276	12,903
1962	15,898	277	16,175	1995	NA	NA	18,116
1963	10,024	176	10,200	1996	NA	NA	NA
1964	14,502	352	14,854				

Almanac Insights

Bucks Prefer Sweet-Smelling Trees

A three-year study at Clemson University in South Carolina showed that bucks preferred to rub their antlers on aromatic trees rather than non-aromatic species. The most commonly rubbed trees were sassafras, Southern magnolia and Eastern red cedar.

Virginia

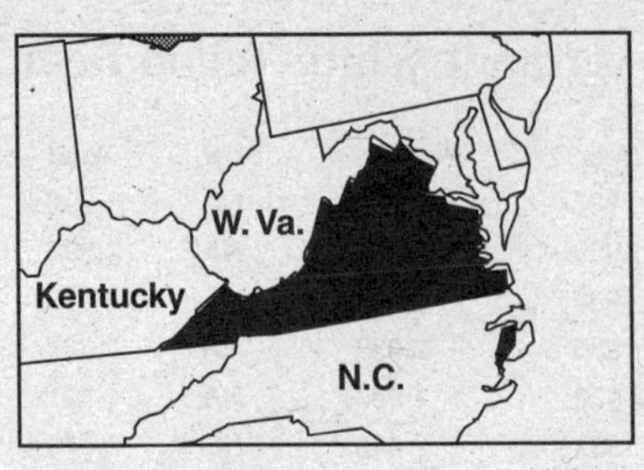

Year	Firearm	Bow	Total	Year	Firearm	Bow	Total
1935	NA	NA	1,158	1969	NA	NA	34,150
1936	NA	NA	1,475	1970	NA	NA	38,138
1937	NA	NA	1,526	1971	NA	NA	42,369
1938	NA	NA	1,391	1972	NA	NA	48,775
1939	NA	NA	1,365	1973	NA	NA	60,789
1940	NA	NA	1,691	1974	NA	NA	61,989
1941	NA	NA	1,901	1975	NA	NA	63,443
1942	NA	NA	1,448	1976	NA	NA	63,671
1943	NA	NA	2,282	1977	NA	NA	67,059
1944	NA	NA	3,433	1978	NA	NA	72,545
1945	NA	NA	4,545	1979	NA	NA	69,940
1946	NA	NA	6,543	1980	NA	NA	75,208
1947	NA	NA	4,019	1981	NA	NA	78,388
1948	NA	NA	5,162	1982	NA	NA	88,540
1949	NA	NA	6,910	1983	NA	NA	85,739
1950	NA	NA	5,699	1984	NA	NA	84,432
1951	NA	NA	7,230	1985	NA	NA	101,425
1952	NA	NA	10,874	1986	NA	NA	121,801
1953	NA	NA	11,797	1987	NA	NA	119,309
1954	NA	NA	14,079	1988	NA	NA	114,562
1955	NA	NA	14,227	1989	NA	NA	135,094
1956	NA	NA	20,855	1990	NA	NA	160,411
1957	NA	NA	22,473	1991	NA	NA	179,344
1958	NA	NA	26,841	1992	NA	NA	200,446
1959	NA	NA	28,969	1993	185,222	15,900	201,122
1960	NA	NA	36,145	1994	190,673	18,700	209,373
1961	NA	NA	32,875	1995	202,277	16,199	218,476
1962	NA	NA	38,838	1996	191,647	15,913	207,560
1963	NA	NA	38,391				
1964	NA	NA	31,179				
1965	NA	NA	27,983				
1966	NA	NA	25,920				
1967	NA	NA	24,934				
1968	NA	NA	28,041				

How Big is Vermont's Herd?

Despite having the eighth-lowest deer population in the United States (110,000), Vermont is one of the most storied deer hunting states in the country.

Virginia Deer Hunters Benefit State's Economy with Serious Dedication

White-tailed deer are the most popular game species in Virginia. During the 1994 season, more than 240,000 deer hunters spent nearly 4.1 million days afield in pursuit of whitetails.

The state's deer herd represents a beneficial economic resource. According to a 1996 hunter survey, 55 percent of all hunter days spent afield were in pursuit of deer.

To put that in dollars, Virginia hunters spend about $140 million annually on deer hunting. This estimate includes only direct hunting expenditures and does not utilize an economic factor or deer-hunting related noncon-sumptive recreation, such as spin-off expenditures.

Virginia's deer management program has been noted for both its success and simplicity. Current objectives of the program are to provide as much recreational deer hunting opportunity as possible without harming the resource and to direct the population control necessary to maintain herd health and to reduce crop depredation.

Consequently, between 1988 and 1992, the total deer harvest increased 75 percent from 114,562 to 200,446.

— 1995 Virginia Deer Harvest Summary

Total Deer Harvest vs. Muzzleloader Harvest

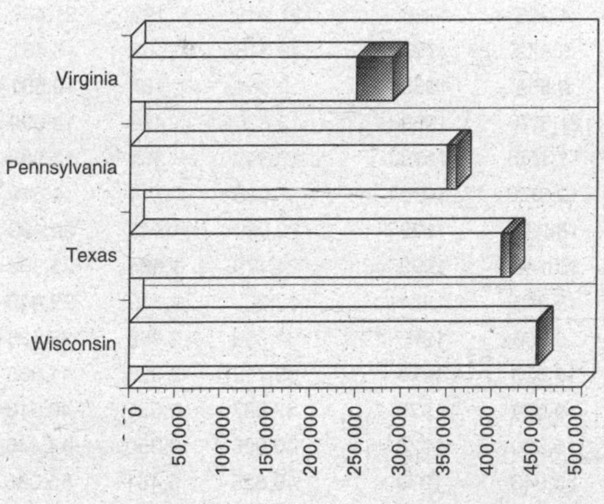

This chart shows the deer harvests for four states and what percentage of the totals are from muzzle-loading hunters (shown in the shaded sections). Virginia muzzle-loading hunters are the most successful, accouting for 16 percent of the state's total harvest.

Washington

Year	Firearm	Bow	Total
1992	10,593	1,007	11,600
1993	7,430	882	8,312
1994	9,709	1,153	10,860
1995	NA	NA	NA

NOTE: Washington does not differentiate between black-tailed deer, mule deer and white-tailed deer in its harvest totals. The total deer kill in 1994 was 46,618 and it is estimated that 23 percent of those animals were white-tailed deer.

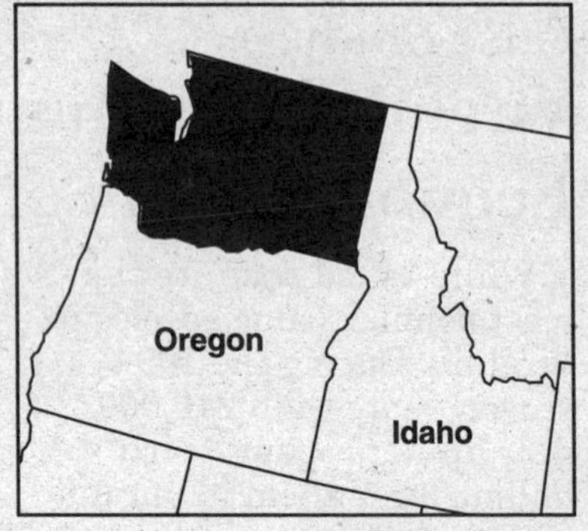

West Virginia

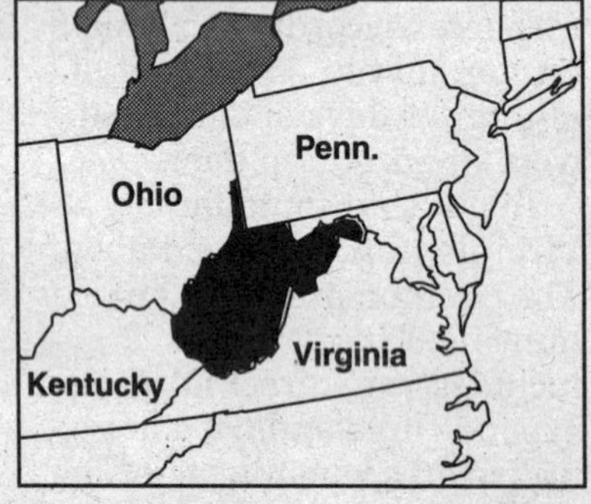

Year	Firearm	Bow	Total
1933	379	0	379
1934	309	0	309
1936	242	0	242
1937	456	0	456
1938	896	0	896
1939	897	0	897
1940	1,116	0	1,116
1941	1,064	0	1,064
1942	1,575	0	1,575
1943	1,827	0	1,827
1947	5,473	2	5,475
1948	4,958	5	4,963
1949	6,466	6	6,472
1950	6,549	10	6,559
1951	21,851	22	21,873
1952	17,140	16	17,156
1953	19,844	13	19,857
1954	16,703	29	16,732
1955	13,081	67	13,148
1956	18,158	87	18,245
1957	6,187	19	6,206
1958	18,436	117	18,553
1959	19,588	90	19,678
1960	15,850	80	15,930
1961	4,930	113	5,043
1962	5,627	152	5,779

Year	Firearm	Bow	Total
1963	7,609	119	7,728
1964	8,474	183	8,657
1965	19,686	226	19,912
1966	21,249	199	21,448
1967	18,318	163	18,481
1968	10,364	187	10,551
1969	13,620	470	14,090
1970	13,399	589	13,988
1971	15,905	714	16,619
1972	20,960	1,443	22,403
1973	24,179	1,684	25,863
1974	27,821	2,119	29,940
1975	32,368	2,968	35,336
1976	38,712	2,323	41,035
1977	37,987	2,531	40,518
1978	40,096	4,350	44,446
1979	49,625	5,461	55,086
1980	47,022	7,144	54,166

West Virginia White-Tailed Deer Harvest Totals, Continued

Year	Firearm	Bow	Total	Year	Firearm	Bow	Total
1981	65,505	9,003	74,508	1989	129,350	16,217	145,567
1982	74,642	13,454	88,096	1990	148,233	21,715	169,948
1983	78,605	11,235	89,840	1991	149,536	27,448	176,984
1984	94,132	12,578	106,710	1992	177,265	28,659	205,924
1985	71,183	13,416	84,599	1993	142,589	26,425	169,014
1986	101,404	17,207	118,611	1994	120,954	24,448	145,402
1987	109,367	19,742	129,109	1995	172,718	26,878	199,596
1988	112,155	16,537	128,692	1996	155,314	28,045	183,359

Wisconsin

Year	Firearm	Bow	Total
1897	2,500	NA	2,500
1898	2,750	NA	2,750
1899	3,000	NA	3,000
1900	3,500	NA	3,500
1901	4,000	NA	4,000
1902	4,000	NA	4,000
1903	4,250	NA	4,250
1904	4,500	NA	4,500
1905	4,250	NA	4,250
1906	4,500	NA	4,500
1907	4,750	NA	4,750
1908	5,000	NA	5,000
1909	5,550	NA	5,550
1910	5,750	NA	5,750
1911	9,750	NA	9,750
1912	8,500	NA	8,500
1913	9,750	NA	9,750
1914	9,850	NA	9,850
1915	5,000	NA	5,000
1916	7,000	NA	7,000
1917	18,000	NA	18,000
1918	17,000	NA	17,000
1919	25,152	NA	25,152
1920	20,025	NA	20,025
1921	14,845	NA	14,845
1922	9,255	NA	9,255
1923	9,000	NA	9,000
1924	7,000	NA	7,000
1926	12,000	NA	12,000

Year	Firearm	Bow	Total
1928	17,000	NA	17,000
1930	23,000	NA	23,000
1932	36,000	NA	36,000
1934	21,251	1	21,252
1936	29,676	1	26,677
1937	14,835	0	14,835
1938	32,855	1	32,856
1939	25,730	6	25,736
1940	33,138	5	33,142
1941	40,403	18	40,421
1942	45,188	15	45,203
1943	128,296	76	128,372
1944	28,537	78	28,615
1945	37,527	160	37,687
1946	55,276	256	55,532
1947	53,520	368	53,888
1948	41,954	279	42,233
1949	159,112	551	159,663
1950	167,911	383	168,294
1951	129,475	188	129,663
1952	27,504	126	27,630
1953	19,823	355	20,178
1954	24,698	743	25,441
1955	35,060	NA	NA

Wisconsin White-Tailed Deer Harvest Totals, Continued

Year	Firearm	Bow	Total	Year	Firearm	Bow	Total
1956	35,562	NA	NA	1977	131,910	16,790	148,700
1957	68,138	NA	NA	1978	150,845	18,113	168,958
1958	95,234	NA	NA	1979	125,570	16,018	141,588
1959	105,596	NA	NA	1980	139,624	20,954	160,578
1960	61,005	NA	NA	1981	166,673	29,083	195,756
1961	38,772	NA	NA	1982	182,715	30,850	213,565
1962	45,835	NA	NA	1983	197,600	32,876	230,476
1963	65,020	NA	NA	1984	255,240	38,891	294,131
1964	93,445	3,164	96,609	1985	274,302	40,744	315,046
1965	98,774	4,995	103,769	1986	259,240	40,490	299,730
1966	110,062	5,986	116,048	1987	250,530	42,651	293,181
1967	128,527	7,592	136,119	1988	263,424	42,393	305,817
1968	119,986	6,934	126,920	1989	310,192	46,394	356,586
1969	98,008	5,987	103,995	1990	350,040	49,291	399,331
1970	72,844	6,520	79,364	1991	352,328	67,005	419,333
1971	70,835	6,522	77,357	1992	288,906	60,479	349,385
1972	74,827	7,087	81,914	1993	217,584	53,008	270,592
1973	82,105	8,456	90,561	1994	307,629	66,254	373,883
1974	100,405	12,514	112,919	1995	397,942	69,158	467,100
1975	117,378	13,588	130,966	1996	388,211	72,313	460,524
1976	122,509	13,636	136,145				

Wyoming

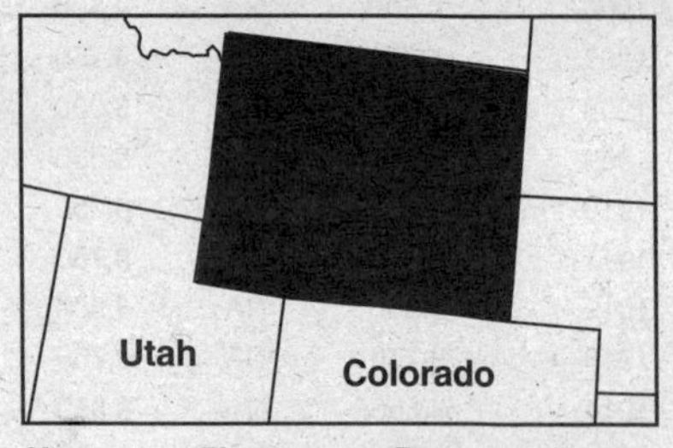

Year	Firearm	Bow	Total
1971	7,806	NA	7,806
1972	4,306	NA	4,306
1973	9,174	NA	9,174
1974	12,832	NA	12,832
1975	14,001	NA	14,001
1976	11,298	NA	11,298
1977	11,049	NA	11,049
1978	7,796	NA	7,796
1979	7,452	NA	7,452
1980	7,014	NA	7,014
1981	7,286	NA	7,286
1982	7,608	NA	7,608
1983	8,498	NA	8,498
1984	9,888	NA	9,888
1985	9,267	NA	9,267

Year	Firearm	Bow	Total
1986	7,983	254	8,237
1987	5,628	192	5,820
1988	7,005	174	7,179
1989	8,903	197	9,100
1990	9,535	147	9,632
1991	10,240	139	10,379
1992	14,533	216	14,749
1993	12,623	1,322	13,945
1994	8,249	228	8,477
1995	6,959	175	7,134

How Accurately Can Hunters Judge White-Tailed Deer Populations?

James Evrard of Grantsburg, Wis., believes a decent correlation exists between a deer herd's size and the number of deer he sees during his state's firearms deer season.

Evrard documents all deer sightings on the property he hunts. As seen in Figure 1 and Figure 2, trends in his deer unit's registered buck kill over 14 years correlate fairly well with changes in the average number of deer he saw per day. Obviously, the average number of deer he saw fluctuated more greatly than the buck harvest, especially in short-term comparisons. For example, from 1980 to 1981, the average number of deer seen per day increased 162 percent, while the buck harvest increased merely 12 percent.

Evrard says his journal made him a better hunter, and it helped him relive enjoyable hunts. "The extra time it takes to jot down information from a day's hunt is well worth the effort," he said. However, journal information is better at gauging deer herd trends than determining actual changes in deer herd number, Evrard wrote.

— *Dan Schmidt*

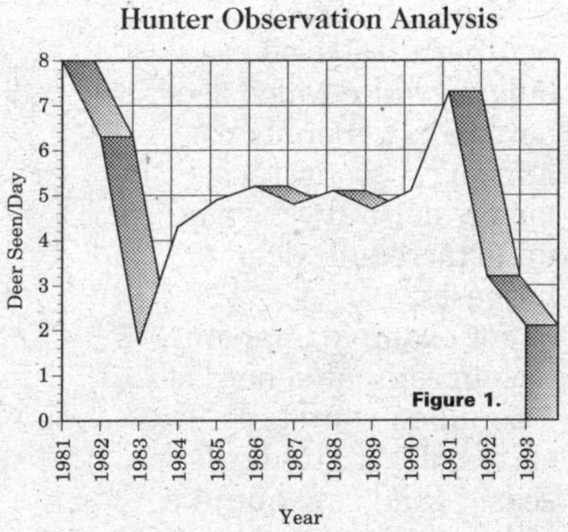

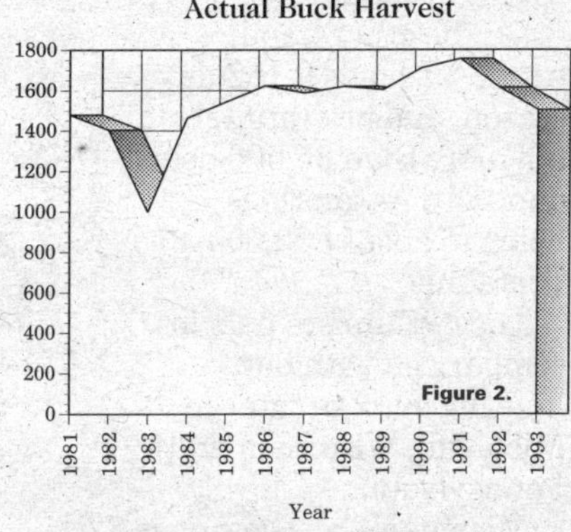

Figures 1 and 2: These charts show the average number of deer James Evrard saw per day on his property and compares it with the deer-management unit's actual buck harvest. Buck-harvest data was used in the comparison because it's a relatively consistent indicator of the deer herd's size. Antlerless harvest can vary greatly, depending on quotas set by state biologists.

Longer Archery Seasons Don't Necessarily Equal Higher Harvests

Although some Southern states offer bulging white-tailed deer herds and generous bow-hunting seasons, those factors don't always add up to incredible deer harvests.

For example, Alabama has an estimated herd of 1.5 million whitetails. The state holds a 110-day bow season, and bow-hunters kill more than 40,000 whitetails annually.

On the other hand, Arkansas holds a 152-day season, and bow-hunters kill more than 35,000 deer annually. Arkansas is home to about 800,000 whitetails.

These numbers pale in comparison with bow-hunting success rates in Michigan, Wisconsin and Pennsylvania.

Michigan's bow season is 77 days — about half as many days as Arkansas' season. However, Michigan bow-hunters kill more than 95,000 deer annually.

Wisconsin is a similar story. Bow-hunters in the Badger State kill more than 70,000 deer annually during an 83-day season.

Why the disparity in the

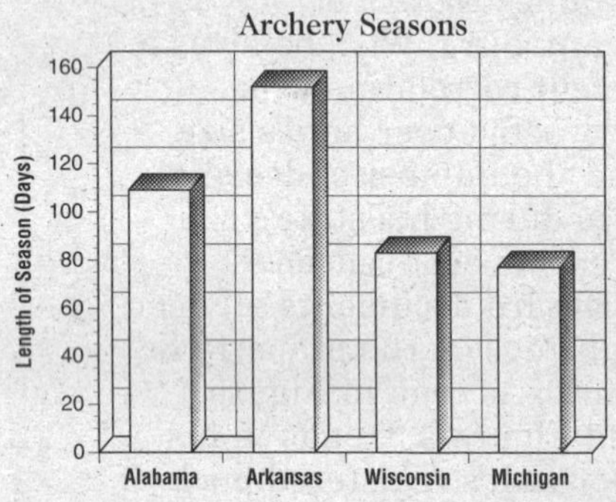

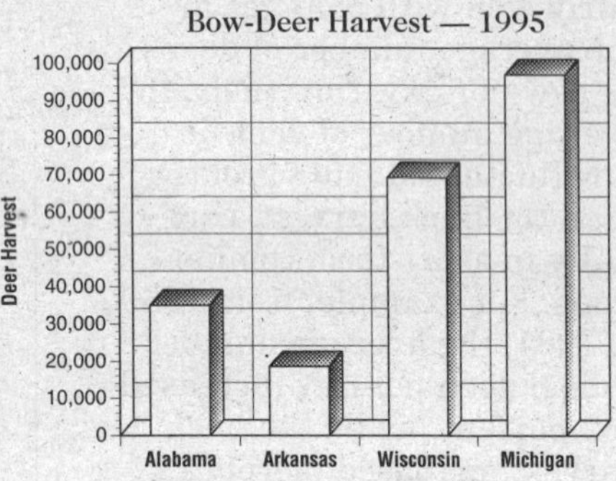

numbers? Land access is one of the reasons.

Nearly all hunting land in Alabama is privately owned, and about 89 percent of the land in Arkansas is also private.

The opposite is true in Michigan and Wisconsin, where thousands of acres are open to public hunting.

— *Dan Schmidt*

Chapter 7

Record Whitetails

It's hard to discuss "trophy class" whitetails in today's modern era of deer hunting without mentioning two respected organizations: the Boone and Crockett Club and the Pope and Young Club.

Unfortunately, the hows and whys of the record-keeping processes of these clubs is grossly misunderstood by many of today's hunters. The clubs document large white-tailed bucks not so much because of the hunters who took them, but rather as a tribute to the incredible animals. For example, one of the founders of P&Y, Dr. Saxton Pope, perhaps best described why we hunt when he said:

"There is no need to battle with the beasts of prey and little necessity to kill wild animals for food; but still the hunting instinct persists.

"The love of the chase still thrills us and all the misty past echoes with the hunter's call.

"In the joy of hunting is intimately woven the love of the great outdoors. The beauty of the woods, valleys, mountains, and skies feeds the soul of the sportsman where the quest of game only whets his appetite.

"After all, it is not the killing that brings satisfaction; it is the contest of skill and cunning. The true hunter counts his achievement in proportion to the effort involved and the fairness of the sport."

Scoring Trophy White-tailed Deer

The Boone and Crockett scoring system, with few changes, is essentially the same one developed by a committee of Boone and Crockett Club members and staff in 1950. A score chart for typical-antlered bucks is included in this chapter.

For B&C record-keeping purposes, official scores can be disputed, even years after the original measurement. Repeat measurements are allowed because of the enduring nature of white-tailed deer antlers.

Scoring a rack begins with careful reading of the official score charts reproduced in this book. Be sure to follow the instructions carefully. After taking a rough measurement, the owner must contact a volunteer B&C measurer to get an official measurement for the records program. An official measurer should be contacted as soon as possible if the rough score is close to the club's minimum "book scores."

Official scorers are not paid — they donate their time as a public service.

An official measurement cannot be made until the rack has dried 60 days after the date of kill. A drying period is necessary to allow for normal shrinkage. The drying period also ensures shrinkage will be relatively the same for all trophies, an impossible condition if "green" scores were allowed.

Typical or Non-Typical?

A non-typical rack is usually defined as one that includes abnormal points —

Typical Antlers

Non-Typical Antlers

"extra" tines that protrude from a standard 4-by-4, 5-by-5 or 6-by-6 frame. If a non-typical rack is entered under the typical category, such points are subtracted as a penalty from the rack's final score. However, these points are added into the final score if the owner decides to classify the antlers as non-typical.

The owner, with the assistance from an official measurer, determines how to classify his or her rack. In these borderline cases, the owner usually has the rack measured under both categories, and chooses the one that allows it to have a higher overall score.

B&C sets no definition for how many non-typical points must be present to call a trophy "non-typical."

Typical and non-typical Coues' white-tailed deer use the same score chart as the more common white-tailed deer. However, to qualify as a B&C Coues' whitetail, the animal must come from one of the following North American locations: all of southwestern New Mexico, west of the Rio Grande River and northward to Interstate Highway 40; central and southern Arizona; or the Mexican states of Sonora and Chihuahua. The trophy must also meet the minimum score and other requirements for entry as a Coues' whitetail.

Whitetail Records Included in Book

The Boone and Crockett Club introduces *Records of North American Whitetail Deer, 3rd Edition*. The book lists the largest whitetails taken from each state, Canadian province, and Mexico.

The 4,000 entries are sorted by state or province and ranked from highest to lowest.

Records of North American Whitetail Deer, 3rd Edition includes more than 150 photographs of award-winning white-tailed deer trophies. Also included are first-time whitetail listings for Delaware, Massachusetts and New Hampshire. The book spans 448 pages.

The score chart of the new World's Record typical whitetail from Canada, scoring 213⅝ points, is reproduced along with the score chart of the largest non-typical whitetail taken in the last three years, which scored 281⅝ points.

An introduction by Jack and Susan Reneau of Montana traces the history of the book and how it was first compiled.

— *For more information, contact **Boone and Crockett Club**, 250 Station Drive, Dept. DDH, Missoula, MT 59801.*

Boone and Crockett Club Whitetails
Category: All-Time Typical

Rank/Location	Hunter	Year	Score
1 *Saskatchewan*	Milo Hansen	1993	213⅝
2 *Wisconsin*	James Jordan	1914	206⅛
3 *Missouri*	Larry Gibson	1971	205
4 *Illinois*	Mel Johnson	1965	204⅝
5 *Alberta*	Steven Stephen	1967	204⅔

Boone and Crockett Club Whitetails
Category: All-Time Non-Typical

Rank/Location	Hunter	Year	Score
1 *Missouri*	(Picked Up)	1981	333⅞
2 *Ohio*	(Picked Up)	1940	328⅖
3 *Texas*	Unknown	1892	284⅜
4 *Iowa*	Larry Raveling	1973	282
5 *Louisiana*	James McMurray	1994	281⅝

Number of Boone & Crockett White-Tailed Deer Entries by State and Year Taken

State	1830 to 1993	1984 to 1993	1991 to 1993
Alabama	11	4	0
Arkansas	50	17	10
Colorado	15	12	5
Connecticut	4	3	1
Delaware	3	2	1
Florida	1	0	0
Georgia	65	24	7
Idaho	35	19	7
Illinois	224	175	81
Indiana	50	38	15
Iowa	317	190	56
Kansas	128	89	29
Louisiana	27	5	1
Maine	62	16	4
Maryland	21	11	2
Massachusetts	1	1	1
Michigan	77	38	13
Minnesota	420	125	42
Mississippi	28	8	0
Missouri	119	69	29
Montana	78	24	11
Nebraska	77	213	6
New York	34	5	2
New Hampshire	4	3	3
North Carolina	5	5	1
North Dakota	34	11	5
Ohio	109	60	24
Oklahoma	23	14	4
Oregon	1	0	0
Pennsylvania	19	3	1
South Carolina	1	0	0
South Dakota	67	10	3
Tennessee	16	6	2
Texas	203	52	28
Vermont	2	1	0
Virginia	26	13	3
Washington	36	11	5
West Virginia	7	1	0
Wisconsin	272	97	28
Wyoming	27	13	5
Totals	**2,699**	**1,198**	**435**

Scoring Instructions for Typical

(Sample — Not for Official Use)

I certify that I have measured this trophy on _________________________________ 19 _______

at .(address) _________________________ City _________________ State ________
and that these measurements and data are, to the best of my knowledge and belief, made in
accordance with the instructions given.

Witness: _________________________________ Signature: ______________________

B&C Official Measurer   □□□□

I.D. Number

INSTRUCTIONS FOR MEASURING TYPICAL WHITETAIL AND COUES' DEER

All measurements must be made with a 1/4-inch wide flexible steel tape to the nearest
one-eighth of an inch. (Note: A flexible steel cable can be used to measure points and main beams
only.) Enter fractional figures in eighths, without reduction. Official measurements cannot be
taken until the antlers have air dried for at least 60 days after the animal was killed.

A. Number of Points on Each Antler: To be counted a point, the projection must be at least one
inch long, with the length exceeding width at one inch or more of length. All points are measured
from tip of point to nearest edge of beam as illustrated. Beam tip is counted as a point but not
measured as a point.

B. Tip to Tip Spread is measured between tips of main beams.

C. Greatest Spread is measured between perpendiculars at a right angle to the center line of
the skull at widest part, whether across main beams or points.

D. Inside Spread of Main Beams is measured at a right angle to the center line of the skull at
widest point between main beams. Enter this measurement again as the Spread Credit if it is less
than or equal to the length of the longer antler; if greater, enter longer antler length for
Spread Credit.

E. Total of Lengths of all Abnormal Points: Abnormal Points are those non-typical in location
(such as points originating from a point or from bottom or sides of main beam) or extra points
beyond the normal pattern of points. Measure in usual manner and enter in appropriate blanks.

F. Length of Main Beam is measured from the center of the lowest outside edge of burr over
outer side to the most distant point of the main beam. The point of beginning is that point on
the burr where the center line along the outer side of the beam intersects the burr, then
following generally the line of the illustration.

G-1-2-3-4-5-6-7. Length of Normal Points: Normal points project from the top of the main
beam. They are measured from nearest edge of main beam over outer curve to tip. Lay the tape
along the outer curve of the beam so that the top edge of the tape coincides with the top edge of
the beam on both sides of the point to determine the baseline for point measurements. Record
point lengths in appropriate blanks.

H-1-2-3-4. Circumferences are taken as detailed for each measurement. If brow point is
missing, take H-1 and H-2 at smallest place between burr and G-2. If G-4 is missing, take H-4
halfway between G-3 and tip of main beam.

FAIR CHASE STATEMENT FOR ALL HUNTER-TAKEN TROPHIES

FAIR CHASE, as defined by the Boone and Crockett Club®, is the ethical, sportsmanlike and
lawful pursuit and taking of any free-ranging wild game animal in a manner that does not give
the hunter an improper or unfair advantage over such game animals.

Use of any of the following methods in the taking of game shall be deemed **UNFAIR CHASE**
and unsportsmanlike:

    I.   Spotting or herding game from the air, followed by landing in its vicinity for the
purpose of pursuit and shooting;

   II.   Herding, pursuing, or shooting game from any motorboat or motor vehicle;

 III.   Use of electronic devices for attracting, locating, or observing game, or for guiding
the hunter to such game;

  IV.   Hunting game confined by artificial barriers, including escape-proof fenced
enclosures, or hunting game transplanted for the purpose of commercial shooting;

   V.   Taking of game in a manner not in full compliance with the game laws or regulations
of the federal government or of any state, province, territory, or tribal council on
reservations or tribal lands;

  VI.   Or as may otherwise be deemed unfair or unsportsmanlike by the Executive Committee of
the Boone and Crockett Club.

I certify that the trophy scored on this chart was taken in **FAIR CHASE** as defined above by the
Boone and Crockett Club. In signing this statement, I understand that if the information
provided on this entry is found to be misrepresented or fraudulent in any respect, it will not
be accepted into the Awards Program and all of my prior entries are subject to deletion from
future editions of **Records of North American Big Game** and future entries may not be accepted.

Date: __________ Signature of Hunter:____

(Signature must be witnessed by an Official Measurer or
a Notary Public.)

Date: __________ Signature of Notary or Official Measurer:__________________________

White-Tailed Deer Antlers

(Sample — Not for Official Use)

OFFICIAL SCORING SYSTEM FOR NORTH AMERICAN BIG GAME TROPHIES

ecords of North American
ig Game

BOONE AND CROCKETT CLUB®

250 Station Drive
Missoula, MT 59801
(406) 542-1888

inimum Score: Awards All-time

	Awards	All-time
whitetail	160	170
Coues'	100	110

TYPICAL
WHITETAIL AND COUES' DEER

Kind of Deer: ______________

Abnormal Points	
Right Antler	Left Antler
Subtotals	
Total to E	

Detail of Point Measurement

SEE OTHER SIDE FOR INSTRUCTIONS

				Column 1	Column 2	Column 3	Column 4
				Spread Credit	Right Antler	Left Antler	Difference
A. No. Points on Right Antler		No. Points on Left Antler					
B. Tip to Tip Spread		C. Greatest Spread					
D. Inside Spread of Main Beams		(Credit May Equal But Not Exceed Longer Antler)					
E. Total of Lengths of Abnormal Points							
F. Length of Main Beam							
G-1. Length of First Point							
G-2. Length of Second Point							
G-3. Length of Third Point							
G-4. Length of Fourth Point, If Present							
G-5. Length of Fifth Point, If Present							
G-6. Length of Sixth Point, If Present							
G-7. Length of Seventh Point, If Present							
H-1. Circumference at Smallest Place Between Burr and First Point							
H-2. Circumference at Smallest Place Between First and Second Points							
H-3. Circumference at Smallest Place Between Second and Third Points							
H-4. Circumference at Smallest Place Between Third and Fourth Points							
			TOTALS				

ADD	Column 1		Exact Locality Where Killed:
	Column 2		Date Killed: Hunter:
	Column 3		Owner: Telephone #:
	Subtotal		Owner's Address:
SUBTRACT Column 4			Guide's Name and Address:
			Remarks: (Mention Any Abnormalities or Unique Qualities)
FINAL SCORE			

Copyright © 1997 by Boone and Crockett Club®

P&Y Documents the Evolution of Deer Hunting

The formation of the Pope and Young Club arose from a need to show the world the bow was an effective, viable hunting tool. Most hunters and state game agencies of the 1940s and 1950s believed the bow was little more than a toy, and few recognized it as a serious hunting weapon.

It was Glenn St. Charles and a small group of dedicated bow-hunters who conceived the idea of pulling together all the nationwide bow-hunting successes they could document. Their idea was to bring all of the information together and hold it up to those who believed bow-hunting was ineffective. In effect, they wanted to say, "Look, see how big these animals are. These big animals were taken with the bow and arrow. The bow works just fine, thank you."

After convincing the non-believers the bow was an effective hunting tool, the group lobbied for bow seasons that preceded rifle seasons. The rest, as they say, is history.

Today, the bow is accepted by every game agency in the country, and droves of hunters continue answering its call.

The underlying principle behind the formation of the Pope and Young Club was its goal of helping bow-hunting and the bow-hunter. The club's philosophy is to improve the image of today's hunter and communicate the fact that hunters are America's most concerned conservationists. In fact, the club believes these tasks loom every bit as large and challenging as those that bow-hunters faced 40 years ago.

Although few people in the non-hunting world think of the hunter as a conservationist, the hunter has always been that. Aldo Leopold, the father of the modern conservation ethic, was a bow-hunter and advocate of stewardship of the land.

It was Theodore Roosevelt — an avid hunter — who conceived the idea of the Boone and Crockett Club, of which P&Y is modeled after, and Roosevelt initiated the national park system.

Unfortunately, hunters haven't been very successful conveying their message to the non-hunting public. That is perhaps because hunters have taken too much for granted. Hunters have probably become somewhat insensitive to the fact that much of today's urban population does not understand what hunters do and why they do it.

— Taken from Bowhunting Big Game Records of North America. *Reprinted with permission of the **Pope and Young Club**, 15 E. Second St., Box 548, Dept. DDH, Chatfield, MN 55923.*

Pope and Young Club Whitetails
Category: All-Time Typical

Rank/Location		Hunter	Year	Score
1	*Illinois*	M.J. Johnson	1965	204⅛
2	*Iowa*	Lloyd Goad	1962	197⅝
3	*Minnesota*	Curt Van Lith	1966	197⅜
4	*Alberta*	Don McGarvey	1961	197⅛
5	*Iowa*	Robert Miller	1977	194⅔
6	*Colorado*	Stuart Clodfielder	1981	194⅐
7	*Michigan*	Craig Calderone	1986	193⅔
8	*Iowa*	Richard Swim	1981	190⅝
9	*Indiana*	B. Dodd Porter	1985	190⅛
10	*Nebraska*	Robert Vrbsky	1978	189⅛

Pope and Young Club Whitetails
Category: All-Time Non-Typical

Rank/Location		Hunter	Year	Score
1	*Nebraska*	Del Austin	1962	279⅞
2	*Kansas*	Ken Flowler	1988	257⅝
3	*Kansas*	Clifford Pickell	1968	249⅝
4	*Illinois*	Robert Chestnut	1981	245⅝
5	*Kansas*	Douglas Siebert	1988	245⅛
6	*Alberta*	Dean Dwernuchuk	1984	241⅞
7	*Ohio*	Ronald Osborne	1986	238⅝
8	*Kansas*	Gilbert Boss	1986	237⅝
9	*Kansas*	Randy Young	1989	233⅞
10	*Kansas*	Royce Frazier	1978	232⅞

Learn How to Use Stands

Deer hunters don't have to look far these days when seeking new material for their deer hunting libraries. When it comes to books on white-tailed deer, there seems to be a never-ending stream. Finding comprehensive works, however, is difficult. Such is not the case with Richard P. Smith's *Stand Hunting for Whitetails.* Smith's book is an A-to-Z work that deals with all of the important aspects hunters address when hunting from tree stands and ground blinds.

Of course, stand-hunting is hardly a new topic. However, Smith sheds new light on the subject by blending a truckload of insight on everything from stand selection and tree stand options to scent control and shot placement. A noted hunter, photographer and outdoor writer, Smith packs this information into a 256-page book that includes more than 175 photos.

Some of the book's best chapters are at the beginning. Chapter 3, "When Tree Stands Don't Stack Up," is an excellent discussion on why hunters are sometimes better off on the ground. For example, Smith describes how ground blinds sometimes offer more productive hunting options. He then follows up with tips on how to hunt from natural blinds like blow-downs and brush piles.

If you're an avid tree-stand hunter, you'll enjoy "Tree Stand Options," and "How High to Go." The first chapter describes which stands are best for various situations and how to maximize comfort and safety. The chapter on stand height tells bow-hunters how

Richard P. Smith, *Stand Hunting for Whitetails*. Iola, Wis.: Krause Publications, 1996. Pp. 256. Illustrated. Soft cover. $14.95. From Krause Publications, 700 E. State St., Iola, WI 54990-0001.

to position their stands to increase their chances of making double-lung hits on whitetails. Then, in Chapter 8, Smith details how to get the most out of stand sites through location, camouflage and pre-season preparations for shooting lanes.

Other useful chapters include "How to Wait for Whitetails," "Bait Hunting," "Hunting in the Rain," and "Tree Stand Safety."

Overall, *Stand Hunting for Whitetails* includes more practical, comprehensive information on stand hunting than one could ask for.

— *Dan Schmidt*

Chapter 8

Deer Hunting Information, Regulations & Statistics

Traveling deer hunters can use this chapter to answer important questions about such topics as bag limits, deer season dates, minimum hunting ages and hunter education requirements.

Whitetail enthusiasts can learn how their state ranks nationally in several categories, including deer hunters, deer population and deer harvest. In addition, we've disected each state, listing their numbers of gun- and bow-hunters. Helpful maps show which states lead in each category.

Trivia buffs can use this chapter to track deer hunting trends. Which states have the most problems with poachers? Which states have an increasing number of women hunters? And, which states have experienced decreases in car-deer accidents? Read on, because the answers are here — in easy-to-read charts.

KEY DEER HUNTING STATISTICS
Descending Numerical Order By State

State[1]	Estimated Deer Population[2]
Texas[9]	3,748,000
Michigan	1,900,000
Mississippi	1,750,000
Wisconsin	1,600,000
Alabama	1,500,000
Pennsylvania	1,180,000
Louisiana	1,000,000
Minnesota	1,000,000
Georgia	936,657
Virginia	900,000
North Carolina	850,000
Tennessee	850,000
Florida	820,000
Arkansas	800,000
West Virginia	800,000
Missouri	777,383
New York	750,000
South Carolina	750,000
California[8,9]	700,000
Illinois	700,000
Oregon[8,9,10]	631,200
Colorado[8,9]	530,400
Wyoming[8,9]	525,000
Ohio	500,000
Kentucky	436,192
Washington[8,9,10]	400,000
Oklahoma[9]	327,500
Iowa	325,000
Kansas[9]	N/A
South Dakota[9]	286,000
Maine	285,000
Nebraska[9]	265,000
New Mexico[8,9]	250,000
Utah[8,9]	249,000
North Dakota[9]	243,750
Maryland	225,000
Idaho[8,9]	220,000
Arizona[8,9]	195,000
New Jersey	150,000
Nevada[8,9]	137,000
Vermont	110,000
Connecticut	75,000
Massachusetts	75,000
New Hampshire	73,000
Delaware	25,000
Rhode Island	10,000
Indiana	Unknown
Montana[9]	Unknown
TOTAL	**29,861,082**

State	Total Deer Harvest[3]
Wisconsin	468,000
Texas	454,550
Michigan	440,000
Pennsylvania	430,583
Georgia	335,000
Alabama	325,000
Mississippi	310,000
Virginia	218,476
Minnesota	215,166
West Virginia	201,625
Louisiana	200,000
New York	188,284
Missouri	181,760
North Carolina	180,000
Ohio	179,543
Arkansas	163,000
South Carolina	148,123
Tennessee	145,132
Illinois	140,154
Montana	137,843
Indiana	117,700
Kentucky	106,116
Iowa	97,251
Florida	84,408
North Dakota	71,539
Oklahoma	65,886
Oregon	60,628
Maryland	60,602
New Jersey	59,769
South Dakota	58,360
Idaho	56,900
Colorado	52,144
Washington	47,000
Nebraska	45,530
Wyoming	39,069
Kansas	
Maine	27,384
Utah	24,723
Vermont	18,116
California	17,273
Arizona	15,508
New Mexico	14,300
Connecticut	13,734
Massachusetts	11,343
New Hampshire	11,207
Delaware	8,748
Nevada	8,114
Rhode Island	1,788
TOTAL	**6,257,379**

State	Resident Deer Hunters[4]	Non-Resident Deer Hunters[5]	Season Bag Limit[6]
Pennsylvania	1,299,372	72,693	1/day
Michigan	1,005,000	25,000	2
Wisconsin	894,543	33,810	2
New York	812,446	30,752	2
Texas	645,000	Unknown	6
Minnesota	523,056	10,571	1
Ohio	490,000	10,000	2
Georgia	421,106	22,000	5
Missouri	409,710	13,023	2
West Virginia	329,568	58,393	1
Virginia	301,000	16,000	3
Illinois	296,600	Unknown	7
Indiana	282,000	Unknown	5
Alabama	265,000	27,800	1/day
Kentucky	263,850	Unknown	3
Tennessee	244,323	8,107	1
Louisiana	230,400	2,567	2
Oregon	227,478	Unknown	1
Mississippi	225,000	22,000	5
Oklahoma	197,568	Unknown	2
Washington	175,054	1,206	20
South Carolina	172,500	34,000	6
Maine	172,200	30,200	1
Idaho	166,200	Unknown	8
Florida	157,919	Unknown	2
New Jersey	156,000	7,000	2
Maryland	152,000	21,000	1
Iowa	144,559	2,710	1
Massachusetts	143,000	Unknown	13
Colorado	117,945	68,400	2/day
Vermont	110,109	19,823	1
New Hampshire	100,974	17,359	20+
North Dakota	97,627	1,481	7
Arizona	87,000	4,000	1
Utah	86,747	5,341	3
South Dakota	82,736	5,507	25
Nebraska	72,409	2,877	2
New Mexico	54,750	5,702	2
Nevada	52,933	2,370	2
Wyoming	49,993	27,493	1
Delaware	22,989	2,171	1
Rhode Island	8,251	699	
Arkansas	Unknown	Unknown	5
California	Unknown	Unknown	12
Connecticut	Unknown	Unknown	1
Kansas	Unknown	Unknown	2
Montana	Unknown	Unknown	2
North Carolina	Unknown	Unknown	2
TOTALS	**11,746,915**	**622,055**	

Leading Deer Hunting States
Licensed Resident Deer Hunters

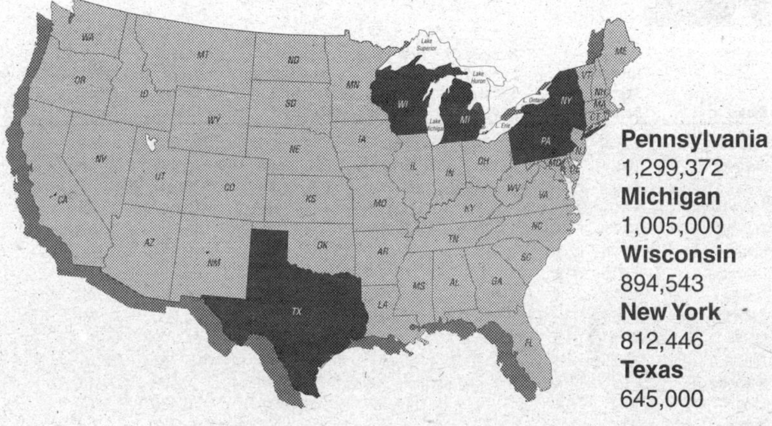

Pennsylvania
1,299,372
Michigan
1,005,000
Wisconsin
894,543
New York
812,446
Texas
645,000

Leading White-Tailed Deer States
Estimated Whitetail Populations

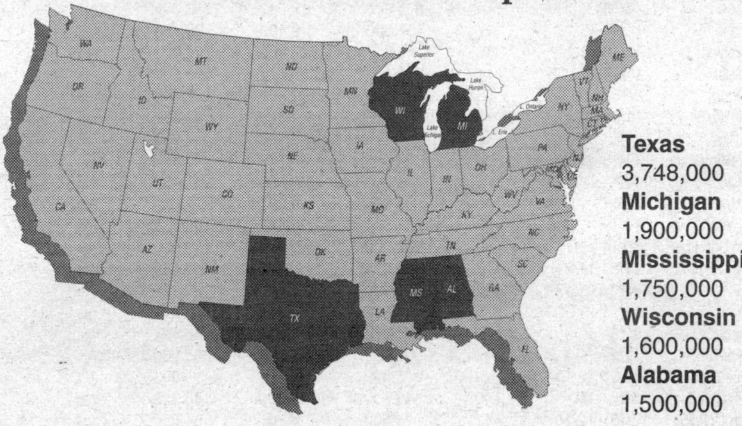

Texas
3,748,000
Michigan
1,900,000
Mississippi
1,750,000
Wisconsin
1,600,000
Alabama
1,500,000

Firearm Hunting Information
Alphabetical Order By State

State	Firearm Season Dates[1]	Number Of Firearm Season Days[2]	How Many Resident Firearms Hunters?	How Many Non-Resident Firearms Hunters?[3]	Number Of Deer Harvested By Firearms	Are Rifles Permitted?[4]
Alabama	11/18 - 1/31	75	205,000	21,500	290,000	Yes
Arizona	10/27 - 12/31	66	65,000	2,500	13,895	Yes
Arkansas	11/11 - 12/16	36	Unknown	Unknown	120,000	Yes
California	8/10 - 10/6	58	Unknown	Unknown	16,057	Yes
Colorado	10/12 - 11/10	26	105,000	60,300	45,700	Yes
Connecticut	11/20 - 12/10	18	24,000	1,500	8,854	Yes
Delaware	11/15 - 1/18	20	16,622	1,618	6,834	No
Florida	10/28 - 2/14	110	126,477	3,480	84,408	Yes
Georgia[5]	10/21 - 1/7	79	325,000	20,000	335,000	Yes
Idaho	9/15 - 11/18	65	146,200	12,869	54,100	Yes
Illinois	11/22 - 12/8	7	186,600	143	107,742	No
Indiana	11/18 - 12/3	16	174,000	Combined	76,400	No
Iowa	12/2 - 12/17	14	111,184	1,684	78,436	No
Kansas	N/A	N/A	N/A	N/A	N/A	N/A
Kentucky	11/11 - 11/20	10	166,430	Unknown	87,121	Yes
Louisiana	10/21 - 1/21	69	181,400	2,184	221,075	Yes
Maine	10/28 - 11/25	25	160,000	29,000	25,710	Yes
Maryland	11/25 - 12/9	13	106,000	14,000	38,725	Yes
Massachusetts	12/2 - 12/14	12	110,000	5,000	8,415	No
Michigan	11/15 - 11/30	16	675,000	25,000	318,000	Yes
Minnesota	11/9 - 11/29	21	453,000	9,400	198,193	Yes
Mississippi	11/18 - 1/17	47	165,000	17,000	230,000	Yes
Missouri	11/16 - 11/26	11	314,115	11,177	160,156	Yes
Montana[5]	9/15 -12/31	36	145,118	32,801	137,843	Yes
Nebraska	11/9 - 11/17	9	57,666	2,060	37,591	Yes
Nevada	10/5 - 11/3	32	47,415	1,756	7,269	Yes
New Hampshire	11/13 - 12/8	26	82,435	13,743	6,790	Yes
New Jersey	12/4 - 1/27	21	105,000	5,000	31,430	No
New Mexico	10/17 - 11/15	33	49,500	5,227	12,300	Yes
New York	10/19 - 12/10	53	643,534	28,447	166,430	Yes
North Carolina	10/14 - 1/1	69	220,000	Unknown	180,000	Yes
North Dakota	11/8 - 11/24	17	86,574	797	67,183	Yes
Ohio	11/27 - 12/9	12	300,000	7,500	137,174	No
Oklahoma	11/18 - 11/26	9	138,128	Unknown	40,877	Yes
Oregon[5]	9/28 - 11/6	40	201,976	Combined	58,621	Yes
Pennsylvania	12/2 - 1/11	32	1,000,000	50,000	365,960	Yes
Rhode Island	12/2 - 12/10	9	5,499	259	603	No
South Carolina[5]	8/15 - 1/1	140	147,500	29,000	148,123	Yes
South Dakota	9/16 - 12/10	47	71,500	4,707	54,850	Yes
Tennessee	11/18 - 1/7	36	149,323	4,610	124,179	Yes
Texas	11/4 - 2/4	94	570,000	18,000	441,000	Yes
Utah	10/19 - 10/27	9	73,819	4,701	20,995	Yes
Vermont	11/16 - 12/1	16	83,965	14,313	10,936	Yes
Virginia	11/20 - 1/6	42	240,000	14,000	161,500	Yes
Washington	10/12 - 11/24	44	153,241	1,041	39,093	Yes
West Virginia	11/20 - 12/9	15	222,568	40,393	159,710	Yes
Wisconsin	10/24 - 12/8	20	656,154	28,335	398,002	Yes
Wyoming[5]	9/10 - 11/30	82	43,090	25,428	37,869	Yes
TOTALS			**9,310,043**	**570,473**	**5,371,149**	

DEER HUNTERS' 1998 ALMANAC

Leading Deer-Kill States
Total Whitetail Kill, Gun and Bow

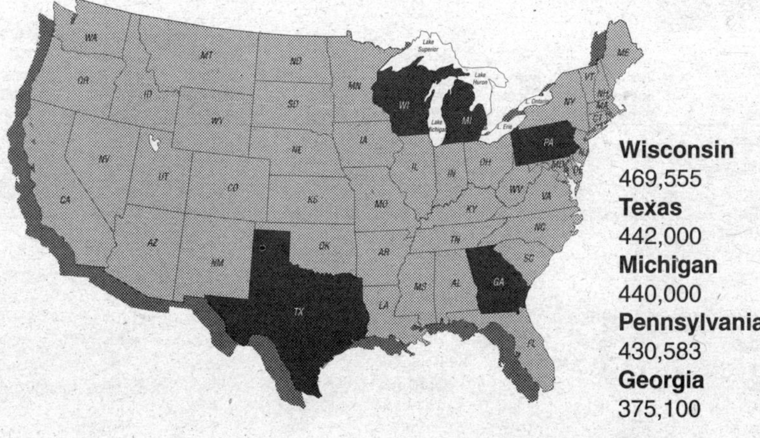

Leading Firearm Hunting States
Licensed Resident Gun-Hunters

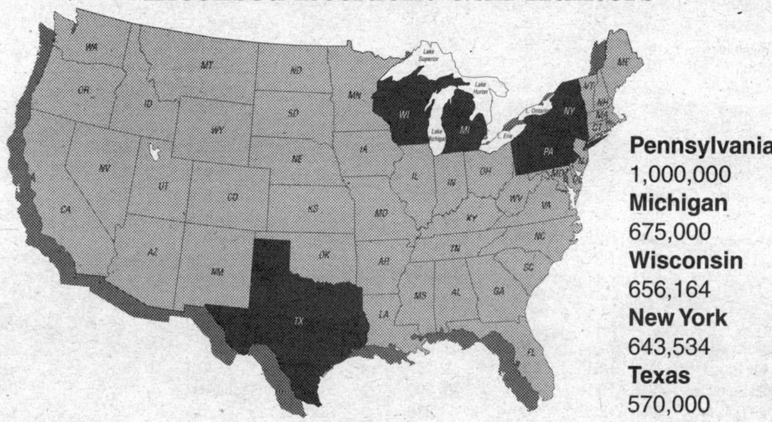

Bow-Hunting Information
Alphabetical Order By State

State	Bow Season Dates[1]	Bow Season Days[2]	How Many Resident Bow Hunters?	How Many Non-Resident Bow Hunters?[3]	Number Of Deer Harvested By Bow[4]	May General Public Hunt Deer With A Crossbow?[5]	May You Hunt Deer With A Crossbow If Handicapped And Have Perm
Alabama	10/14 - 1/31	110	60,000	6,300	35,000	No	Yes
Arizona	8/25 - 1/31	76	22,000	1,500	1,330	Yes	Yes
Arkansas	10/1 - 2/29	152	Unknown	Unknown	18,500	Yes	Yes
California	7/13 - 9/15	65	Unknown	Unknown	1,216	Yes	Yes
Colorado	8/24 - 12/31	118	12,945	8,100	4,505	Yes	Yes
Connecticut	9/16 - 12/31	107	Unknown	Unknown	2,698	No	Yes
Delaware	9/1 - 1/31	131	6,367	553	728	No	Yes
Florida	9/9 - 11/12	65	31,442	Combined	Combined	Yes	Yes
Georgia	9/16 - 10/20	35	96,106	2,000	40,000	No	Yes
Idaho	8/30 - 12/31	24	20,000	Combined	1,900	Yes	Yes
Illinois	10/1 - 1/16	101	110,000	Combined	34,404	No	Yes
Indiana	10/1 - 12/31	87	108,000	Combined	25,200	No	Yes
Iowa	10/1 - 1/10	86	33,375	1,026	13,372	No	Yes
Kansas	N/A	N/A	N/A	N/A	N/A	N/A	
Kentucky	10/1 - 1/15	107	97,420	Unknown	9,833	Yes	Yes
Louisiana	10/1 - 1/31	123	49,000	383	24,700	No	Yes
Maine	9/27 - 10/27	27	12,200	1,200	1,151	No	No
Maryland	9/15 - 1/31	90	46,000	7,000	12,247	No	Yes
Massachusetts	11/4 - 11/23	18	33,000	Unknown	1,901	No	No
Michigan	10/1 - 1/1	77	330,000	10,000	97,000	No	Yes
Minnesota	9/14 - 12/31	109	70,056	1,171	14,521	No	Yes
Mississippi	10/1 - 1/31	62	60,000	5,000	40,000	No	Yes
Missouri	10/1 - 1/15	107	95,595	1,846	17,136	Yes	Yes
Montana[9]	9/3 - 10/16	44	Unknown	Unknown	Unknown	Yes	No
Nebraska	9/15 - 12/31	99	14,743	817	4,451	No	Yes
Nevada	8/10 - 9/6	26	5,518	614	308	No	No
New Hampshire	9/15 - 12/15	92	18,539	3,616	1,580	No	Yes
New Jersey	9/30 - 1/31	82	51,000	2,000	20,593	No	No
New Mexico	9/1 - 1/15	137	5,250	475	610	No	No
New York	9/27 - 12/15	96	168,912	2,305	21,854	No	Yes
North Carolina	9/9 - 11/23	66	Unknown	Unknown	Unknown	No	Yes
North Dakota	8/30 - 12/31	124	11,053	684	4,078	Yes	Yes
Ohio	10/7 - 1/31	91	190,000	2,500	27,299	Yes	Yes
Oklahoma	10/1 - 12/31	78	59,440	Unknown	9,116	No	Yes
Oregon	8/24 - 9/22	30	25,502	Combined	4,186	No	No
Pennsylvania	10/5 - 1/11	51	299,372	22,693	54,622	No	Yes
Rhode Island	10/1 - 1/31	123	2,752	440	415	No	No
South Carolina[9]	8/15 - 10/10	41	25,000	5,000	Combined	Yes	No
South Dakota	9/23 - 12/31	100	11,236	800	3,510	No	Yes
Tennessee	9/30 - 11/12	39	95,000	3,497	20,953	No	Yes
Texas	9/30 - 10/31	32	75,000	Unknown	15,000	No	Yes
Utah	8/17 - 9/6	21	12,928	640	1,959	No	Yes
Vermont	10/5 - 12/15	32	26,144	5,510	5,046	No	Yes
Virginia	10/1 - 1/6	77	61,000	2,000	16,200	No	Yes
Washington	9/1 - 12/31	86	21,813	165	4,948	No	No
West Virginia	10/14 - 12/30	67	107,000	18,000	28,072	No	No
Wisconsin	9/21 - 12/31	83	238,379	5,475	69,269	No	Yes
Wyoming	9/1 - 9/30	30	6,903	2,065	1,200	Yes	Yes
TOTALS			**2,825,990**	**125,375**	**712,611**		

Leading Bow-Hunting States
Licensed Resident Bow-Hunters

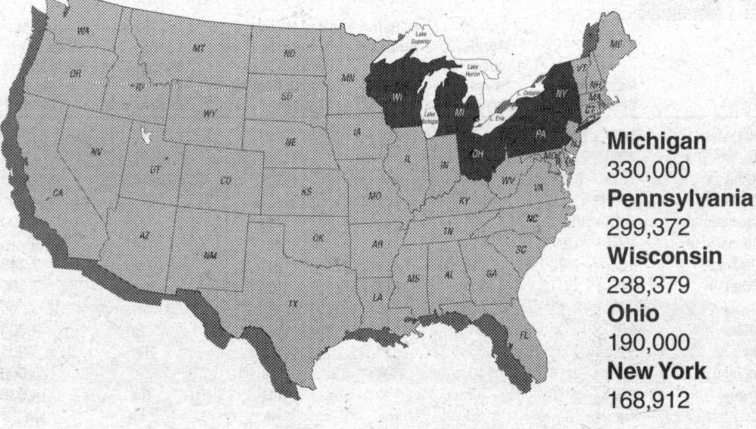

Leading Bow-Deer Kill States
Total Whitetail Kill With Bows

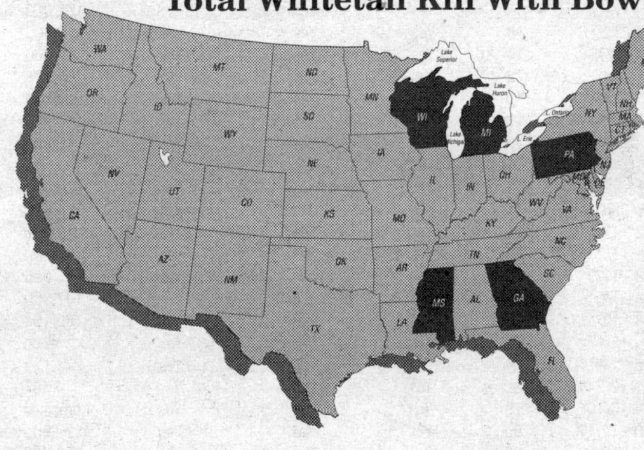

MUZZLELOADER-HUNTING INFORMATION
Alphabetical Order By State•

State	Muzzleloader Season Dates[1]	Special Muzzleloader Season Days[2]	Is There A Special Muzzleloader Season?[3]	May Muzzleloaders Be Used To Hunt Deer During Regular Firearms Season?[4]	Are There Special Muzzleloader Restrictions?[5]	How Many Resident Muzzleloader Hunters?[6]
Alabama	1/25 - 1/31	7	Yes	Yes	Yes	14,000
Arizona	10/27 - 12/31	34	Yes	Yes	Yes	1,400
Arkansas	10/21 - 12/31	21	Yes	Yes	Yes	Unknown
California	10/26 - 1/26	51	Yes	Yes	Yes	Unknown
Colorado	9/14 - 9/22	9	Yes	Yes	Yes	6,100
Connecticut	12/11 - 12/24	12	Yes	No	Yes	Combined
Delaware	10/14 - 1/22	9	Yes	Yes	Yes	7,245
Florida	10/14 - 11/12	20	Yes	Yes	Yes	17,109
Georgia	10/21 - 1/7	0	No	Yes	Yes	Combined
Idaho	10/5 - 12/9	20	Yes	Yes	Yes	4,900
Illinois	12/13 - 12/15	3	Yes	Yes	No	5,500
Indiana	12/9 - 12/24	16	Yes	Yes	No	80,000
Iowa	10/14 - 1/10	33	Yes	Yes	Yes	14,038
Kansas	NA	NA	NA	NA	NA	NA
Kentucky	10/20 - 12/19	9	Yes	Yes	No	Unknown
Louisiana	12/2 - 12/8	7	Yes	Yes	Yes	5,363
Maine	11/27 - 12/9	12	Yes	Yes	Yes	8,800
Maryland	10/19 - 1/6	16	Yes	Yes	Yes	34,717
Massachusetts	12/16 - 12/18	3	Yes	Yes	Yes	22,000
Michigan	12/1 - 12/17	17	Yes	Yes	No	173,000
Minnesota	11/30 - 12/15	16	Yes	Yes	Yes	7,300
Mississippi	12/2 - 12/15	14	Yes	Yes	Yes	58,000
Missouri	11/16 - 1/5	22	Yes	Yes	No	14,775
Montana	9/15 - 12/31	0	No	Yes	Yes	Combined
Nebraska	12/2 - 12/17	16	Yes	Yes	Yes	7,944
Nevada	9/7 - 9/22	15	Yes	Yes	Yes	1,194
New Hampshire	11/2 - 11/12	11	Yes	Yes	Yes	22,334
New Jersey	12/11 - 12/30	14	Yes	Yes	Yes	20,000
New Mexico	9/10 - 9/20	11	Yes	No	Yes	4,400
New York	10/12 - 12/17	14	Yes	Yes	Yes	49,386
North Carolina	10/7 - 11/23	18	Yes	Yes	No	Unknown
North Dakota	11/29 - 12/9	7	Yes	Yes	Yes	695
Ohio	10/23 - 1/6	9	Yes	Yes	Yes	107,300
Oklahoma	10/28 - 11/5	9	Yes	Yes	Yes	55,107
Oregon	10/1 - 12/15	76	Yes	Yes	Yes	Combined
Pennsylvania	12/26 - 1/11	14	Yes	Yes	Yes	74,120
Rhode Island	11/6 - 12/24	30	Yes	No	Yes	4,567
South Carolina	10/1 - 10/10	10	Yes	Yes	Yes	Combined
South Dakota	10/10 - 12/17	55	Yes	Yes	Yes	965
Tennessee	10/21 - 12/10	23	Yes	Yes	Yes	99,500
Texas	1/13 - 1/21	9	Yes	Yes	Yes	2,500
Utah	10/30 - 11/7	9	Yes	Yes	Yes	10,691
Vermont	12/7 - 12/15	9	Yes	Yes	Yes	17,553
Virginia	11/6 - 1/6	30	Yes	Yes	Yes	83,000
Washington	10/1 - 12/31	49	Yes	Yes	Yes	10,278
West Virginia	12/11 - 12/16	6	Yes	Yes	Yes	70,000
Wisconsin	12/2 - 12/8	7	Yes	Yes	Yes	Combined
Wyoming	9/10 - 11/30	0	No	Yes	Yes	Combined
TOTALS						**1,115,781**

Each year, more hunters take to the woods to hunt whitetails with muzzleloaders. Michigan leads the nation with 173,000 muzzle-loading hunters.

STATE DEER HUNTING TRENDS
Alphabetical Order By State

Deer Vehicle Collisions	Deer Crop Damage	Number Of Youth Hunters	Total Number Of Hunters	Number Of Male Hunters	Number Of Female Hunters	Hunting With Rifles
INCREASED	**INCREASED**	**INCREASED**	**INCREASED**	**INCREASED**	**INCREASED**	**INCREASED**
Arkansas	Delaware	Idaho	Connecticut	Delaware	Arizona	Connecticut
Delaware	Maryland	Iowa	Delaware	Illinois	Delaware	Idaho
Georgia	Massachusetts	Nebraska	Idaho	Wisconsin	Georgia	Louisiana
Idaho	Missouri	North Dakota	Illinois	**CONSTANT**	Illinois	North Carolina
Illinois	New Hampshire	Oregon	North Dakota	Arizona	Kentucky	North Dakota
Maine	New Jersey	Wisconsin	South Carolina	Georgia	Louisiana	Wisconsin
Mississippi	North Dakota	**CONSTANT**	South Dakota	Indiana	Missouri	**CONSTANT**
Missouri	Ohio	Arizona	Wisconsin	Louisiana	Nevada	Alabama
Nebraska	Oregon	Indiana	**CONSTANT**	Missouri	New Jersey	Arizona
New Hampshire	Rhode Island	Maine	Alabama	Nevada	Rhode Island	Arkansas
New York	Vermont	Nevada	Georgia	Pennsylvania	Wisconsin	Colorado
North Carolina	West Virginia	North Carolina	Indiana	Rhode Island	**CONSTANT**	Georgia
North Dakota	Wisconsin	Pennsylvania	Iowa	West Virginia	Colorado	Kansas
Ohio	**CONSTANT**	Rhode Island	Kansas	**DECREASED**	Indiana	Kentucky
Oklahoma	Arkansas	South Carolina	Kentucky	Colorado	Pennsylvania	Maryland
Rhode Island	Colorado	Texas	Louisiana	Kentucky	West Virginia	Minnesota
South Carolina	Connecticut	Utah	Maine	Michigan	**DECREASED**	Mississippi
Tennessee	Indiana	Vermont	Maryland	New Jersey	Michigan	Missouri
Vermont	Kentucky	Virginia	Massachusetts	Wyoming	Wyoming	Nebraska
West Virginia	Nebraska	**DECREASED**	Minnesota	**UNKNOWN**	**UNKNOWN**	Nevada
Wisconsin	North Carolina	Kentucky	Mississippi	Alabama	Alabama	New Hampshire
CONSTANT	South Carolina	Maryland	Missouri	Arkansas	Arkansas	Oklahoma
Connecticut	Tennessee	Missouri	Nebraska	California	California	Pennsylvania
Indiana	**DECREASED**	South Dakota	Nevada	Connecticut	Connecticut	South Carolina
Iowa	Alabama	Tennessee	New Hampshire	Florida	Florida	Texas
Kentucky	Georgia	West Virginia	North Carolina	Idaho	Idaho	Utah
Minnesota	Idaho	Wyoming	Ohio	Iowa	Iowa	Vermont
New Jersey	Kansas	**UNKNOWN**	Oklahoma	Kansas	Kansas	West Virginia
Pennsylvania	Montana	Alabama	Pennsylvania	Maine	Maine	**DECREASED**
DECREASED	Nevada	Arkansas	Rhode Island	Maryland	Maryland	California
Maryland	New York	California	Texas	Massachusetts	Massachusetts	Maine
Utah	Utah	Colorado	Utah	Minnesota	Minnesota	Michigan
Wyoming	Wyoming	Connecticut	Virginia	Mississippi	Mississippi	New Mexico
UNKNOWN	**UNKNOWN**	Delaware	West Virginia	Montana	Montana	New York
Alabama	Arizona	Florida	**DECREASED**	Nebraska	Nebraska	Oregon
Arizona	California	Georgia	Arizona	New Hampshire	New Hampshire	Tennessee
California	Florida	Illinois	California	New Mexico	New Mexico	Washington
Colorado	Illinois	Kansas	Florida	New York	New York	Wyoming
Florida	Iowa	Louisiana	Michigan	North Carolina	North Carolina	**UNKNOWN**
Kansas	Louisiana	Massachusetts	Montana	North Dakota	North Dakota	Florida
Louisiana	Maine	Michigan	New Jersey	Ohio	Ohio	Montana
Massachusetts	Michigan	Minnesota	New Mexico	Oklahoma	Oklahoma	South Dakota
Michigan	Minnesota	Mississippi	New York	Oregon	Oregon	Virginia
Montana	Mississippi	Montana	Oregon	South Carolina	South Carolina	**NOT ALLOWED**
Nevada	New Mexico	New Hampshire	Tennessee	South Dakota	South Dakota	Delaware
New Mexico	Oklahoma	New Jersey	Washington	Tennessee	Tennessee	Illinois
Oregon	Pennsylvania	New Mexico	Wyoming	Texas	Texas	Indiana
South Dakota	South Dakota	New York	**UNKNOWN**	Utah	Utah	Iowa
Texas	Texas	Ohio	Arkansas	Vermont	Vermont	Massachusetts
Virginia	Virginia	Oklahoma	Colorado	Virginia	Virginia	New Jersey
Washington	Washington	Washington	Vermont	Washington	Washington	Ohio

Hunting With Shotguns	Hunting With Handguns	Hunting With Muzzle-loaders	Hunting With Bows	Coyote Pressure On Deer Herd	Anti-Hunting Pressure	Problems With Poaching	Interest In Quality Deer Management
INCREASED	**INCREASED**	**INCREASED**	**INCREASED**	**INCREASED**	**INCREASED**	**INCREASED**	**INCREASED**
Delaware	Arizona	Colorado	Alabama	Kentucky	Connecticut	Kentucky	Alabama
Illinois	Illinois	Delaware	Arizona	Montana	Delaware	Wyoming	Arkansas
Maine	Minnesota	Illinois	Colorado	Nebraska	Idaho	**CONSTANT**	Colorado
CONSTANT	Nevada	Indiana	Connecticut	New Jersey	Kentucky	Alabama	Georgia
Alabama	New York	Kansas	Delaware	Oklahoma	Maine	Arizona	Idaho
Arizona	North Carolina	Kentucky	Illinois	Texas	Massachusetts	Arkansas	Illinois
Arkansas	Washington	Louisiana	Iowa	Wisconsin	Minnesota	Colorado	Kansas
Connecticut	**CONSTANT**	Maine	Louisiana	**CONSTANT**	New Jersey	Georgia	Louisiana
Georgia	Alabama	Maryland	Maine	Colorado	Oregon	Illinois	Maryland
Indiana	Arkansas	Massachusetts	Maryland	Connecticut	South Carolina	Indiana	Minnesota
Iowa	Georgia	Minnesota	Massachusetts	Georgia	Virginia	Iowa	Mississippi
Kansas	Indiana	Missouri	Missouri	Indiana	Washington	Kansas	Montana
Kentucky	Kansas	Nebraska	Nebraska	Iowa	Wisconsin	Maine	Nebraska
Maryland	Kentucky	Nevada	Nevada	Louisiana	**CONSTANT**	Maryland	New York
Massachusetts	Louisiana	New Hampshire	New Hampshire	Maine	Alabama	Massachusetts	North Carolina
Michigan	Maryland	New Jersey	New Jersey	Mississippi	Colorado	Mississippi	Oklahoma
Minnesota	Michigan	New York	North Carolina	Nevada	Georgia	Missouri	Oregon
Mississippi	Mississippi	North Carolina	Oklahoma	New Hampshire	Illinois	New Hampshire	Pennsylvania
New Hampshire	New Hampshire	North Dakota	Pennsylvania	North Dakota	Indiana	North Carolina	South Dakota
North Dakota	North Dakota	Oklahoma	Rhode Island	Oregon	Iowa	North Dakota	Tennessee
Ohio	Ohio	Oregon	South Carolina	Pennsylvania	Kansas	Ohio	Utah
Oklahoma	Oklahoma	Rhode Island	Vermont	Vermont	Louisiana	Oklahoma	Virginia
Oregon	Oregon	South Dakota	Washington	Washington	Maryland	Pennsylvania	Washington
Pennsylvania	Pennsylvania	Texas	Wisconsin	**DECREASED**	Mississippi	Rhode Island	West Virginia
Rhode Island	South Carolina	Vermont	**CONSTANT**	Wyoming	Missouri	South Carolina	Wisconsin
South Carolina	Tennessee	Virginia	Arkansas	**UNKNOWN**	Nebraska	South Dakota	**CONSTANT**
Tennessee	Texas	Washington	Georgia	Alabama	Nevada	Tennessee	Arizona
Texas	Vermont	West Virginia	Indiana	Arizona	New Hampshire	Texas	Indiana
Vermont	West Virginia	Wisconsin	Kansas	Arkansas	New York	Utah	Iowa
West Virginia	**DECREASED**	**CONSTANT**	Kentucky	California	North Carolina	Vermont	Kentucky
DECREASED	Wyoming	Alabama	Michigan	Delaware	North Dakota	Washington	Maine
Louisiana	**UNKNOWN**	Arizona	Minnesota	Florida	Ohio	West Virginia	Nevada
New Jersey	California	Arkansas	Mississippi	Idaho	Oklahoma	Wisconsin	New Jersey
New York	Colorado	Connecticut	Ohio	Illinois	Pennsylvania	**DECREASED**	Ohio
North Carolina	Florida	Georgia	Oregon	Kansas	Rhode Island	Delaware	South Carolina
Washington	Idaho	Iowa	Tennessee	Maryland	South Dakota	Louisiana	Vermont
Wyoming	Maine	Michigan	Texas	Massachusetts	Tennessee	New Jersey	Wyoming
UNKNOWN	Missouri	Mississippi	Virginia	Michigan	Texas	**UNKNOWN**	**DECREASED**
California	Montana	Ohio	West Virginia	Minnesota	Utah	California	Rhode Island
Colorado	Nebraska	Pennsylvania	**DECREASED**	Missouri	Wyoming	Connecticut	**UNKNOWN**
Florida	New Mexico	Tennessee	New Mexico	New Mexico	**UNKNOWN**	Florida	California
Idaho	South Dakota	Utah	New York	New York	Arizona	Idaho	Connecticut
Missouri	Utah	**DECREASED**	North Dakota	North Carolina	Arkansas	Michigan	Delaware
Montana	Virginia	New Mexico	South Dakota	Ohio	California	Minnesota	Florida
Nebraska	Wisconsin	South Carolina	Utah	Rhode Island	Florida	Montana	Massachusetts
Nevada	**NOT ALLOWED**	Wyoming	Wyoming	South Carolina	Michigan	Nebraska	Michigan
New Mexico	Connecticut	**UNKNOWN**	**UNKNOWN**	South Dakota	Montana	Nevada	Missouri
South Dakota	Delaware	California	California	Tennessee	New Mexico	New Mexico	New Hampshire
Utah	Iowa	Florida	Florida	Utah	Vermont	New York	New Mexico
Virginia	Massachusetts	Idaho	Idaho	Virginia	West Virginia	Oregon	North Dakota
Wisconsin	New Jersey	Montana	Montana	West Virginia		Virginia	Texas

STATE DEER HUNTING REGULATIONS
Alphabetical Order By State

State	Minimum Hunting Age[1]	Is General Hunter Education Mandatory?[2]	Is Bow Hunting Education Mandatory?[3]	Is A Separate Bow Hunting Education Class Offered?	Is Bow Hunting From An Elevated Stand Allowed?	Is Gun Hunting From An Elevated Stand Allowed?
Alabama	None	Yes	No	No	Yes	Yes
Arizona	10	Yes	No	No	Yes	Yes
Arkansas	None	Yes	No	No	Yes	Yes
California	12	Yes	No	No	Yes	Yes
Colorado	12	Yes	No	No	Yes	Yes
Connecticut	12	Yes	Yes	Yes	Yes	Yes
Delaware	None	Yes	No	Yes	Yes	Yes
Florida	None	Yes	Yes	No	Yes	Yes
Georgia	None	Yes	No	No	Yes	Yes
Idaho	12	Yes	Yes	Yes	Yes	Yes
Illinois	None	Yes	Yes	No	Yes	Yes
Indiana	None	Yes	No	No	Yes	Yes
Iowa	None	Yes	No	Yes	Yes	Yes
Kansas	N/A	N/A	N/A	N/A	N/A	N/A
Kentucky	None	Yes	No	No	Yes	Yes
Louisiana	None	Yes	No	Yes	Yes	Yes
Maine	10	Yes	Yes	Yes	Yes	Yes
Maryland	None	Yes	No	No	Yes	Yes
Massachusetts	12	Yes	No	No	Yes	Yes
Michigan	12	Yes	No	No	Yes	No
Minnesota	12	Yes	No	Yes	Yes	Yes
Mississippi	None	Yes	No	No	Yes	Yes
Missouri	11	Yes	No	Yes	Yes	Yes
Montana	12	Yes	Yes	Yes	Yes	Yes
Nebraska	12	Yes	Yes	Yes	Yes	Yes
Nevada	12	Yes	No	No	Yes	Yes
New Hampshire	None	Yes	Yes	Yes	Yes	Yes
New Jersey	10	Yes	Yes	Yes	Yes	Yes
New Mexico	None	Yes	No	Yes	Yes	Yes
New York	14	Yes	Yes	Yes	Yes	Yes
North Carolina	None	Yes	No	No	Yes	Yes
North Dakota	14	Yes	No	No	Yes	Yes
Ohio	None	Yes	No	No	Yes	Yes
Oklahoma	None	Yes	No	No	Yes	Yes
Oregon	12	Yes	No	No	Yes	Yes
Pennsylvania	12	Yes	No	No	Yes	Yes
Rhode Island	12	Yes	Yes	Yes	Yes	Yes
South Carolina	None	Yes	No	No	Yes	Yes
South Dakota	12	Yes	Yes	Yes	Yes	Yes
Tennessee	None	Yes	No	No	Yes	Yes
Texas	None	Yes	No	No	Yes	Yes
Utah	14	Yes	No	No	Yes	Yes
Vermont	None	Yes	No	No	Yes	Yes
Virginia	None	Yes	No	No	Yes	Yes
Washington	None	Yes	No	No	Yes	Yes
West Virginia	None	Yes	No	No	Yes	Yes
Wisconsin	12	Yes	No	Yes	Yes	Yes
Wyoming	14	Yes	No	No	Yes	Yes

1. In many states, a youth must be accompanied by an adult or pass a hunter education course to qualify for hunting privileges.
2. Mandatory general hunter education usually applies to first-time hunters, or all those born after a designated date.
3. Bow hunting education is mandatory in only twelve states, but it is briefly covered in the general hunter education course in most states.
4. Indicates whether or not dogs may be used at any time to assist in the hunt. "Yes" signifies that dogs may be used in at least some parts of the state, but not necessarily all parts. Check regulations for restrictions.

Is Blaze Orange Required?	May Food Bait Be Used?	May You Hunt Over Salt Blocks?	May You Hunt Over Mineral Blocks?	May Dogs Be Used To Hunt Deer?[4]	May Dogs Be Used To Trail Wounded Deer?[5]	May You Shine For Deer?[6]	Are "Bonus" Deer Tags Available?
Yes	No	Yes	No	Yes	Yes	Yes	Yes
No	No	No	No	No	No	Yes	No
Yes	Yes	Yes	Yes	Yes	Yes	No	Yes
No	No	Yes	Yes	Yes	Yes	No	No
Yes	No	No	No	No	No	No	Yes
Yes	No	No	No	No	No	No	Yes
Yes	No	No	No	No	No	No	Yes
Yes	Yes	Yes	Yes	Yes	Yes	Yes	No
Yes	No	No	No	Yes	Yes	No	No
No	No	No	No	No	No	No	No
Yes	No	No	No	No	No	No	Yes
Yes	No	No	No	No	Yes	Yes	Yes
Yes	No	No	No	No	No	Yes	Yes
N/A	N/A	N/A	N/A	N/A	N/A	N/A	N/A
Yes	Yes	Yes	Yes	No	No	Yes	Yes
Yes	Yes	Yes	Yes	Yes	No	No	No
Yes	No	No	No	No	No	Yes	No
Yes	Yes	Yes	Yes	No	No	No	Yes
Yes	No	No	No	No	No	No	No
Yes	Yes	Yes	Yes	No	No	Yes	Yes
Yes	No	Yes	Yes	No	No	Yes	Yes
Yes	No	No	No	Yes	Yes	No	No
Yes	No	Yes	Yes	No	No	No	Yes
Yes	No	No	No	No	No	No	No
Yes	Yes	Yes	Yes	Yes	Yes	Yes	No
No	No	No	No	No	No	No	No
No	Yes	No	No	No	No	Yes	No
Yes	No	No	No	No	No	No	Yes
No	No	No	No	No	No	No	No
No	No	No	No	No	No	No	Yes
Yes	Yes	Yes	Yes	Yes	Yes	Yes	Yes
Yes	Yes	Yes	Yes	No	No	No	No
Yes	Yes	Yes	Yes	No	No	No	Yes
Yes	Yes	Yes	Yes	No	Yes	No	Yes
No	Yes	No	No	No	No	No	No
Yes	No	No	No	No	No	Yes	Yes
Yes	No	No	No	No	No	No	Yes
Yes	Yes	Yes	Yes	Yes	Yes	Yes	Yes
Yes	No	No	No	No	No	No	No
Yes	No	Yes	Yes	No	Yes	No	Yes
No	Yes	Yes	Yes	No	Yes	Yes	No
Yes	No	Yes	Yes	No	No	No	No
No	Yes	No	No	No	Yes	No	No
Yes	No	No	No	Yes	Yes	Yes	Yes
Yes	Yes	Yes	Yes	No	No	No	No
Yes	Yes	Yes	Yes	No	No	No	No
Yes	Yes	Yes	Yes	No	No	Yes	Yes
Yes	Yes	Yes	Yes	No	No	No	Yes

5. "Yes" signifies that dogs may be used in at least some parts of the state to help trail wounded deer, but not necessarily all parts of the state. Check regulations for restrictions.

6. Restrictions usually apply in states that permit shining for deer, such as time restrictions, no weapon in possession, or being restricted to private property.

Contacts for Hunting Information

<table>
<tr><td>

**STATE
DEPT/ADDRESS**

Alabama
Dept. of Conservation
64 North Union St.
Montgomery, AL 36130

Alaska
Dept. of Fish & Game
Div. of Fish & Wildlife Protection
Box 3-2000
Juneau, AK 99802

Arizona
Game & Fish Dept.
2221 W. Greenway Road
Phoenix, AZ 85023

Arkansas
Game & Fish Commission
No. 2 Natural Resources Drive
Little Rock, AR 72205

California
California Fish & Game
Box 944209
Sacramento, CA 94244

Colorado
Dept. of Natural Resources
Division of Wildlife
6060 Broadway
Denver, CO 80216

Connecticut
Dept. of Environment Protection
391 Route 32
North Franklin, CT 06254

Delaware
Dept. of Natural Resources
89 Kings Hwy.
Box 1401
Dover, DE 19903

</td><td>

**STATE
DEPT/ADDRESS**

Florida
Game & Fresh Water Fish Comm.
Bureau Staff Office
620 S. Meridian
Farris Bryant Blvd.
Tallahassee, FL 32399

Georgia
Dept. of Natural Resources
Wildlife Resources Division
Game Management Section
2070 US Hwy. 278 SE
Social Circle, GA 30279

Hawaii
Dept. of Land & Natural
Resources
Div. of Forestry & Wildlife
1151 Punchbowl St.
Honolulu, HI 96813

Idaho
Dept. of Fish & Game
600 S Walnut St.
Box 25
Boise, ID 83707

Illinois
Dept. of Conservation
524 S Second St.
Springfield, IL 62701

Indiana
Dept. of Natural Resources
402 W. Washington
Room 255D
Indianapolis, IN 46204

Iowa
Dept. of Natural Resources
Wallace State Office Bldg.
Des Moines, IA 50319

</td></tr>
</table>

Kansas
Dept. of Wildlife & Parks
Route 2 Box 54A
Pratt, KS 67124

Kentucky
Dept. of Fish & Wildlife
#1 Game Farm Road
Frankfort, KY 40601

Louisiana
Dept. of Wildlife & Fisheries
Box 98000
Baton Rouge, LA 70898

Maine
Dept. of Inland Fisheries
284 State St.
State House Station 41
Augusta, ME 04333

Maryland
Department of
Natural Resources
3 Pershing St., Room 110
Cumberland, MD 21502

Massachusetts
Division of Fisheries
& Wildlife
100 Nashua St.
Boston, MA 02114

Michigan
Department of Natural Resources
Wildlife Division
Box 30028
Lansing, MI 48909

Minnesota
Dept. of Natural Resources
Division of Fish & Wildlife
Box 7 DNR Bldg.
500 Lafayette
St. Paul, MN 55155

Mississippi
Dept. of Wildlife Conservation
Southport Mall
Box 451
Jackson, MS 39205

Missouri
Dept. of Conservation
1110 S. College Avenue
Columbia, MO 65203

Montana
Department of Wildlife
1420 E. 6th Avenue
Helena, MT 59620

Nebraska
Game & Parks Commission
2200 N 33rd St.
Box 30370
Lincoln, NE 68508

Nevada
Department of Wildlife
Box 10678
1100 Valley Road
Reno, NV 89520

New Hampshire
Fish & Game Dept.
Region 1 Ofc, Rd 2
Route 3N, Box 241
Lancaster, NH 03584

New Jersey
Division of Fish,
Game &Wildlife
5 Station Plaza CN400
Trenton, NJ 08625

New Mexico
Department of
Natural Resources
Villagra Bldg 408 Galisteo
Santa Fe, NM 87503

Contacts for Hunting Information

**STATE
DEPT/ADDRESS**

New York
Dept. of Environ. Conservation
50 Wolf Road
Albany, NY 12233

North Carolina
Wildlife Resources Commission
512 N. Salisburg St.
Raleigh, NC 27604-1188

North Dakota
Game & Fish Dept.
100 N. Bismarck Expy.
Bismarck, ND 58501

Ohio
Dept. of Natural Resources
1840 Belcher Drive
Columbus, OH 43224

Oklahoma
Dept. of Wildlife Conservation
1801 N. Lincoln, Box 53465
Oklahoma City, OK 73105

Oregon
Dept. of Fish & Wildlife
400 Public Service Bldg.
Salem, OR 97310

Pennsylvania
Pennsylvania Game Commission
2001 Elmerton Avenue
Harrisburg, PA 17110

Rhode Island
Dept. of Environmental Mgmt.
83 Park St.
Providence, RI 02903

South Carolina
Dept. of Natural Resources
Box 167, Columbia, SC 29202

**STATE
DEPT/ADDRESS**

South Dakota
Division of Wildlife
Bldg. 445 E. Capital
Pierre, SD 57501

Tennessee
Wildlife Resources, Box 40747
Nashville, TN 37204

Texas
Parks & Wildlife Dept.
4200 Smith School Road
Austin, TX 78744

Utah
Division of Wildlife Resources
1596 W. N. Temple
Salt Lake City, UT 84116

Vermont
Dept. of Fish & Wildlife
103 S. Main St., 10 S.
Waterbury, VT 05671

Virginia
VA Dept. of Game and Fish
4010 W. Broad St., Box 11104
Richmond, VA 23230

Washington
Dept. of Wildlife
600 Capitol Way N.
Olympia, WA 98501

West Virginia
Wildlife Resources
State Capital Complex, Bldg. 3
Charleston, WV 25305

Wisconsin
Dept. of Natural Resources
101 S. Webster St.
Madison, WI 53707

Wyoming
Game & Fish Department
5400 Bishop Blvd.
Cheyenne, WY 82002

Canada
Alberta Fish & Wildlife
Bramalea Building
9920 108th St.
Edmonton AB T5K 2M4
CANADA

Dept. of Natural Resources
Box 6000
Fredericton NB E3B 5H1
CANADA

Quebec
Jean-Yves Desbiens 150 Blvd.
Rene LaVefque E. 5th Floor
Quebec City PQ G1R 4Y1
CANADA

British Columbia
Fish & Wildlife Branch
Parliament Bldgs.
Victoria BC V8V 1X5
CANADA

Provincial Building
136 Exhibition St.
Kentville, King Country
Novia Scotia B4N 4E5

QUEBEC Wildlife Federation
Castelneau St. La Tuque PQ G9X
2P4
CANADA

Energy & Natural Resources
Mail Floor, N. Tower 9945-108 St.
Edmonton AB T5K 2G6
CANADA

Wildlife Branch
Dept. of Natural Resources
Box 24, 1495 St. James St.
Winnipeg MB R3H OW9
CANADA

ON Federation of
Anglers and Hunters
2740 Queensview Drive
Ottawa ON K2B 1A2
CANADA

SK Dept. of Environment &
Resource Management
Box 3003
Prince Albert, SK S6V 6G1
CANADA

Almanac Insights

Find Deer, and You'll Find Hunters

More than 83 percent of all hunters live in the prime
white-tailed deer areas of the eastern two-thirds of the
country. This accounts for more than 12.6 million hunters.
Plus, seven of 11 Western states are home to an increasing
number of whitetail hunters.

Lucky Oaks

■ *Mike Moutoux*

For 70 summers, the white oak had been gathering sunlight, converting it to sugars and combining it with water and nutrients from the soil. It grew thicker and taller along the pasture fence, free from competition. Oaks are long-lived, slow growing trees. Some have lived longer than 600 years. This old oak, however, grew fast, and most years produced a good crop of acorns. But two consecutive years of drought had taken its toll, and this year the crop could be collected in a baseball cap.

Still, where there were acorns, there would be deer, and that's why a deer stand was hung among the tree's first layer of branches.

Three acorns grew from a branch 15 feet above the stand and dangled above the deer trail. The trail paralleled the old pasture, now overgrown from 20 years of non-use.

A Lawyer, a Logger, a Buck

The woodlot was recently purchased by a lawyer from Cleveland, who sold off the timber before the ink was dry on the title transfer. The old trees that grew along the pasture's border were spared because the property line had not been surveyed for two generations, and no one was quite sure who owned them.

The logger was a deer hunter, and it wasn't hard for him to get the lawyer's written permission to hunt the land.

The buck, who alternated his time between the old pasture and the woods, knew nothing about contracts or permission slips. He only knew these woods provided sustenance and security. It was these acorns that would bring deer and the logger to the same tree on a cool October morning.

Squirrels at Work

The day started out mild with just a trace of westerly winds. On the eastern horizon, clouds had collected like dust-bunnies under a bed until they swallowed the sun's rays.

The logger was vaguely aware of all of this, but his focus was directed to the trail that connected the old pasture and the woods. A noise behind him made him grip his bow a little tighter, and his right hand felt for the leather shooting tab nestled in a coat pocket. The next time he heard the leaves rustling, it was followed by a twitter and more rustling. He relaxed his grip. "Chipmunks," he thought to himself.

The next sound was a gray squirrel climbing the tree next to the white oak. It stopped halfway up and eyed the

Patrick Durkin

strange lump in the oak. Satisfied the lump wasn't dangerous, the squirrel scrambled up the tree and leaped into the old oak's top branches. Directly above the logger's head, the squirrel began searching for acorns.

The buck was bedded in the field when the sound of falling nuts roused him. When squirrels are felling acorns, it's first come, first served. He made a beeline for the old oak.

The deer approached head-on as the man narrowed his eyes to slits. He was afraid the buck would see him. With the buck facing him, the logger dared not move or try to draw.

The buck approached the tree and began sniffing the leaves for fallen nuts, but the race was already on.

The chipmunks had each stolen an acorn, and the squirrel was coming down to claim the rest.

After finding only two acorns, the buck pawed the leaves in

Find White-Tailed Deer by Lo

Find oaks, and you'll likely find white-tailed deer. Deer rely on acorns as a high-protein staple in their diet.

The easiest way to identify an oak tree is by its leaves. While most oak leaves have easy-to-identify "fingers," some oaks,

Live Oak

The Live Oak can be found in most Coastal Plains states. The tree is common in Texas, Florida, Alabama, Mississippi and Oklahoma.

Its acorn is small but oblong, and its leaf is round with a tough skin.

Water Oak

The water oak can be found in the Coastal Plains and adjacent areas. The tree is common in New Jersey, Florida, Texas, Missouri, Oklahoma and Mississippi.

Its thin leaf is oblong, featuring three rounded points.

frustration. With the buck less than 10 yards away, but facing directly away, the logger came to full draw and waited for the buck to move. Instead of turning, the buck settled down below the oak, dropping his knees and then his hindquarters, leaving his back end toward the oak.

It was a shot angle the hunter had never thought about. He knew he could put an arrow between the buck's shoulder blades, but was uncomfortable with the margin of error. Quietly, he eased his arrow forward and squeezed the arrow holder back onto the shaft.

Twenty minutes passed, and the squirrel resumed his search for nuts. Spying three acorns just above the logger, the squirrel climbed through the branches until it was just above them. It reached for a nut and pulled. As the acorn snapped off, a second one fell, landing squarely in the man's lap. The

eating Productive Oak Trees

such as the water, shingle and willow varieties, feature round, narrow and oblong shapes.

More than 20 species of oaks thrive in whitetail country. Acorns from white, water, red and live oaks are among the whitetail's favorite foods.

Red Oak

The red oak is common in the North, including Michigan, Wisconsin, Illinois and Minnesota, and in the Canadian provinces of Nova Scotia and Quebec.

Its leaf features corresponding points that are jagged.

White Oak

The white oak is most common in the woods of the Canadian provinces of Ontario and Quebec. In the United States, it's common south and east from Minnesota to Florida.

Its leaf features non-corresponding rounded points.

oak's seed gave the logger an idea.

Holding the bow with his left hand, the man pitched the acorn toward the bedded buck. He hoped the deer would move to where the nut fell. Unfortunately, it hit a branch and ricocheted in front of the buck's nose. He picked it up by just stretching his neck, never having to get up.

One More Chance

By now, low clouds hinted at rain. The logger studied the space between the buck's shoulders again, but bit the thought short.

Then a last acorn fell without warning. The logger drew his arrow back immediately, moving the top pin of his bow sight toward the buck. The buck looked toward the spot where the nut fell, stood and stretched like a cat. When he turned, the archer followed, but a small sapling was now in the way. Still at full draw, the logger double-checked his anchor point and locked his left elbow.

The buck picked up the acorn, took one step, and the man let the arrow fly. The buck took six steps and fell with a grunt.

The logger climbed down and examined the buck, finding the acorn unbroken in the animal's mouth. He pulled it out and put it in his pocket.

Spare the Oaks

From that winter on, the logger never looked at oak trees quite the same. While cutting new timber, he began to find excuses to spare a few oaks each trip. Some, he claimed, had nails in them or part of an old wire fence that could ruin his saw. Others had dry rot or some other disease that made them worthless for lumber.

Some he spared just for luck.

Hunting Supports Wildlife Refuges

The National Wildlife Refuge System has long recognized hunting as a legitimate and traditional form of wildlife-dependent recreation and, in some locations, as an effective wildlife population management tool.

Refuges open to white-tailed deer hunting include the Tamarac Refuge near Detroit Lakes, Minn., Twaukon Refuge near Fargo, N.D., Tishomingo Refuge in central Oklahoma and the Wichita Mountains Refuge in Indiahoma, Okla.

Hunters have contributed funding to the acquisition and management of refuges through excise taxes on guns and ammunition. This program has returned over $2.5 billion to states for wildlife and habitat manage-

Chapter 9

Meat Processing

Tasty venison results from proper handling from the moment you kill a deer to the time you place the packaged cuts in the freezer. Proper care includes field dressing, hanging, skinning, butchering and storage.

Field dressing ("gutting") a deer is an extremely important step in the handling of venison. Removing the paunch, intestines and other inedible internal tissue permits the deer's body heat to dissipate quickly, thus cooling the meat. This step remains important in either warm or cool weather.

Equally important, field dressing eliminates the possibility of stomach acids and expanding gases tainting the venison. It also helps to completely drain blood from the body cavity.

As a side benefit of field-dressing, you reduce the weight of the deer by about 20 percent, making it easier to transport. Although novice hunters think this process is complicated, it's rather easy. After working on a deer or two, you will be able to complete the chore in less than 10 minutes.

In fact, your greatest concern should be the safety of your own fingers working in proximity to a sharp hunting knife.

Whether you transport your deer home or leave it in camp, the deer should be hung shortly after being killed. Hanging a deer accomplishes two things: it facilitates cooling, and it puts the deer in a good position for skinning. Propping the body cavity open with a stick promotes even faster cooling.

Some hunters prefer to hang a deer head up, but the head-down position remains better for several reasons. First, it allows heat to rise freely from the chest cavity. Second, it makes it easier to skin the head out, an important consideration if the deer is a trophy. Third, it reduces the amount of hair you get on the meat. Naturally, if you do not intend to save the cape, or if skinning will be done elsewhere, hanging deer by the head is fine in camp.

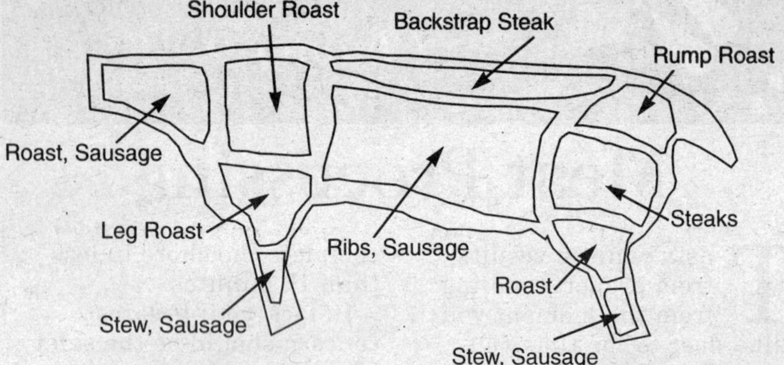

Palatability of Venison

Many factors affect the taste and tenderness of venison:
- ✓ age of deer
- ✓ sex of deer
- ✓ the deer's diet
- ✓ winter severity
- ✓ parasites
- ✓ stress on animal before the shot
- ✓ shot placement
- ✓ stress on animal while trailing
- ✓ field-dressing technique

Other factors include the immediacy of:
- ✓ handling from field to home
- ✓ hanging
- ✓ aging of meat
- ✓ butchering method
- ✓ packaging, freezing and duration of storage
- ✓ length and manner of cooking.

Butchering Basics

In the absence of experience or a willing instructor, most hunters take their deer to a local processor to have it butchered, for a fee. In most cases, however, even the novice ends up with better quality venison when he butchers his deer himself. Several reasons apply.

For one, when you butcher a deer that you harvested, you know the meat comes from your deer. Also, you can take as much time as you like to remove hair, blood, gristle and fat in order to make the finished product more enjoyable. Further, you can debone the deer as much as you wish, thus saving valuable freezer space.

Completely removing all bones represents the easiest way to butcher a deer. Surprisingly, it takes very little to become proficient at "boning," and you don't need any special tools other than a sharp, stiff knife and a steel to keep it sharp. With the deer hung, remove the front legs and shoulders first. Then remove the loin or back strap. Next cut off rib meat for grinding. Finally, remove the hind quarter and cut into round steaks and rump roasts.

Butchering an animal you personally harvested provides satisfaction. As the completion of an age-old ritual, when the steaks are sizzling or the stew is bubbling, you will know exactly where that meat came from.

As a side benefit, the butchering process also offers an opportunity for you to become familiar with deer physiology. This knowledge naturally translates into better understanding of shot placement, thus ensuring future clean kills.

General Suggestions

✓ Cool venison as quickly as possible after killing a deer.

✓ After returning to camp, immediately remove the tenderloins found inside the deer's body cavity.

✓ Trim venison of all fat, membranes and connecting tissue before freezing or cooking.

✓ Freezing meat in chunks

> *When you butcher a deer that you harvested, you know the meat comes from your deer. Also, you can take as much time as you like to remove hair, blood, gristle and fat in order to make the finished product more enjoyable.*

or sections, as opposed to individual steaks, helps to retain moisture. Further, well-chilled or semi-frozen meat is also easier to slice than room-temperature meat. For these reasons, divide each loin strap into four or five sections, wrap and freeze. Do the same with the round. To determine the size of the chunks, use a scale or try to visualize the number of steaks you will slice from a section.

✓ Venison should thaw slowly to prevent toughness. Venison roast, stew and casseroles should cook slowly and with a cover.

✓ Venison steaks, roast and stew must be served hot and the balance kept hot without burning. It prevents a waxy taste.

Taste Factors are Hard to Identify

The factors that affect venison seldom — if ever — occur under controlled conditions. As a result, even if we could identify all the factors, it would be impossible to consistently predict which individual deer will produce venison with the best taste and texture.

Weights and Heart Girth

To calculate live or hog-dressed weight, first measure heart girth, the circumference of the body just behind the front legs. Then consult this chart to convert girth into a close estimate of weight.

Heart girth inches (cm)	Hog-dressed weight Adults pounds (kg)	Live weight Adults pounds (kg)
26 (66.0)	46 (20.9)	69 (27.2)
27 (68.6)	52 (23.6)	68 (30.8)
28 (71.1)	58 (26.3)	75 (34.0)
29 (73.7)	64 (29.0)	83 (37.6)
30 (76.2)	70 (31.8)	90 (40.8)
31 (78.7)	76 (34.5)	98 (44.5)
32 (81.3)	82 (37.2)	106 (48.1)
33 (83.8)	88 (39.9)	113 (51.3)
34 (86.4)	94 (42.6)	121 (54.9)
35 (88.9)	101 (45.8)	128 (58.1)
36 (91.4)	107 (48.5)	136 (61.7)
37 (94.0)	113 (51.3)	144 (65.3)
38 (96.5)	119 (54.0)	151 (68.5)
39 (99.1)	125 (56.7)	159 (72.1)
40 (101.6)	131 (59.2)	166 (75.3)
41 (104.1)	137 (62.1)	174 (78.9)
42 (106.7)	143 (64.9)	182 (82.6)
43 (109.2)	149 (67.6)	190 (86.2)
44 (111.8)	155 (70.3)	197 (89.4)
45 (114.3)	161 (73.0)	205 (93.0)

Virginia Polytechnic Institute & State University

Venison Recipes

Country-Fried Venison Steaks

2 pounds venison steak (round or sirloin tip) ½- to 1-inch thick
½ cup flour
3 tablespoons shortening
2 cans condensed cream of mushroom soup
Water
Salt and pepper

Trim all fat from the steaks, and cut into pieces approximately 3 inches square. Using a meat mallet, pound flour into both sides of the steaks.

Melt shortening in a large skillet and brown meat slowly over medium heat (15 to 20 minutes). Season to taste with salt and pepper. As pieces are browned, transfer them to a 2- to 3-quart casserole dish.

Blend the 2 cans of mushroom soup in a blender until creamy. Pour this mixture over the steak. Add enough water to cover all pieces of steak. Cover and bake until tender (approximately 2½ hours) in 350-degree oven, adding water as necessary.
— *Valorie D. Bailey, Hixson, Tenn.*

TNT Pepper Steak over Noodles

2 pounds cubed venison
2 cups barbecue sauce
1 cup of honey
1 teaspoon garlic powder
3 to 4 cups egg noodles
6 diced cayenne peppers
6 diced jalapeno peppers
1 large onion (diced)
1 small can mushrooms (sliced)
1 tablespoon butter or shortening

Cut 2 pounds of venison into 1-inch cubes. Brown in 10- to 12-inch skillet with butter or shortening. Add mushrooms, diced onion and garlic powder to venison in skillet. Mix barbecue sauce, honey, cayenne and jalapeno peppers in a large bowl. Mix well. Pour sauce in skillet and cook until meat is done, stirring occasionally.

Boil about 6 cups of water in large pot. Add noodles and cook as

directed on package. Drain noodles. Serve venison over noodles.
— *Lonny R. Robertson, McDonald, Pa.*

Bacon and Wine Marinated Steaks

Marinade:
¼ pound cooked and crumbled bacon (save fat for frying later)
½ cup red wine
¼ cup oil
1 green pepper, diced
1 onion, diced
Garlic salt
Italian seasoning

Marinate two deer steaks (¾-inch thick) for 24 hours, turning occasionally. Remove and drain on plate. Sprinkle with garlic salt and pepper.

With burner on high heat, saute meat in hot bacon fat, 3 to 4 minutes per side.

(Meanwhile, cook onions, green pepper and mushrooms). Pile on steaks.
— *Mary Scott, Rochester, N.H.*

Venison Loins In Gravy

1 pound venison cut ½-inch to 1-inch thick
⅓ cup margarine
2 tablespoons vegetable oil
¾ cup flour
1 teaspoon salt
1 tablespoon black pepper
1 teaspoon garlic powder
1 (4 ounce) can mushrooms, drained
1 10½-ounce can cream of mushroom soup
1 can water

Rinse venison with cold water and drain. Mix remaining dry ingredients in a bowl large enough so the venison can be added. Cover bowl and shake until venison is coated with flour mixture. Place meat in skillet. Brown on medium heat 5 minutes per side. Remove from skillet and brown remaining venison, if necessary. Drain skillet. Place all venison in skillet. Add mushrooms, cream of mushroom soup and water — in that order. Bring to a boil, while stirring in soup mix. Reduce heat to low,

cover and simmer 45 minutes to 1 hour. Serve hot.
— *Barry McCombs, Williamsburg, Iowa*

JC's Super-Simple Sandwich

2 pounds venison chops/steaks
3 teaspoons Worcestershire sauce
¼ cup ketchup
1 tablespoon soy sauce
¼ cup vinegar
Salt, pepper

Cut venison into ¾-inch cubes. Place venison, Worcestershire sauce, ketchup, soy sauce and vinegar in covered bowl and microwave for 4 to 5 minutes. Serve on buns or bread as sandwiches.
— *Jack and Zack Courtright, Spring Lake, Mich.*

High Speed Venison

2 to 3 pound venison steak
1 package onion soup mix
1 can cream of mushroom soup
Salt and pepper
2 beef bouillon cubes
2 onions, sliced
¾ cup milk

Brown meat in skillet. Add rest of ingredients and simmer for 1 hour. Salt and pepper to taste. Serve over rice. Serves 4.

Sour Mash Venison

2 large venison steaks, 2-inches thick

Sour Mash Whiskey Marinade:

1 cup whiskey
1 teaspoon celery seeds
6 whole peppercorns
Garlic to taste
1 12-ounce can concentrated orange juice
3 tablespoons concentrated liquid smoke

Venison Recipes

Combine the marinade ingredients in a large pan. Put the venison in a pan, spoon marinade on top. Cover and refrigerate for 24-36 hours, occasionally turning the meat in the marinade.

Lightly oil the barbecue grill and place the meat on grill. Baste the venison with marinade. Grill for 10 minutes on each side.

Quick and Easy Venison Strips

1¼ to 1½ pounds venison round steak
2 tablespoons butter
1 green pepper, cut into thin rounds
1 large onion, sliced
1 teaspoon game seasoning

With sharp, thin-bladed knife, cut steak into paper-thin slices. In a large, heavy skillet, heat the butter over medium heat. Add pepper and onions, cook for about 5 minutes, until they are lightly browned and limp. Remove the vegetables and place on a preheated plate. Add more butter to the skillet if necessary and place the meat strips on a single layer in the skillet. Fry over medium-high heat for 12 minutes on the first side and 2 minutes on the other. While the meat is frying, sprinkle it with seasonings. Add the vegetables, then stir and heat for a few seconds. Don't overcook! Serve immediately on heated plates. Serve with baked potatoes and green salad. Serves 4.

Borden's Sloppy Bucks

3 to 4 pounds venison
1 bag crab boil
Black pepper
2 packages onion soup mix
3 medium bottles of barbecue sauce
Meat tenderizer

Place venison and crab boil in pot and sprinkle with black pepper and meat tenderizer. Cover with plenty of water and boil slowly until meat is done. Let meat cool. Slice meat into small chunks, then using your fingers, shred the meat into small pieces. Place meat in large mixing bowl, pour the onion soup mix over it and mix well. Next pour the barbecue sauce over the mixture. Take each bottle and rinse with about ⅓ bottle of water and pour over the mixture. Stir this up real good. Place in crock pot and simmer on high for about 2 hours, then turn to low and

simmer for about 2 hours. Spoon into buns.
— *Borden Crawford, Meridian, Miss.*

Venison and Barbecue Sauce

4- to 6-pound roast
¼ cup brown sugar
½ cup vinegar
Salt and pepper to taste
½ cup melted butter
1 cup catsup
5 tablespoons chopped onions
2 tablespoons Worcestershire sauce
1 cup water
1 clove garlic, mashed
Flour

Rub meat with combined sugar and vinegar, and marinate 3 to 4 hours.
Rub meat with salt and pepper and dust with flour, then brown in skillet. Combine all remaining ingredients for sauce.
Place roast in pan and add small amount of water, baste with sauce. Roast at 350 degrees for 30 minutes per pound. Baste occasionally, then remove roast and thicken sauce for gravy.
— *Michael Ramach, Jacksonville, N.C.*

Venison Ribs

3 pounds venison ribs or one rack
2 tablespoons cooking oil
1 teaspoon salt
⅛ teaspoon pepper
2 bouillon cubes
2 tablespoons vinegar
1 teaspoon Worcestershire sauce
2 medium onions, slice thin

Brown ribs in oil and pour off drippings. Sprinkle with salt and pepper. Add bouillon cubes, vinegar, Worcestershire sauce, onions and 1½ cups water. Cover and cook slowly until meat is tender (about 2 hours). Drain off liquid and make into gravy. Serve over ribs.

Venison Pot Roast

3- to 4-pound top round or shoulder roast
Flour
2 tablespoons cooking oil
Pepper
1 clove garlic
1 envelope onion-mushroom soup mix
5 large carrots
5 potatoes with skin, quartered
1 tablespoon cornstarch

Roll roast in flour. Heat oil in a Dutch oven and brown the roast in oil. Sprinkle roast with pepper. Add garlic and contents of the soup envelope to the pot, along with 2 cups of hot water. Cover the Dutch oven and simmer until the meat is nearly tender, from 1½ to 2 hours. Turn the roast a couple of times during cooking. Add vegetables to the pot. Simmer another 30 minutes. Remove the meat and vegetables to a heated platter. Thicken the sauce with cornstarch dissolved in ½ cup of cold water.

Leg of Venison in Mustard and Pepper Sauce

5-pound leg of venison
5 ounces lard, cut into 2-inch by ⅛-inch strips
1 tablespoon mustard powder
1 teaspoon black peppercorns, crushed
Salt to taste
4 ounces margarine
1 large onion, chopped
1 carrot, chopped
1 parsnip, chopped
1 cup beef broth

Marinade:
1 carrot, chopped
2 medium onions, chopped
1 teaspoon black peppercorns, crushed
1 cup red wine vinegar
1 cup red wine
¼ cup brandy
1 cup beef stock

Sauce:
3 ounces honey bread, ground
6 tablespoons marinade
4 tablespoons red currant jelly
1 tablespoon mustard powder

Rinse venison in cold water. Remove skin. Mix ingredients for marinade in a deep bowl. Submerge venison completely (if necessary, add water). Cover with a lid and refrigerate 5 hours.

Remove venison from marinade. Save 1 cup. Spread lard mixture across the fibers of the leg of venison. Rub with mixture of salt, crushed pepper and mustard powder.

Heat margarine in pot, then brown venison for 10 minutes, flipping it occasionally. Add onion and carrot. Brown for 5 minutes. Add beef broth, cover with a lid and cook in preheated oven (lowest rack) for approximately 90 minutes at 350 degrees. Replace evaporated fluid with water. Remove venison from pot and place on warm plate.

For sauce, strain all pan juices. Mix well with ingredients for sauce. Add salt, pepper or vinegar to taste. Bring to a short boil. Pour ⅕ of the sauce over leg of venison and serve the remainder in a gravy boat. Serve with potato dumplings. Serves 6 to 8.

Venison Cider Stew

2 pounds venison, cut into 1-inch cubes
3 tablespoons all-purpose floor
2 teaspoons salt
¼ teaspoon dried thyme
¼ teaspoon pepper
3 tablespoons cooking oil
2 cups apple cider or apple juice
1 to 2 tablespoons vinegar
3 potatoes, quartered
4 carrots, quartered
2 onions, sliced
1 stalk celery, sliced

Coat meat with flour, salt, pepper and thyme. Pour hot oil in a large Dutch oven, and brown meat. Drain off fat. Stir in apple cider or juice, vinegar and ½ cup of water. Cook and stir until mixture boils. Reduce heat, cover and simmer about 1 hour or until meat is nearly tender. Stir in vegetables. Cook 20 minutes or until vegetables are done.

VENISON RECIPES

Hot Spicy Stew
2 pounds venison, cubed
2 tablespoons cooking oil
1 cup beer
2 large onions, diced
2 tablespoons steak sauce
1 teaspoon Tabasco
Salt and pepper
Cooked noodles

Heat oil in large skillet, add meat and brown. Add ingredients, simmer covered one hour. Serve over hot noodles.

Venison Curry

1 pound venison stew meat
¼ cup flour
1 medium onion, thinly sliced
¼ teaspoon powdered ginger
1½ teaspoons curry powder
1 large can tomatoes, with liquid
1 beef bouillon cube, dissolved in 1 cup boiling water

Toss meat in flour, shaking off excess. In a cast iron or other heavy Dutch oven, saute venison in hot oil until browned. Add onion, ginger, curry, tomatoes with liquid (break up tomatoes) and beef bouillon. Cover and cook on low simmer for 1½ hours or until meat is tender. Serve over hot rice. If you wish to thicken sauce, add one or two tablespoons cornstarch dissolved in small amount of cold water.
Serves 3.

Forty Below Chili

4 pounds ground venison
2 cans beer
2 medium onions, chopped
1 24-ounce can tomato paste
2 tablespoons vinegar
1 to 2 tablespoons chili powder
1 teaspoon Tabasco
1 pound bacon, chopped
2 tablespoons cumin, ground

1 dash red pepper, crushed
1 tablespoon MSG
1 to 2 cloves garlic, minced
1 tablespoon oregano
1 teaspoon Worcestershire sauce
2 tablespoons bacon drippings
1 tablespoon black pepper
1 can kidney beans

In a large chili pot, combine tomato sauce, tomato paste, beer, chopped peppers, chili powder, vinegar, Tabasco sauce, cumin, crushed red pepper, oregano, Worcestershire sauce, salt and pepper. Bring to a simmer. In a large frying pan, cook bacon until crisp, then add it and 2 tablespoons drippings to chili pot. Brown meat, onions, garlic and MSG, and add to chili pot. Cover pot and simmer for one hour. Add kidney beans with liquid. Simmer for ½ hour.

Heavy-Duty Chili

3 pounds venison, ground or small cubes
1 teaspoon Tabasco sauce
1 tablespoon chili powder (or ground chili peppers)
1 tablespoon cumin
1 teaspoon cayenne pepper
2 cans tomato sauce
10 cloves garlic
1 teaspoon salt
6 large onions
4 large green peppers
1 dozen red peppers
5 chili peppers
1 can red kidney beans
1 can white beans

Brown venison, green peppers and onions in large heavy skillet. Add all ingredients except beans and simmer 45 minutes. Add beans with juice and simmer an additional 15 minutes.

Venison Spanish Rice

1 pound ground venison
2 large onions, chopped

2 large green bell peppers, chopped
1 32-ounce jar spaghetti sauce
3 bags boil-in-bag rice, cooked
4 tablespoons butter

Saute venison, onions, peppers in large Dutch oven. Dot top with butter. Bake, uncovered in a 350-degree oven for 45 minutes. If you prefer it a little moister, add another ½-jar spaghetti sauce or an 8-ounce can tomato sauce.
— *H.F. Coleman, Norwich, N.Y.*

Venison Parmesan

2 15-ounce cans tomato sauce
2 tablespoons butter
2 tablespoons brown sugar
1 tablespoon Worcestershire sauce
½ teaspoon Season All
1 teaspoon dried whole oregano
1 teaspoon dried whole basil
½ teaspoon garlic powder
½ teaspoon white pepper

2 eggs
½ teaspoon white pepper
1 teaspoon Season All

2 pounds venison (cube steak cut or flank pounded) cut into serving-size pieces
¼ cup freshly grated Parmesan cheese
2 8-ounce packages mozzarella cheese
4 cups Italian-style bread crumbs
½ cup olive oil

To make sauce, combine the first nine ingredients in saucepan over medium heat for 5 to 10 minutes, stirring occasionally — set aside.

Beat eggs and add 1 teaspoon Season All, ½ teaspoon white pepper. Dredge venison in crumbs. Saute venison in the olive oil 4 to 5 minutes (until brown). Place venison in lightly greased baking dish — pour sauce over meat and sprinkle with Parmesan. Bake an additional 5 to 10 minutes in 350-degree oven until cheese melts. Serves 4 to 6.
— *Janeann Dailey, Duluth, Ga.*

Venison Zucchini Bake

2½ cups of ¼-inch thick zucchini slices
2 cups cooked leftover venison, cut up
1 large can condensed cream of chicken soup
2 tablespoons milk
⅛ teaspoon ground nutmeg
1 cup biscuit baking powder
¼ cup grated Parmesan cheese
1 egg
¼ cup margarine, melted

Heat oven to 350 degrees. Arrange zucchini in 8-inch by 10-inch baking dish. Top with meat. Mix soup, milk and nutmeg; spread over meat. Drizzle with margarine. Bake until golden brown, 25 to 30 minutes. Makes 4 servings.

Venison Vegetable Braid

½ cup mayonnaise
2 teaspoons Dijon mustard
2 cups cooked leftover venison, cubed
8-ounce can refrigerated crescent dinner rolls
⅓ cup finely chopped celery
2 cups mixed vegetables, cooked and drained

Heat oven to 350 degrees. In medium-size bowl, combine mayonnaise and mustard; stir in leftover meat, celery and vegetables. Roll dough into 2 long rectangles. Place on ungreased cookie sheet with long sides overlapping ½-inch; firmly press edges and perforations to seal. Press or roll to form a 10-inch by 15-inch rectangle. Spoon mixture to form a 4-inch strip lengthwise down center of dough. Make cuts 1 inch apart on each side of rectangle. To give braided appearance, fold strips of dough at an angle halfway across filling, alternating from side to side. Bake for 25 minutes or until golden brown. Makes 6 servings.

Big Game Pie

4 large potatoes (mashed) or packaged instant mashed potatoes
½ cup celery, finely chopped
1 tablespoon chopped onion
3 tablespoons flour
3 tablespoons butter or oleo

Venison Recipes

½ cup milk
¾ cup beef broth
2½ cups venison, cubed and browned
¼ teaspoon browning sauce
¼ cup grated cheddar cheese

Prepare mashed potatoes according to the package directions. In a skillet, saute celery and onion in butter until tender but not brown. Blend in flour and gradually add milk and broth. Cook and stir until mixture thickens and bubbles. Stir in cooked meat, browning sauce and season with salt and pepper. Pour meat mixture into a 1½-quart casserole dish and top evenly with mashed potatoes. Sprinkle with cheese and bake at 400 degrees for 20 to 25 minutes or until brown. Serves 4.

Cajun Venison and Wild Rice

¾ pound venison steaks cut 1-inch thick
½ teaspoon garlic powder
½ teaspoon thyme
¼ teaspoon cayenne pepper
1 or 2 tablespoons vegetable oil
¼ cup sliced celery
1¾ cups water
1 package (5 ounces) Uncle Ben's Long Grain & Wild Rice
Beef stock sauce with vegetables
¼ cup thinly sliced green bell pepper strips
1 small tomato, coarsely chopped
2 tablespoons chopped green onion

Cut meat into 1-inch cubes. Combine garlic powder, thyme and cayenne in a medium bowl. Add meat, and toss to coat. Heat oil in a 10-inch skillet over medium-high heat. Add meat and cook, stirring until no longer pink. About 2½ minutes. Drain excess fat. Add celery, water and contents of rice and seasoning packet to skillet with meat. Bring to a vigorous boil. Cover tightly and simmer 5 minutes, or until rice is desired consistency. Stir in bell pepper and tomato. Sprinkle with green onion. Serves 4.
— *Cheryl Markham, Morganfield, Ky.*

Greek Style Venison and Scallops

1½ pounds of venison cubed

1 pound scallops
2 large carrots, grated
6-10 plum tomatoes chopped
6 ounces clam juice
½ stick of butter

Marinade:
½ bottle of Madeira wine
Juice of ½ lemon
½ teaspoon rosemary
½ teaspoon black pepper
2 cloves pressed garlic

Combine marinade ingredients and add venison, let it sit for 24 hours.

In a heavy skillet over medium heat, combine clam juice, any juice from the scallops and drained marinade. Reduce sauce by ¾, stirring occasionally. When sauce is reduced, add butter and stir until combined.

In a separate pan, brown venison in a little olive oil. Add carrots and chopped tomatoes and heat through. Add scallops and cook until they turn white. Be careful not to overcook the scallops.

Serve at once over noodles, pilaf or yellow rice. Top off with your sauce.
— *Daryl Lotecka, Philadelphia, Pa.*

Venison Sauerbraten

4-pound venison roast
2 onions, sliced
1 bay leaf
10 black whole peppercorns
10 juniper berries
6 cloves
2 teaspoons salt
6 cups boiling water
½ cup red wine vinegar
2 tablespoons oil
1 medium-sized red cabbage, cut into 8 wedges

Caraway Sauce:
15 gingersnaps, crushed
2 teaspoons sugar

Caraway Dumplings:
1½ cups sifted four

1 cup milk or water
7 cups boiling water

Place meat in bowl with onions, bay leaves, cloves, juniper berries, salt, water and vinegar. Cover and marinate 6 to 8 hours. Drain the venison and reserve the marinade. In a heavy Dutch oven, heat the oil over medium-high heat and brown the venison on all sides. Add the reserve marinade, then cover, lower heat and simmer 2 hours or until tender. Drain venison and keep it warm.

Strain and measure the marinade (add water if needed) to equal 4 cups and return to the Dutch oven.

Combine the dumpling ingredients with a fork. Mold 2 tablespoons of dumpling mixture into balls and drop them into boiling water. Cook 10 minutes, remove and rinse with hot water and drain. Bring the marinade to a boil, then add the cabbage wedges and place the dumplings on top. Cover to steam and cook over medium heat for 10 minutes or until the cabbage is tender. Mix the crushed gingersnaps and sugar and stir into cabbage liquid. Simmer for 3 minutes. Serve on a platter topped with gingersnap sauce.

This authentic dish makes a great after-the-hunt meal. As always, follow the recipe exactly the first time you make the dish — don't leave out the gingersnaps or use green cabbage instead of red! It needs no side dish.

Italian Venison

3 cups meat — cooked and chopped
1½ cups spaghetti broken into 2-inch pieces
½ cup onion, chopped
½ cup green pepper, chopped
1 can cream of mushroom soup
1 cup chicken broth
Salt and pepper
1½ cup grated sharp cheddar cheese
1 cup sliced mushrooms

Cook the spaghetti as directed and drain. Brown meat, and place it with pepper and onion in 2-quart casserole dish. Pour the soup, broth, 1½ cups cheese and spaghetti in the casserole with a little salt and pepper. Toss lightly. Add remaining cheese on top, cover and place in preheated 350-degree oven for 30 minutes until bubbly. Serves 6.

Venison Pocket Pizza

Venison steak
Pizza sauce (or a reasonable substitute)
Bread dough (homemade or frozen)
Mozzarella cheese

Optional ingredients:
Lawry's seasoning salt
Beef bouillon
Parmesan cheese
Italian seasonings
Pizza toppings
Garlic salt

Tenderize steak with a meat hammer (loins or "breakfast steaks" work well. Cut the steaks into ½- to ¾-inch squares.

Fry meat in pan with butter (or margarine) to your liking. You might also season it with Lawry's seasoned salt and/or crushed beef bouillon.

Buy some frozen raw bread dough loaves, and allow them to rise per instructions. Do not cover the loaves with butter or margarine. (The bread doesn't need to rise completely but needs to thaw.) When thawed, flatten the bread into a pizza-like crust.

In the center of the crust place the following: 8-ounces mozzarella cheese, 4-ounces pizza sauce, additional pizza toppings and precooked meat.

You can fold the crust two ways. One way is to fold the dough in half from one side to another, forming a half circle. Another way is to bring both sides to the top over the middle, which forms a fat half circle with the "seam" on top. Be sure to keep butter away from the outer 1-inch of the crust, otherwise the pocket won't seal properly. Pinch the seams together. For extra flavor and coloring, sprinkle Parmesan cheese, Italian seasonings and garlic salt on the outside surface of the bread. Bake in oven at 350 degrees, until golden brown.
— *Gary Sisk, Darien, Wis.*

How to Sharpen Knives

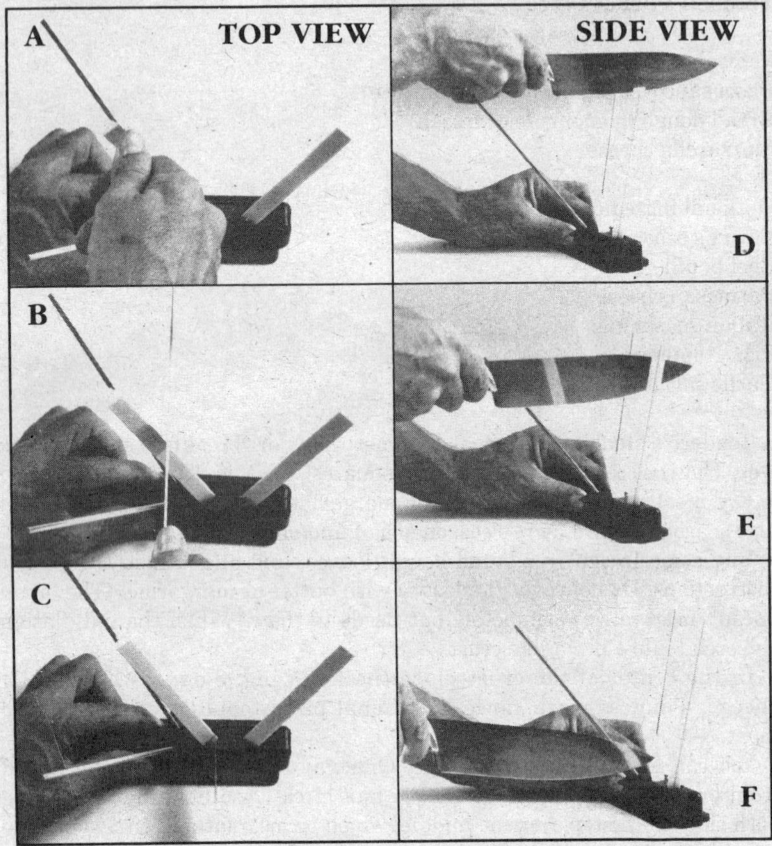

1. Stick-type sharpeners work best on straight-edge knives. Always use both safety guards, and keep your hands behind the guards.

2. Press hard enough to remove metal. Excess pressure will not serve the knive.

3. Always keep the blade perpendicular to the sharpener's base.

4. Always sharpen the entire blade. Draw the blade toward you as you "slice" down on the stone. See A, B, C, D, E and F.

5. When one area of the stone is loaded with steel, to where it is no longer cutting metal, rotate the stone in base to a fresh area.

6. Sharpen the blade by giving 20 strokes on each side, alternating strokes from right to left. Repeat the same number of strokes with grey stones positioned as in Step 2. Continue the sharpening process with white stones (Step 3), and finish with Step 4.

7. Repeat the process if the knife doesn't reach desired sharpness.

Serrated and Scalloped-Edge Knives

1. Sharpening serrated knives requires the same process as straight knives, but you should only use the corners of the stones to hone the knife edges. This allows the serrations to slide easily across the sharpener's surface.

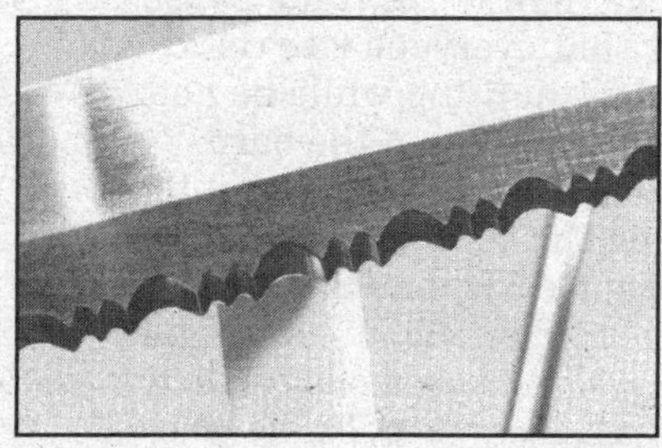

2. Sharpen both sides of all serrations, even if original sharpening was only performed on one side. This will allow for straighter cuts.

Fillet Knives and Other Sharp, Flexible Knives

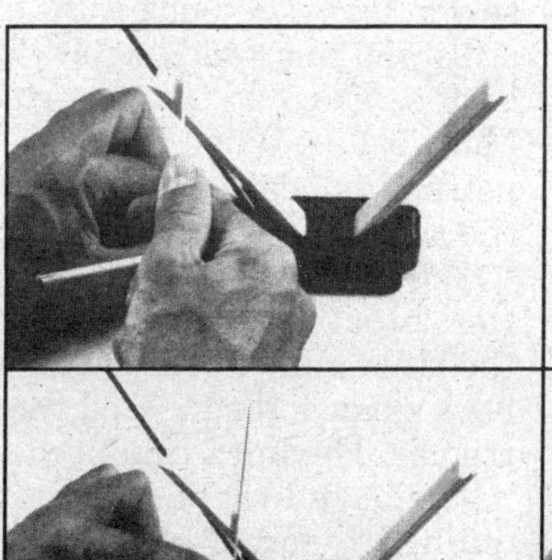

1. Sharpen fillet knives and long, flexible knives in the same manner as rigid knives. However, flexible knives require sufficient side pressure

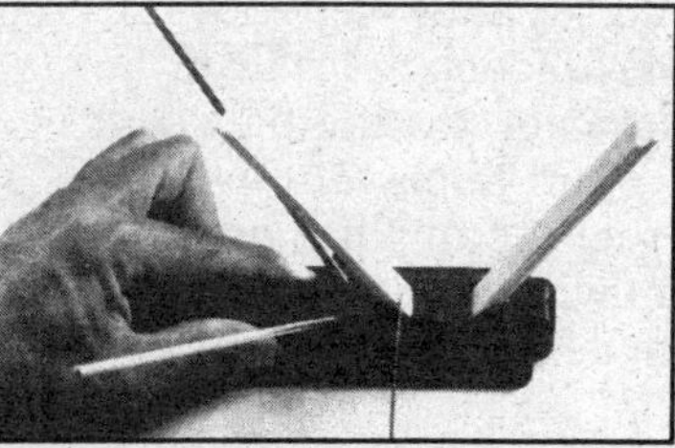

Man Enough

■ *Bryce M. Towsley*

The kid was as mad as a wet rooster. And the way he saw things, he had every right to be. It just wasn't fair that everyone else could go deer hunting while he had to stay and clean the barn.

Sometimes it really stunk being the youngest. He hated being treated like he was never old enough. To his figuring, if he was old enough to do chores, then by golly, he was old enough to hunt deer. Of course, his dad and older brother didn't see it that way.

But he had a plan. He would show them that he was not only old enough to go deer hunting, he could also get a buck by himself.

When his chores were done, he picked up the old Stevens Crack Shot .22 that was kept in the barn for shooting rats. He searched for bullets, but all he could find were a handful of shorts. Those were fine for killing rats, but most folks would say they were not powerful enough for deer.

However, the kid figured it was more important where he hit them than what he hit them with. Besides, it was all he had. Shorts would have to do.

On the post by the last stall hung a coil of hemp rope. With the rifle tucked under his arm, the kid snatched the "drag" rope and hung it over his head and shoulder. He was ready to go deer hunting.

Approaching the Orchard

The climb up the back pasture was steep. The rocky shale bedrock that showed through the thin soil made for a poor pasture and for tough walking. The kid didn't think about that, though, as he scaled the hill. He thought about what his dad once told him: Deer like to eat apples.

He knew exactly where to hunt. There was a lone apple tree high in the back pasture. Surely the deer would come there to feed.

As he topped the hill and looked down at the tree, he saw a deer. The buck was straining and reaching as high as he could to reach ripe McIntoshes. When the deer moved his head, a big part of the tree moved with it.

The kid was having a hard time breathing. He steadied the rifle, aimed behind the buck's ear and squeezed the trigger. The buck collapsed.

The boy's luck started fading. He forgot his knife and realized his dad and brother were not home. He would have to drag the buck home — alone. Although the buck outweighed him by three or four times, he tied the rope

Patrick Durkin

to its antlers and started pulling. Then the unthinkable happened.

The buck opened his eyes, let out a gut-wrenching bawl, lunged up, and stood on all fours.

The scared kid dodged around the apple tree and tied the end of the rope to a limb. He then grabbed his rifle and shot at the thrashing buck.

By now the kid was bawling and carrying on just as loud as the buck was. He didn't even aim as he loaded shell after shell into the little single shot. Most of the bullets missed, and those that hit the deer were inflicting little damage.

Luckily, his neighbor was hunting just over the hill. The man heard the commotion and raced over.

"He's my deer. Don't you shoot him!" the kid yelled.

"I wouldn't think of it," the neighbor said. "But, here, use my rifle."

The shot from the .30-30 carbine knocked the deer and the kid to the ground. They laid there quietly. The buck was dead, and the kid was emotionally and physically drained.

All is Still

The neighbor knew this was not the time to talk. He quietly took over and started

> *As he topped the hill and looked down at the tree, he saw a deer. The buck was straining and reaching as high as he could to reach ripe McIntoshes. When the deer moved his head, a big part of the tree moved with it.*

field-dressing the buck. Without saying a word, the man dragged the buck back to the barn while the kid followed behind, carrying the rifles.

The neighbor even handed the kid his handkerchief so he could wipe his face. He wouldn't want his dad and brother to know he'd been crying. While they were waiting, the neighbor picked up the kid's rifle and studied it.

"I can see how you had trouble killing that big fella with the little pop-gun you got here, Bub," the neighbor said.

"But tell me, I'm quite puzzled about it all. How did you manage to get him hitched in the first place?"

In the many times he told me this story, my grandfather never said if he answered the man.

Book Details Deer Behavior

There's a saying in the business world that goes "You get what you pay for."

Well, in the case of Charles Alsheimer's book, *Whitetail: Behavior Through the Seasons*, that saying doesn't ring true.

You get a whole lot more.

To Alsheimer, the white-tailed deer is the crown jewel of American wildlife. Maybe that's why he's been photographing and writing about whitetails for more than 20 years. That experience shines in this book. The deer behavior insights and 166 color photos in this 10-chapter book are simply spectacular.

Chapter 1 of *Behavior Through the Seasons* gives an overview on the whitetail's past and how it has survived over the centuries.

Spring ranks second only to fall as Alsheimer's favorite season. "Few things in nature can top the fresh smell of the forest as the last snows vanish, hearing the first peepers, seeing the gradual budding of leaves, or witnessing the birth of a fawn," he said. He captures this magical time in Chapter 2, "Blossom Time," which includes precious photos of doe-fawn relationships.

Alsheimer packs a lifetime of fall hunting and photographing experience in the chapter "Autumn's Splendor." Learn what leads up to the chase phase, and discover why doe family groups steer clear of bucks during this time. Also, discover how to determine deer behavior by examining rubs. What does a buck with a 26-inch

Charles J. Alsheimer, *Whitetail: Behavior Through the Seasons*. Krause Publications, 1996. Pg. 208. Illustrated. Hard cover. From Krause Publications, 700 E. State St., Iola, WI 54990-0001. $34.95.

spread look like? You'll find out in Chapter 6, "The Lure of Antlers." Also included are before-and-after photos of bucks that show their development over several years. The most impressive comparison starts on Page 122, which shows a massive non-typical buck that later grew a rack only vaguely similar to his original headgear.

There's no doubt, *Whitetail: Behavior Through the Seasons* is the best deer hunting book to hit the market in years, and it will no doubt rise to the status of an all-time classic.

— *Dan Schmidt*

GET THE MOST FROM YOUR WHITETAIL HUNTS

PROVEN WHITE-TAIL TACTICS
by Greg Miller
In his latest book, one of America's best-known hunters shares more secrets for locating and bagging big whitetails in the less-than-exotic locales that most hunters find close to home. This volume will entertain and educate as it explains strategies for scouting, calling and stalking deer. 6x9 SC • 224 pages • 100 b&w photos • **AWH02 $19.95**

Bowhunter Handbook
Expert Strategies & Techniques
by M.R. James with Fred Asbell, Dave Holt, Dwight Shuh & Dr. Dave Samuel
Take your bowhunting to the next level using these vital tips from bowhunting's top experts. You'll learn how to select the right equipment, plan strategies and pick the best method to take North American game from whitetails to Arctic musk ox and polar bear. 8-1/2x11 SC • 256p • 500 photos • **BHH $19.95**

301 Venison Recipes: The Ultimate Deer Hunter's Cookbook sizzles with succulent, mouth-watering recipes you can't be without. If you need to feed a hungry bunch at deer camp, or serve special guests in your home, look no further. 6x9 Comb-bound •128p •**VR01 $10.95**

Whitetail: Behavior Through the Seasons offers in-depth coverage of whitetail behavior through striking portraits by award-winning photographer and author Charles J. Alsheimer. His in-the-field observations will help you better understand this spectacular game animal. 9x11-1/2 HC • 208p • 166 color photos • **WHIT $34.95**

Stand Hunting for Whitetails Author Richard Smith teaches you the best places, times and conditions for stand hunting. Get the scoop on commercial blinds, camouflage and essential safety precautions. 6x9 SC • 256p • 100+ photos • **GSH01 $14.95**

Deer & Deer Hunting: A Hunter's Guide to Deer Behavior & Hunting Techniques is written with you in mind. One of the finest deer hunting guides available, this book provides tips and insights on antlers, communication, activity, rubs and scrapes, the rut, hunting styles and techniques, guns, plus much more. Al Hofacker, Editor. Includes 100 color photos! 8-1/2x11 HC • 208p • full color • **DD01 $34.95**

Credit Card Calls Toll-free

800-258-0929 Dept. OAS8

Mon-Fri, 7 a.m. - 8 p.m. • Sat, 8 a.m. - 2 p.m., CST
Visit our web site: http://www.krause.com

JUST $13.95 BRINGS YOU A FULL YEAR OF

TURKEY & TURKEY HUNTING
MAGAZINE

Turkey hunters know special technical skills and hunting abilities are essential to bagging a prize gobbler. Whether you're a seasoned turkey hunter, or new to the sport, **TURKEY & TURKEY HUNTING** will bring you the tips, tactics and know-how to bag your gobbler. It's the nation's leading magazine exclusively for turkey hunters.

Subscribe today to get six exciting issues and find out what we mean. Our money-back guarantee assures you that if you're not satisfied you can cancel and receive your money back on all unmailed issues. This risk-free offer puts cutting edge turkey hunting know-how in your hands.

Please begin my 1-year subscription to TURKEY & TURKEY HUNTING MAGAZINE for only $13.95

Check or Money Order Enclosed (Payable to **Turkey & Turkey Hunting Magazine**)

Mail Today to:
TURKEY & TURKEY HUNTING
Circ. Dept. ABARAL
700 E. State St.,
Iola, WI 54990-0001

Name______________________
Address______________________
City______________________
State/Zip______________________

MASTERCARD, VISA, AMEX, DISCOVER CUSTOMERS CALL TOLL-FREE

800-258-0929 Dept. ABARAL
M-F 7 am - 8 pm, Sat 8 am - 2 pm CT
Visit our web site: www.krause.com/outdoors